THOMAS NOAKES

DIARY OF WAR,
DROUGHT AND HARD TIMES

EDITED BY
MURPHY GIVENS

THOMAS NOAKES

DIARY OF WAR, DROUGHT AND HARD TIMES

EDITED BY MURPHY GIVENS

NUECES PRESS

Corpus Christi, Texas

Library of Congress Control Number 20200902172

Noakes, Thomas J. — The Diary of Thomas Noakes

Edited by: Givens, Murphy — The Diary of Thomas Noakes

Includes index.

1. South Texas — History.
2. Nueces County — History.
3. Corpus Christi, Texas — History.
4. Nuecestown, Texas — History
5. Civil War — History

ISBN   978-1-7339524-2-2

Published by Nueces Press, Corpus Christi, Texas.

Cover design by Jeff Chilcoat

www.nuecespress.com

TABLE OF CONTENTS

PUBLISHER'S NOTE

For years I have read of the life of Thomas Noakes when Murphy Givens has written about the Civil War in South Texas. When we published Perilous Trails of Texas, Red Dunn described the Mexican bandit attack and burning of Thomas Noakes' store.

With the publication of this book, I am able to read of Thomas J. Noakes experiences in South Texas. The life Noakes lived is hard to imagine. He was poor and life was difficult. Corpus Christi and Nuecestown were mere settlements on the Texas frontier in 1858 when this diary begins. Noakes was a single man, living alone in a settlement on the Nueces River, west of Corpus Christi.

Thomas Noakes would be a forgotten man, possibly known for his painting of the Civil War Battle of Corpus Christi or the 1875 bandit raid on his Nuecestown store. But he kept a diary of his mundane life, telling of his struggles to exist in South Texas during the hard years of the Civil War.

Over the years, Murphy Givens has relied on Thomas Noakes diary in his documentation of Corpus Christi's history. Through the diary we can imagine the difficulty of Civil War times. We are very pleased to bring you the extraordinary life to this forgotten man through his documented life. We hope you find this diary as compelling and interesting as we have in publishing it.

We are indebted to Charles Butt and Courtney Robinson for the copy of Noakes' painting of the Civil War skirmish at Corpus Christi Pass.

Jim Moloney
Nueces Press

INTRODUCTION

This diary is a fascinating document, surprising in many ways and at the same time studiously authentic. The authenticity is a gift of Murphy Givens, who has followed up almost every person and event cited with detailed verification; he offers more validity with explanatory and primary source appendices at the end.

But the surprises lie in the recollections of Thomas Noakes, author, painter, poet, and transplanted Texan scrimping a living along the Nueces River.

To readers more accustomed to hearing about life amidst the bays and estuaries of the Coastal Bend, the trials of those choosing to live westward are unique. Building shelters, penning livestock, securing meat, planting vegetables—all were as vital to survival as the endless forays into the brush to recover bolting horses. These Noakes makes vivid, along with almost constant cattle-hunting and hide skinning.

His experiences during the Civil War are no less enlightening, bypassing the Texans' triumphant victory over Union bombardment in 1862 to describe the aftermath: a drought so devastating animals died in harness or bogged down at dried up watering holes. Noakes's desperate trip down the Cotton Road for supplies, occasioned by the blockade, mirrored his futile salvage expedition on Padre Island during Reconstruction—both as discouraging as South Texas existence at the time.

Most inspiring, however unexpected, is Noakes' iron dedication. As morose as he is and sickly (malaria seems to be just one of his maladies), the Englishman strives on, making stools for his son, buying a hat for his wife (when he has funds), teaching children, exchanging books, hoarding newspapers, and writing poems. One can almost hope he found some solace in the general store he established years later, an achievement not covered in these pages but only attained through the struggles described in them.

The diary of Thomas Noakes gives us a whole different perspective on what a hard and brutal life it was in South Texas in the mid-1800s, before, during and after the Civil War.

—Mary Jo O'Rear,
author of "Storm Over the Bay"

FOREWORD

Thomas John Noakes left his home in Sussex, England when he was 18, crossed the Atlantic and reached Corpus Christi in 1848. He worked as a ranch hand for Henry Kinney and on a dredge boat digging a channel across the bay. He built a home in Corpus Christi then, in 1857, moved to up the river and worked to establish his own ranch. It was a poor life. A hard life. He was often miserable.

We know a lot about Noakes. He kept a diary, written in the manner of ship's log in which he noted the weather and major events of the day. Through his diary, we see a community trying to cope with the ravages of one of the worst droughts ever and the havoc caused by the war. We see what it was like to live in those turbulent and trying times. We see people who lived a lot closer to the elements, closer to nature, closer to the ground.

Noakes' small holding, whether called a farm or ranch, was at Nuecestown, usually called the Motts, or Twelve-Mile Motts. It was 12 miles up the river from Corpus Christi. The settlement was founded by Henry Kinney and the settlers were mainly English immigrants like Noakes.

The Motts was a close-knit community. Noakes and neighbors visited freely from house to house, they held dances and picnics, and when beeves or hogs were slaughtered, they shared the meat. They also shared the work, helping one another to plow a field, brand yearlings or search for strayed livestock. It was not an easy life, as these journals make clear, it was a life of toil and endurance. In Noakes' case, it was a life without comfort and luxury and he never quite became reconciled to it. He missed the England of his youth, the Sunday roast beef, the Sussex pudding, the green and gentle landscape.

If life was hard for Noakes and his neighbors before the war, their tenuous way of life was made worse by a terrible drought, one of the worst in living memory, and by the hardships caused by the Union blockade and the insatiable demands of, as Noakes called it, "the war fiend." For the people at the Motts, these were hard times in which their existence was stripped to the bone.

Noakes' journal begins in January 1858. An earlier book, the green book, was lost. We begin with the second volume and continue with subsequent volumes for the next 10 years. Later volumes were also lost. There are long gaps in time but Noakes' diaries tell us much about life on the raw frontier before, during and after the Civil War. We learn something from Noakes. We go where he goes and see what he sees. It is like immersing oneself in a world long past.

On Jan. 7, 1858, Noakes intended to go to Corpus Christi with his cart but a cold sleet kept him home. He boiled a pot of rice, which he mixed with a fish, for his puppy named Peter. Noakes spent much of January on organized cattle hunts, riding with George Reynolds, Joseph Wright and neighbors to find strayed cows and calves.

Noakes rode to Corpus Christi on Feb. 5 to try to collect $160 owed him for his past employment with a dredging company. Noakes called the people who owned him back wages "the mudflat people" but he couldn't collect a penny due him. He also checked on his house in town which he rented out.

On Sunday, Feb. 14, an English sailor named Peter Kershaw moved in with Noakes. They agreed to plant a field of corn and began to build a fence around the field. As he worked on his fence, Noakes killed, on average, a rattlesnake a day. Each morning, his first task was to search for his horse then search for his cattle. Noakes and neighbors tracked down and killed a panther and Noakes wrote an account of the hunt for the Nueces Valley newspaper.

At the end of September Noakes noted that the river was rising and they would have fresh water again. When the river was down, saltwater from the bay advanced up the Nueces and river water became unfit for man and stock.

Noakes was sick at the end of 1858 and his troubles rested heavily on him. He thought he had suffered the limits of ill fortune. He wrote in his diary that he was "out of grub, out of money, out of health, my horse dead, my steers vanished, no one knows where. I will let my cattle drift and be off, as I am no good at home."

He moved to Corpus Christi and stayed with the Joseph Almond family (paying for his room and board) until January. It was bitterly cold when Noakes returned home in the first week of January 1859 to find that his chickens had been killed, a heifer calf he had raised drowned in the river, and his dog Peter was shot to death by a neighbor.

In the summer of 1859, because of the newspaper article Noakes wrote about the panther hunt, Richard King at King Ranch invited Noakes and his fellow hunters to bring their dogs and go after panthers that were killing his colts. In a week of hunting they killed one panther and several bobcats and King gave each man a mare in appreciation.

In August, Noakes joined a company of cattle hunters rounding up southwest of Corpus Christi around today's Flour Bluff. They rounded up several thousand head and cut out more than 500 head belonging to the Motts crowd.

On a trip to Corpus Christi on Nov. 9, 1859, Noakes found the town excited over rumors that Juan Cortina was headed north with an army of border raiders. Martial law was declared and male inhabitants organized into the Corpus Christi Guards. Noakes decided not to do anything but keep his guns loaded and close at hand.

Noakes noted on July 26, 1860 that cattle, already weak, would begin to die because of the drought. In early August there were still no signs of rain. Noakes rode up the river with George Reynolds to rescue cattle bogged in the mud. They pulled out eight cows, a yoke of steers and a horse. They were too tired to pull out others and headed home.

Heavy rains near the end of August put the river in full flood and overflowed the bottoms. Noakes dug a ditch to drain his yard. People at the Motts celebrated their improved prospects by holding a dance, which was almost broken up uninvited guests — voracious mosquitoes.

Noakes gained new neighbors in 1860, an older German couple named Ludewig with two grown daughters. Noakes became a frequent visitor of the Misses Ludewig. In choosing between the two girls, Noakes makes it clear that while the older sister, Ellen, was better-looking, he needed a wife who knew how to work and could help him with roping, branding, and other farm chores. He described the younger daughter as a veritable Amazon who could ride and rope as well if not better than himself.

The weather was cold and frosty on Feb. 11, 1861 when Noakes rode to Corpus Christi to procure a marriage license. He left a notice of his marriage at the newspaper office. That night, he and Marie Ludewig were married by the justice of the peace at the home of her parents. Noakes wrote in his diary that he couldn't have a party because the only cash he had amounted to 30 cents. The newlyweds settled down to domestic life and hard work.

On March 18, 1861 a late frost damaged Noakes' vegetable gardens. He and Marie went fishing in the evenings and caught large catfish. On March 27, with a gray fog, Noakes joined a large party of cattle hunters. They rode around the Encinal Ranch and along the Oso Creek. Noakes afterwards criticized the excessive cruelty practiced by the cattle hunters. When he returned home, Noakes was annoyed that Marie was not there to greet him, with a hot meal ready and waiting.

The news in early 1861 was not encouraging, with war and a blockade threatened. Corpus Christi intended to raise three companies, one of which would consist of mounted riflemen from area ranches. Noakes joined this company. Frank Byler was elected captain and Noakes first lieutenant. In 1862, Noakes joined John Ireland's regular infantry company and on May 9 they marched into Corpus Christi, through nearly empty streets, and passed by where the bodies of two deserters were left hanging from a tree.

There is a gap in Noakes diary from May 1862 until late 1863. On Christmas Day 1863 Noakes, on medical leave, and Marie visited his in-laws and celebrated the holiday with an eggnog. They heard that a Yankee cavalry force had raided King Ranch. On Dec. 31, Noakes wrote that it was the end of a miserable year.

On New Year's Day 1864, Noakes noted that water inside the house froze and he had to bring his horse inside to keep him from perishing. Noakes counted 42 cows bogged in the river, mired in mud, too weak to pull out, and slowly dying. Noakes would skin dead animals for their hides, for which he had many uses. He wrote that there had been no rain worth mentioning since the previous July and that dead animals could be seen everywhere, "look which way you will."

At the end of January 1864, Noakes, not having a barrel to hold water, put up four posts and strung a deer hide between them to use as a waterproof sack to make soap. Noakes wrote that they could get no news of the war, but heard rumors that Yankees on Mustang Island would soon make a raid on the Motts. Noakes buried his valuables and slept away from the house.

Noakes and other men of the Motts gathered wagon-loads of salt at the Laguna Madre and Baffin Bay to take to inland to trade for corn, flour, bacon, whatever food they could get. The trips were hard for Noakes, who had a bad lung and was spitting up blood.

Noakes was so poor during this time that he could rarely afford to buy clothes for himself or his family. He learned to make his own shirts from buckskin, which he dyed orange, and learned how to make shoes for himself and Marie out of his own dressed leather.

On April 13, 1864 Noakes was making a saddle when it rained, the water running like a river in the hollows, and it rained again the next day. The rain changed the look of everything, with a cover of green spreading over the land. Noakes wrote that no country in the world could revive so quickly after a rain.

Noakes was a handy man. He could fix a clock, make a saddle, do carpentry work, write poetry, and paint a scene. Because manufactured goods were almost impossible to buy during the war, Noakes made his own lye soap, he made shot to kill small game by beating lead into sheets and cutting it into small squares, and he made his own sacks and "square buckets" framed of rawhide.

Noakes went to Banquete to get paid for one of his beeves that was killed to feed Confederate troops. He thought the beef was worth $15 but he was paid $2 in Confederate money. In December 1864 Noakes moved his family from the Motts to Corpus Christi where they lived until after the end of the war.

In July 1865, Noakes and three others traveled to Padre Island to salvage a boat washed up on the beach which, after much effort, sank. Back in Corpus Christi, Noakes heard the Yankees were in town and saw two regiments of black soldiers. Noakes loafed around town, hanging out at Schubert's store.

That August, Noakes prepared to move back to the farm. He hired a team and wagon driven by a man named Uncle Ned to move their furnishings to the Motts. Back at the farm Noakes took no pleasure in the resumption of his old chores. George Reynolds asked him to teach school at the Motts and Noakes began teaching on Oct. 1, 1865.

When Noakes' friend John Williams died, he expected to be named executor of the estate, which would entitle him to a percentage of the sale. But George Reynolds and James Bryden took it on themselves. A furious Noakes gave up the teaching post.

In early June 1866, Noakes went on a cattle hunt and when he returned home, he found that Marie, besides attending three horses, a mule, cows and pigs, made a pig pen and a hen house out of old fence pickets. They got a hog and three hens and Noakes noted that they were getting an extensive establishment.

It was a blowing a gale on New Year's Day 1867 and freezing cold inside, even with a blazing fire. About noon it began to sleet and from that to snow. At dusk everything was white. The river froze with ice nearly an inch thick. What is left of Noakes' diary ends on June 18, 1867 with the notation that he was engaged in doing the same chores "as every other day."

Noakes' struggles to achieve financial independence long eluded him until he opened his own store at Nuecestown. How and when Noakes' acquired a stock of merchandise and opened the store would have been detailed in another of his missing diaries. He sold land he inherited in Polegate, England and perhaps the proceeds were used to open a store at Nuecestown. Noakes' store was a well-established concern when it was burned in the bandit raid that began in the last week of March 1875. As the building burned, Noakes watched as the flames "were licking up everything except ourselves that I valued in the world."

—*Murphy Givens*

Should accident or other cause deprive me of life, I wish that the written part of this book together with the earlier part of my diary which is contained in a green book which many be found among my belongings, may be sent to England to my friends, not that I expect they will reap much benefit of either amusement or instruction from it, but that it may compensate somewhat for the neglect I have shown in not writing to them oftener. Address to Mrs. Noakes, Wannsch Farm, Willingdon, near Hurst Green, Sussex, England.

—Thomas John Noakes

Thomas J. Noakes

Found my horse sick. He cannot live another day. If I can get away anywhere, I will be off, being no good at home — out of grub, out of money, out of health, my horse dead, my steers vanished, no one knows where. I will let my cattle drift and be off, as I am no good at home.

—Dec. 3, 1858

BEFORE THE WAR
1858

January 10 (Sunday)

On Monday last it was too wet to do anything. Tuesday, January 5, and Wednesday, January 6, I helped a neighbor fix his cattle pen, making and hanging a gate for him. Thursday, January 7, I intended to go to Corpus with my cart to fetch some things but a cold driving sleet prevented me. Up till today the bad weather prevented me from doing anything but jobbing around, planting a few seeds in the garden and such like performances.

Yesterday I hunted a horse and cow which strayed from my herd. I have been hard-pressed for meat during the last week. Peter, my pet pup, has been on short rations. Having very little but milk to give him, and two or three quarts of that, Peter receives nothing more to whet his appetite. However, I boiled him a large pot of rice and with that and part of a good-sized fish I caught in the Nueces River he now feels that he is in better condition to go on living. Peter is now in the giddy stage of youth, loose limbed and big boned, and has an appetite like a lion.

He manages to keep himself fairly comfortable except in cold weather, which he eschews beyond everything. He gets as close to the fire as he possibly can, without burning his skin, not minding to burn his whiskers and eyebrows, which have been burned off so often that I believe that the fire has stopped their growth until the warm weather sets in. At this season, Peter and I are more apt to come to blows, or rather kicks, as he seems to think that the fire was created especially for overgrown pointer pups and that human beings like myself have no right to it whatever, and he is determined to stand his ground to the very last, let the consequences (the kicks) be what they may.

He would rather sacrifice a toe or two to a hot coal that has rolled from the fire than to relinquish one inch of ground. If at length after sundry hard kicks, I succeed in dislodging him from the warm spot, he immediately takes up his position close to me on one side and when routed from there he goes to the other side, and when beaten from there makes a stand between my legs.

This is going on at a time when I am cooking on the coals from the fireplace. Sometimes when I go away and leave the fire to go out, I find him on my return curled up between the firedogs among the warm ashes. He has one more failing peculiar to dogs of his age and class and that is the useless pursuit of birds which the foolish ideas of his youth lead him to think he can catch.

At one time he considered it particularly absurd that my chickens should go to roost and under that impression he placed himself beneath the hen-roost at roosting time, while I was milking and seeing to the cattle, and it was the uproarious orgy the rooster was carrying on that attracted my attention. I gave him to understand at once that his interference was unnecessary and I so impressed it upon him that he never presumed to do it again only when he felt sure I was away.

2

Peter seems to have a great respect for horses but is strongly prejudiced against cows, especially if they have young calves with them, and for sows and little pigs he has a perfect disgust — this latter is owing, no doubt, to a severe fright he sustained when a little puppy from one of those brutes. But altogether I have every reason to suppose that by the time he has reached the years of discretion he will make as fine a dog as any in Texas.

January 11 (Monday)

Went to Corpus with George Reynolds, he borrowing my steers and driving his wagon.[1] My principal object in going was to get young trees and cuttings to plant in my garden. I camped at my home in Corpus, keeping plenty of wood and water there for that purpose.

January 12 (Tuesday)

I came to an understanding with Robert Adams about my cattle wherein he proved himself like some others I have favored here, taking advantage of me in every way he could and getting as much as he possibly could out of me .[2] He has acted unjustly toward me.

January 13 (Wednesday)

Another dreary wet day. Went about five miles on the Corpus road to fetch home a mare I had bought on the day previous. She is a little gray mare, four years old and very well-made, a nice little thing.

January 14 (Thursday)

Went in the afternoon with Mr. Orchard and three others to a prairie beyond the neighboring wide strip of timber to

---

[1] George Reynolds and wife Hannah came to Texas from Oxfordshire in 1854. He got work cutting hay for the U.S. Army, which had a supply depot in Corpus Christi, then worked for Richard King on King Ranch. Reynolds lived at Nuecestown before he established his own ranch, Palo Ventana, in 1869.
[2] Robert Adams Sr. brought his family to Texas from England in 1852. He worked as a butcher in Corpus Christi. His sons, Robert Jr. and William, would later become prominent sheep and cattle ranchers in the Nueces Valley.

hunt some cows of theirs with young calves.[3] Mr. Orchard and I got parted from the rest and took a long way out where we fell in with two of his cows and we started for home. Ere we reached the timber, darkness set in and we could see nothing of the road.

Orchard grew uneasy and anxious to get through the thick bush and unless we could strike a trail, we could by no means get through that night. I must confess our prospects for that night appeared gloomy. I had nothing on but shirt and pants and the wind by this time had veered around to the northeast and was growing cold. The night set in very dark and the repeated flashes of lightning in the quarter from which the wind was blowing told us plainly that a storm was gathering. The prairie was covered with water, our horses were sinking halfway to their bellies, and between us and home was a thickly wooded mott.

We tried to find a trail for some time and we were about to give up when I luckily struck one, but we had nothing to go by until the storm cleared. By the assistance of the few stars that were visible to give us the direction, we were able to strike a trail which I knew would lead us through the next timber and so home, and our reaching there depended entirely upon taking the trail. The sky was covered by a thick canopy of clouds so that I could steer only by insight.

We floundered on, keeping the cows before us, sometimes being able to see them and sometimes not. Mr. Orchard at length began to express his doubts as to our course but I told him we could do nothing better than to hold it as nothing intervened to stop us and I felt quite sure about the direction being right.

At length, to our delight, we struck just the point to which I had been steering and soon we were at his home with the cows in the pen. Mr. Orchard's family was looking

---

[3] Stephen C. Orchard, a Baptist preacher from England, settled at Nuecestown near Noakes' place. He farmed, taught school for a time and preached on a circuit around.

4

for him with great anxiety, fearing we were lost. I took supper with them and then steered for my lonely home. I had not been there long before the thunderstorm came up and we had a rough night. I laid down and thanked my lucky stars I was not out on the wet prairie.

January 16 (Saturday)

I have done very little today as I did not feel well after the hardship we experienced when we were lost on Thursday. I shall do nothing until I rest up.

January 23 (Saturday)

On Monday last [January 18] I was seeing to my cattle. Tuesday I was putting up a gate on Reynolds pen up to dinner time and while at dinner John Orchard came running in.[4] He asked us to go shoot a panther which he thought his father's dogs had treed a short way off.

Reynolds took his revolver and I rammed a bullet into an old musket he had in the house and took it but when we reached the spot, we found it was nothing but two wild cats which the dogs had treed. I sent my bullet through the first and then reloaded and served the other the same way. I took their skins which I now have drying.

January 20 (Wednesday)

I was principally occupied getting ready for the next day.

January 21 (Thursday)

I started with George Reynolds and a neighbor named Wright for a three-day cattle hunt, returning home this evening (Saturday, Jan. 23).[5] I should think that during that time we went over upwards of ninety miles and that without getting a single head of mine, although we brought in several of the others. We met with no particular

---

[4] He was the son of the minister, Stephen Orchard.
[5] Joseph Wright and wife Seana emigrated from England in 1853.

adventures this trip, beyond the common occurrences of camping out.[6]

January 25 (Monday)

Weather wet and cold. I was unwell from painful piles (hemorrhoids) on my stern.

January 26 (Tuesday)

My piles were no better but having agreed to go on a cattle hunt with Reynolds and another neighbor, a young man named Binon [Beynon], I determined to start despite them.[7] I rode all day until I was perfectly done up, when we camped in a mott of trees in the middle of a large prairie. We had a Mexican to camp with us who, I suppose, had been to Corpus and was returning to Mexico. He rode a bay mare which had a young colt sucking her and besides himself he must have had a half a hundred-weight of store goods tied on the saddle and to top all, he carried a live hen and some gunpowder. He made himself useful in camp, for which we gave him plenty of coffee, bread and meat.

The night was very damp. Moonlight and my piles prevented me from getting any rest. The next day we were again in the saddle by sunrise, riding hard from that time till late at night, with the exception of about one hour at noon. We reached home with a cow and two heifers of mine, and several of the others, and we were all fairly tired out.

When I reached home, I found an acquaintance of mine waiting for me. His name is Curshaw, an Englishman who has been a sailor.[8] He just purchased a boat to run to

---

[6] In cow hunts, neighbors would go out as a group, generally called a "crowd", looking for each other's branded cattle that had wandered away. The range was unfenced and cattle roamed at will. The organized cow hunts gave way to the general roundup, which in time became outdated with the coming of enclosed pastures and barbed-wire fences. Noakes spent a lot of time and bother searching for strayed horses and cattle. See Appendix 1.

[7] Thomas Beynon later worked for King Ranch, was elected sheriff of Nueces County, and owned a livery stable in Corpus Christi.

[8] The correct spelling is Kershaw.

Corpus and as he owned land here he intended to settle on it and keep his boat near my place, but having no house I had told him to come and stop [stay] with me as long as he liked, so he arrived that evening.

January 28 (Thursday)

I had one of my best cows die. I skinned her and did various things about the home.

January 29 (Friday)

I was jobbing and seeing to my cattle.

February 1 (Monday)

I was riding up my cattle and jobbing at home.

February 2 (Tuesday)

I went riding with Reynolds and a man named Couling on another cattle hunt.[9] Our object was to ride to a ranch about 20 miles away and get a cow of mine which I heard had recently calved there, and then get as many cows of mine as we could find on the way home. We reached there a little before sundown and camped in some bushes about a mile from the ranch, with every prospect of having a wet night.

The owner of the ranch didn't reside on it but employed a man to superintend the cattle for him, and this man I knew, a young single man living with the Mexicans, whose wives cooked for him. He came to us soon after we camped and invited us to bring our blankets inside the house as the weather appeared rainy, but I declined, preferring to remain

---

[9] Samuel Couling, his wife Hester and son Henry lived on a small ranch a mile from the Motts called Rancho Mezquit. Robert Adams in his memoirs recalled that his father apprenticed him, as a young boy, to a freighter at Nuecestown named Samuel Colon. He said that one day when he didn't move fast enough to hitch a team of oxen, Colon threw him across a porch and broke his leg. No "Colon" has been found in the census records or historical narratives of the area. It seems likely that Robert Adams' "Samuel Colon" was Samuel Couling. Ref. Robert Adams in "Recollections of Other Days."

with the horses, but promised him we would do so in case it was very wet.

We collected all the wood we could find and with three or four old trees soon made a large fire. Soon after sundown a nasty driving rain set in, which lasted till towards morning when the wind dropped and a thunderstorm came tearing up from the opposite direction. We had managed to wait it out so far, on our saddles, the ground being too much flooded to admit of laying down but now we saw that we were going to get it beyond all reason. We agreed to make a start for the ranch. We had scarcely moved before the storm was on us and the rain came pouring down. I proceeded some distance when I remembered I left behind my revolver and so returned to get it and then made it back to my companions. We carried our saddlebags and blankets, leaving other things behind.

My companions were in such a hurry to get to the ranch that they determined to strike straight for it, but I thought the safer and surer way was to strike for a road which led to it. In case we became separated, they determined to holler for me to know if I had found the road, but at length I could not hear them in the storm.

I floundered along as well as I could in the direction of the road. The ground was covered with water, up to the top of my high boots, and I could recognize nothing, but I finally reached the road and found it a running creek. By trying to get along by the side of it I was continually falling into holes nearly to my waist. Seeing a hummock of land about the same size as myself, I laid myself down. I could see nothing with the lightning dazzling my eyes and between flashes everything was doubly dark.

I wrapped my blanket around me, determined to wait until the storm was over. The wind coming from the north blew very hard and cold. The rain soaked my clothes and my body started to chill and I began to think I would perish.

Luckily, I remembered I had a small flask of whisky in my saddlebag. I took a good long draught, which saved me as it kept my blood in circulation. When the storm was over, mustering all my strength, I made another attempt to find the ranch. After wading a considerable time, I came in sight of it. Not knowing where my companions were, I took my revolver from its waterproof case and fired two or three times. Being answered from the ranch, I knew they were all right. I found on my arrival that they had been there two or three hours.

It was nearly daybreak. We made a fire and partly dried ourselves. The vaqueros had shot several geese and gave us one. The others agreed to pluck it if I would cook it. After eating the goose and drinking hot coffee we felt a little more alive, but it was bitterly cold and we had an awful day's work before us, with wet clothes and wet blankets load enough for a horse over such ground as was between us and home.

The cold piercing wind was in our faces all the way. Of course, we gave up the cattle we were after, and would only be too glad to reach home ourselves that night. We rode the whole day and most of the time in water up to the bellies of our horses. Toward night my horse gave signs of giving out and we had six miles before us yet. I managed at length to get him home sometime after dark. We were both nearly beat. I made out to get a fire, however, and some supper and got into all the dry clothes and blankets I could muster. Next morning, I was all right again.

February 4 (Thursday)

I was about among my cattle. I had a cow calved but the calf died in the night.

February 5 (Friday)

I rode to Corpus to get some money from the Dredge Company.[10] I camped at my house, and returned the next day.[11] I accomplished nothing more than getting six grape cuttings to plant in my garden.

February 7 (Sunday)

Weather pleasant, another cow calved, but the calf also died, being deformed. I have agreed with a person to rent my town house from the first of March at four dollars a month.[12] Peter Kershaw commenced living with me today.[13]

February 14 (Sunday)

Weather beginning to feel like spring. Kershaw and I agreed to make a small field on shares. Consequently, the greater part of the past week was spent in cutting and fetching home posts for the fence. Yesterday, George Reynolds helped me plow my own field and Mr. Orchard plowed some of the land we intend to fence.

The calf that I reckoned on being dead is still alive and doing well. It was born without an opening from its bowels, but I made what nature neglected and it is now doing well, although soon after the operation I thought it was dead.

I have been waiting impatiently for the balance of the money due to me from the mudflat people.[14] They had been looking and praying for a loan from the state, which would enable them to pay us off, but I hear that they cannot obtain

---

[10] Noakes was trying to collect unpaid salary and other debt he was owed from working for the company dredging a ship channel across Corpus Christi Bay.

[11] He was referring to a house and property he purchased from Henry Kinney when he lived in Corpus Christi.

[12] Equivalent to $123 in today's dollars.

[13] Noakes alternately spelled it Curshaw and Kershaw, but the correct spelling was Kershaw.

[14] The "mudflat people" meant the D. S. Howard Company that contracted to dredge a channel through the mudflats of the bay. A bond issue of $50,000 was authorized in 1854 but costs exceeded $500,000 by 1858.

the loan, so I suppose I shall have to whistle for it [the back pay].

I also find that the title I had with my town lot in Corpus is not good in consequence of a decision of a certain court in favor of a person of the name of Jones against Col. Kinney, from whom the land was originally purchased. I expect I shall have to pay for it again or lose it. It's the same with the whole town.[15]

February 20 (Saturday)

Weather fine. Last Monday I finished plowing my field and partly planted it. On Tuesday Kershaw and I intended fetching home posts but when I found my steers (oxen), one was too lame to work. On the previous day the plow share cut his foot. We set off down the river in the boat and cut a load of wood for filling in the fence [between the posts]. On Wednesday we did the same. On Thursday I hunted my steers to see if they were fit for work; we were very desirous of getting home the posts. But I found the lame one was worse and the other appeared queer so I drove them home and unyoked them.

Towards night I could see my best steer was sick. On Friday the first thing I saw when I went to the pen was the steer lying dead. He died of the same disease as the cows; they call it bloody murrain but I do not know what it is. It appears to be a violent inflammation of the insides which cause them to discharge nothing but blood, or a liquid like it, only darker colored. It happens to the fattest cattle; very rarely a poor one dies from it. It carries them off quickly. I skinned him and took the tallow and then went digging post holes the rest of the day. I am at a loss now to know what to

---

[15] The land claim by Dr. Levi Jones of Galveston and J. Temple Doswell of New Orleans against Henry Kinney was not resolved until another court decision ruled in favor of the Jones-Doswell suit. Litigation in the case continued from 1849 until the final decision in 1873. Many of the town's landowners had to repurchase property they had bought from Kinney.

do. I cannot do the first thing without oxen, and I have no money to buy more.

There is the probability of the lame steer dying also, as he appears sick. We had the promise of a yoke of oxen from a neighbor to get some posts home. I started this morning to hunt my horse to get them but walked myself down and could not find either horse or mare, so went on digging post holes.

February 21 (Sunday)

Weather in the first part of the day very warm but towards evening a cold norther came up.

February 22 (Monday)

Very cold. Did nothing in consequence.

February 23 (Tuesday)

Borrowed a yoke of steers from Mr. Wayde [Wade] and fetched home some posts.[16]

February 24 (Wednesday)

It took me about half the day to get the oxen after which we fetched home two loads of posts.

February 25 (Thursday)

Brought home three loads of posts.

February 26 (Friday)

Did the same.

February 27 (Saturday)

One of the oxen being lame, I was getting filling-in wood from the river bank and fetched one load of posts.[17]

February 28 (Sunday)

Morning very warm but a norther blew up about noon and now it is very cold. Went with Kershaw for a short sail

---

[16] John L. Wade emigrated with his parents from Yorkshire, England in 1852. His father, also John Wade, died soon after they arrived in Corpus Christi. John L. Wade lived at Nuecestown and married Sarah Beynon in 1861. Wade later established a ranch on the old Casa Blanca grant. He died in 1898.

[17] Common fences in Noakes time were constructed of upright posts, set four to eight feet apart, and filled between with smaller poles and mesquite brush interlaced horizontally and tied off with rawhide.

in his boat but when the norther came on we had to leave her four or five miles down the river and walk home.

March 6 (Saturday)

A strong norther is blowing again. It came up in the night accompanied by thunder and rain. We had a nice shower. The balance of the week has been warm. The oxen which I was forced to borrow from Mr. Wade both lamed themselves by some method or other so that I could use them no longer. I was compelled (if I would finish my field, and that is all I have to depend on for a living) to borrow a yoke from Reynolds with which I have been getting posts as fast as I can.

The last two days I have been nearly broke down from a swollen foot; in fact, the whole week my feet have been so sore from blistering that I could hardly walk. Had an old boatman, a chum of Kershaw's, stay here the last two days. He brought us plenty of fine oysters.

March 13 (Saturday)

Weather warm, the trees and shrubs coming into leaf and blossom, showing every indication of spring. Most of the past week has been spent in getting the field furrowed. Mr. [Stephen] Orchard has been plowing it for us and finished today. I have been sadly hindered for the want of oxen, so have done very little to the fence; in fact, most of the days have been spent cooking, as Orchard and his son John have eaten here.

On Thursday I went to look among my cattle but could not find them. I borrowed a horse on Friday with which to catch my own. After dinner I started to seek my herd, but could not find a single head. I have been hunting them the whole day today, but with no better success. I am very much afraid they are gone clear off and if so, I have all my hunting to do over again.

Received a letter from Emily the other day.[18] This week I have sown watermelons, pumpkins, lettuce and squash seed. I hoed up my Irish potatoes and planted shallots and garlic.

March 14 (Sunday)

Fetched home my cattle today from about six miles away.

March 21 (Sunday)

Weather fine, but continued indications of rain. We have not had a real norther for a fortnight.

March 22 (Monday)

On Monday last I attended a cattle gathering at Col. Parkinson's but found none of mine.[19]

March 23 (Tuesday)

I went to Corpus to fetch a steer I had bought from Mr. [Robert] Adams [Sr.]. I made a trade for a horse from him at the same time. I tried to do a little business in town but could not get on, so left disgusted and reached home with the steer about sundown.

The next morning, I took my horse to get in my other steer, turning the fresh one out to feed. I hunted all day but could not find him. When I returned home the other one had left.

March 24 (Wednesday)

My cow died and it took most of the day to skin her, render the tallow, and stretch the hide. I replanted most of my field, the first crop being eaten up by something.

March 25 (Thursday)

My horses were all loose and away so the first thing I had to hunt and catch one of them, after which I hunted the whole day unsuccessfully for the two steers. I came home at night, tired and disheartened.

---

[18] His sister.
[19] Col. H. Parkinson was listed as a rancher and stock-raiser in the Nueces Valley, July 17, 1858.

March 26 (Friday)

We thought, since we could get no steers, we would take Kershaw's boat up the river and bring home a load of wood for the fence. We cut and loaded the boat and had to drag her along with a rope, there being a strong head wind. We dragged her till dark and with the wind getting stronger we had to leave her and walk home.

March 27 (Saturday)

Mr. Orchard lent us a yoke of steers if we could find them. Kershaw and I started early and walked to nearly midday before we found them. In the p. m. we brought home one load of filling-in wood for the fence and that was all that we did worthwhile all week, although we worked every day early and late.

My dog Peter was bit in the head by a large rattlesnake while with us on the prairie. I killed the snake and put some of the fat on the wound, which continued to swell until night, one eye being completely swollen shut. The next day it subsided and he is now all right. I have killed six rattlesnakes in the past week, and have nearly a bottle full of oil from them.

March 28 (Sunday)

Walked all day to find a horse to drive a cow and calf home but came home tired and determined to let things "rip" as they say here.

March 29 (Monday)

Still loading wood for the fence.

March 30 (Tuesday)

Same as Monday.

March 31 (Wednesday)

Started early to sail to Corpus, Kershaw and I in his boat, the weather being fair. We had to go as we were out of everything in the grub line, having no bread or flour. We got aground several times and had to go overboard to lighten her off. I took three hides and some tallow, the proceeds of which went to paying some of my debts. I did as much as I could in the way of business in the town and slept that night in the boat.

April 1 (Thursday)

We started for home with nothing but a bag of Indian corn, not being able to get anything else, as I had no money, although I had owing me in town one hundred and sixty dollars. Just about sundown we ran onto a mud reef and although we were doing our best long after dark to get her off, we had to give it up and turn in on the boat till morning.

April 2 (Friday)

The wind was more aft and after a deal of trouble we got the boat into deep water and ran her into the inner (Corpus Christi) bay where we got some oysters. We had our gun, net, fish spear, line and oyster tongs, so we were ready for anything. We stayed at the island and fished awhile and then made for some more islands farther up the bay, expecting to get some eggs. We ran onto an oyster reef and got stuck. We were compensated with as many oysters as we wanted.

After a time, we regained deep water and made sail with a fresh wind in our favor for home. When we reached the river bar we again grounded and stayed until I caught as many fish as we wanted with my net, which I did in two throws.[20]

I pushed the boat over the bar and we entered the river. Just then a large alligator showed his ugly head within a few yards of the boat. I presented him with the contents of my gun and he disappeared. As we were sailing very fast at the time, we did not stop to see if the shot had taken effect. We made home about sunset.

---

[20] Sandbar at the mouth of the Nueces River in Nueces Bay.

April 3 (Saturday)

Spent the day hunting in vain for steers and horses, hoed my corn in the little field, and put in some seeds for beans, squash, pumpkins and watermelons.

April 4 (Sunday)

Weather warm and dry. Hunted on foot till 12 o'clock and brought home the steers, and this evening a neighbor brought home my horse, so I hope to be all right for tomorrow.

April 5, 6, 7 (Monday, Tuesday, Wednesday)

We were fetching home wood.

April 8 (Thursday)

I had a swelling on the instep of my left foot but I fetched home two loads of wood and then rode out for the third time to try and hunt down two cows which had young calves on the prairie, but this time I could do nothing. One I could not find and the other had hid her calf and would not go to it. The time previous I found them both and had run them off the prairie and was coming by the mesquite tree at the back of my place when they began their dodge. I ran one till her calf dropped when I left her and ran the other which took to the timber and bushes, dodging me in every direction, and every place where she knew I could not follow on a horse. At last I dismounted, tied my horse in a hurry, and ran her out on foot. When I returned for my horse, I could not find him. I didn't take sufficient notice of the spot to remember where it was. I hunted until I was pretty well tired out before I found him.

I commenced another round with the cow who by this time had recovered her wind and ran into the trees. I rode after her for a long time, nearly tearing myself to pieces in the process. At length I had her out in the open and thought I had her beat, when she made another run for the thicket. As I was running her, one of my stirrup leathers broke and that ended the chase. The darned cow was pretty much a mile away before I could fix up the stirrup again. If anybody wants to see animal instinct at work, let them take to driving old cows with calves.

April 9, 10 (Friday and Saturday)

My foot was too bad for walking so I remained at home, mending some broken things. This morning [Saturday] it was hot and sultry until about eight o'clock when a norther came blustering in and now it is quite cool. My foot is very painful. I can hardly touch the ground with it. I have killed, on average, a rattlesnake a day over the past week. We are not on a flourishing footing in the grub line. We have had nothing in the house this week but milk and cornbread.

April 11 (Sunday)

Weather fair. This week has been a busy one.

April 12 (Monday)

Went to a cattle branding about 17 miles from here to get a cow and calf and heifer of mine. On my way I saw one of my horses that was dead. I knew my cow and calf were there. I went with three of my neighbors and, although a friend had seen the cow there, I did not get a sight of her. We went too late. The cattle were all turned loose.

April 15 (Thursday)

We started on a cattle hunt, there being seven of us. We were mounted, armed and fit for anything. We rode the whole day and camped at night about 25 or 30 miles away.

April 16 (Friday)

We were in the saddle a little after daylight and toward night we made the Gregory Ranch.[21] After a good deal of trouble we managed to pen several head of cattle belonging to everybody, among which was my long-sought cow. It was now sundown and we rode to a convenient place and camped, falling in with two more friends and neighbors on the same mission. Nine of us camped together.

---

[21] William S. Gregory, a Nueces County Commissioner in the 1850s, was the superintendent of a 60,000-acre ranch that was 15 miles south of Corpus Christi. The ranch was owned by Brownsville merchant Charles Stillman.

After supper I and one of the other men went to the pen to see if all was right when we found the bars had been let down and all the cattle were out and all our trouble for nothing. We suspected the Mexicans of doing it but we could not be sure enough to do anything about it. I believe they did it to let my cow go, as I found that they had branded and earmarked the calf.[22] The man who superintends the ranch was in Corpus so I could nothing about it then.

April 17 (Saturday)

We hunted in vain for the cattle and at length struck for home with nothing. However, we picked up two or three head as we rode along.

April 18 (Sunday)

I reached home in the middle of the afternoon with my horse fairly broke down. Another week gone and nothing accomplished.

April 19 (Monday)

I went hunting for my steers but could not find them. Rode my horse down, then came home and jobbed about all day.

April 20 (Tuesday)

Kershaw was hunting for the steers all day on foot, without success. I was fencing.

April 21 (Wednesday)

I hunted on foot all day for the strayed steers, without success.

April 22 (Thursday)

I hoed my corn and worked in the small field.

---

[22] A cut made in the ear of livestock to show ownership. A few of the many kinds of earmarks included: crop-eared, dewlap, over-bit or under-bit, jingle-bob, jug-handled, steeple-fork, swallow-fork, under-slope, under-split, wattle. Ref. Ramon Adams, "Western Words."

April 23 (Friday)

Kershaw and I worked on the fence, using all the wood we had fetched home.

April 24 (Saturday)

We could do no more to the fence, so we started with the boat and went up the river to get all the mulberries and dewberries we came across.

April 26 (Monday)

We got back Monday morning with a few mulberries and dewberries. I shot at two turkeys but could not hit one. We were hunting all day Sunday, thinking it was Saturday, and instead of getting home Sunday, as we thought, we found it was Monday. Texas all over this spring is infested with grasshoppers. In some places they have destroyed every growing thing. They have not as yet done much damage to my corn, although they have eaten all my garden stuff.

April 27 (Tuesday)

I was riding in search of my steers again, but could not find them.

April 28 (Wednesday)

I was making a cheese for Mr. Orchard.

April 29 (Thursday)

I finished the fence and rode out to see about my cattle.

April 30 and May 1 (Friday and Saturday)

Mr. Orchard, Kershaw and I started in the boat and went up the river to get some grapes. We gathered about a bushel of grapes by nightfall and camped in the trees by the river. I went to a turkey roost. I was after the turkeys but could not get a shot. I cut and loaded as many palmettoes as I wanted, after which Kershaw and I (Mr. Orchard already having gone home) gathered some more grapes. We then took on board a party of young men and their sisters from

Nuecestown.[23] We let them gather as many grapes as they wanted. They had tied their horses in nearby trees.

The grapes that grow abundantly on this river are called muscadine grapes. They are large black grapes with thick skins that are somewhat sour. The vines grow among the branches of the river trees and hang out over the water, giving the scenery a beautiful appearance, especially when loaded with grapes.

I believe that if we had wanted to take the time, we could have filled the boat with grapes. They were small and green at this time of year and used for making preserves and pies. In this state they resemble green gooseberries and are preferable to the riper ones.

The party of young men and their sisters went ashore and we set sail for home, having to beat the whole way against a head wind. We kept on till dark then came to and cooked supper. We turned in till about 11 o'clock, for the moon to rise. The weather showed evident signs of a coming storm and we wanted to get home before it came on. As soon as the moon rose, we were on our way and after beating about we reached our mooring place just as the storm came up. The lightning and thunder were severe and we had a splendid rain which lasted till morning.

May 2 (Sunday)

Weather cool and pleasant with a norther blowing in and thunder rumbling in the distance.

May 3 (Monday)

Rode to a place eight miles away and at length got my steers and fetched home one load of wood before night fell.

---

[23] Noakes and his neighbors usually referred to Nuecestown as "The Motts." It was founded in the early 1850s by Henry Kinney and settled by immigrants from England. Kinney's land sales scheme offered English settlers a free town lot in Nuecestown for every hundred acres they purchased. See Appendix 2.

May 4 (Tuesday)

Weeding and fencing all day. Hunted home a cow and a calf in the evening.

May 5 (Wednesday)

Mr. Orchard and Reynolds helped us plow and plant the field with corn. Mr. [Joseph] Wright also helped on the condition that I would repair his plow as soon as I could.[24]

May 6 (Thursday)

In the morning I put the plow to right while Mr. Wright took my place at the weeding. After cooking dinner, I went fencing. The reason we planted before we finished the fence was on account of the recent rain and lateness of the season. This will compel us to finish the fence before the corn comes up.

May 7 (Friday)

Weeding and fencing.

May 8 (Saturday)

Got John Williams to cut wood for us. Kershaw drove the steers and I worked on the fence.

May 16 (Sunday)

The past week was spent entirely at the field fence which we were in hopes of finishing yesterday, but one of the wheels of the cart was damaged and will hinder us till we can get it fixed. The other evening [afternoon] I fetched home a young heifer which had calved. She was so spiteful I could do nothing with her. She ran at me several times and it was only by hard fighting that I escaped injury.

For the last few days I have felt very unwell, being so weak that it is a trouble to move, and having a nasty hoarseness on my chest. The weakness I attribute to the want of more nourishing food, and hard work. I have lived

---

[24] Noakes used the British spelling, plough, but we substituted the American usage, plow, both as verb and noun. Noakes doesn't say, but the typical plow at that time and place was fashioned of tough mesquite wood fitted with handles and a point of iron.

now for weeks on corn alone, which we grind ourselves, and eat with milk. Such fare may do to idle on but will not do for heavy work. I cannot get enough money as to buy the necessaries of life, although I have still a good sum owed me by the Dredge Boat Company. To get things on credit is the last thing I will do before starving.

May 23 (Sunday)

On Monday and Tuesday, we worked on the field fence, which we finished on the latter day. We should have finished it on Monday had not the wheel of my cart hindered me, taking a long time to fix, besides feeling very unwell.

May 26 (Wednesday)

I was hunting for my horse the first half of the day without hearing or seeing anything of him. I want him badly to hunt my cattle, which have been neglected while the field has engaged my attention. My other horse is sick and the mare has just foaled, so I have only the missing one to ride. The rest of the day was occupied in getting home firewood.

May 27 (Thursday)

Kershaw and I went to Corpus for provisions. I took my cart and oxen. We started very early in the morning and reached home a little after 12 at night.

May 28 (Friday)

I was hunting again all day for my horse but could not find him. In the evening I drove the mare up, intending to ride her in search of the other one, as it is impossible to go far on foot.

May 29 (Saturday)

I was riding most of the day in search of the horse, attended a sale of cattle in the town and hoed some of the field.

May 31 (Monday)

Found my horse on the prairie and chased him home.

June 1 (Tuesday)

I was cattle hunting, which I have been principally engaged at up till now. The last three days have been very blustery from strong southerly gales. We are beginning to feel the want for rain.

June 6 (Sunday)

I have been principally occupied in the past week at cattle hunting. On Thursday I went out to try and shoot a deer but although I wounded two or three, I did not succeed in getting one.

June 7 (Monday)

I went out in search of a cow and calf, riding my mare. She had not been ridden for a long time and the colt being left at home made her foolish and she managed to throw me twice before I got back.

June 8 (Tuesday)

We commenced to plow the corn in the field but the plow broke as soon as we began and put an end to that.

June 9 (Wednesday)

I found and fetched home the cow and calf. I was all day getting her home, as the calf was very bad with maggots.

June 10 (Thursday)

Today a lot of us started to hunt a panther that has been killing calves, but the dogs could not pick up the scent.

June 12 (Saturday)

I was busy at home. We had a shower Friday and for a short time a tremendous squall of wind.

June 13 (Sunday)

I had a fine lot of watermelons ready to cut and intended to go to Corpus with them to sell tomorrow. They would be worth a good deal. But last night the possums destroyed the whole crop. It is very disheartening.

June 14 (Monday)

I planted some potato vines in the morning. About 10 o'clock a heavy rain and storm came up, which did considerable damage to Wright's home.[25] In the afternoon I rode out to find the steers, but could not do so.

June 15 (Tuesday)

I found the steers and took back the broken plow and was going to get another but found the ground too wet to plow.

June 16 (Wednesday)

I borrowed a plow and team of oxen from Mr. Orchard to try to get the field finished that is plowed between the corn, but we had hardly commenced before that plow also broke. We let the steers out and knocked off.

June 17 (Thursday)

Kershaw and I went up the river in the boat to cut a piece of timber to use to fix the plow. It took us all day to go. I could hardly walk from a bad foot again. My hard boots without socks hurt the instep of my left foot.

June 18 (Friday)

Laid up with my sore foot. Had a calf die, which I skinned.

June 19 (Saturday)

My foot is still too bad to do any heavy work. In the morning I cleaned my clock and worked most of the day on a fishing net I am making.

June 20 (Sunday)

Took a bath in the river, which is running high from a heavy freshet. At most places the river is over its banks.

June 21 (Monday)

The flies this summer are very troublesome, especially among the cows and calves. The cow I lost the other day was because of that. The least sore on an animal becomes

---

[25] Noakes called it a hurricane. No record of a hurricane is shown for June 1858 on the Texas Coast so it may have been a tropical storm. The Nueces Valley on June 19, 1858 reported some damage in the town caused by "a fearful gale, though of short duration."

flyblown and filled with maggots. Mr. Orchard came to help me and we finished plowing the corn.

June 22 (Tuesday)

I was cattle hunting and fetched up the steers to get a plow from Mr. Wade to plow up some ground to plant sweet potatoes, which I did this evening.

June 23 (Wednesday)

We tried all we could to make the steers pull the plow but could not do it. Kershaw knows nothing of driving steers and the steers have been very little worked at the plow. I saw that it was no use trying anymore so we let the steers out.

June 24 (Thursday)

I was jobbing at home and made a fish cage to keep fish alive in the river. It is a kind of box made in the shape of a boat that will let water run through it.

June 25 (Friday)

Kershaw and I started early in the morning in the boat for a day's fishing on the bay. We found that all the fresh water [from the river flooding] was keeping the fish away. We caught only a dozen mullet after trying all day.

June 26 (Saturday)

Kershaw went to Corpus in his boat. I was at home jobbing in the morning. In the afternoon I started to hunt for a missing heifer but the rain stopped me from going very far.

June 27 (Sunday)

Weather wet all day.

June 28, 29 (Monday and Tuesday)

Jobbing at home both days.

June 30 (Wednesday)

Cattle hunting.

July 1 (Thursday)

Panther hunt all day.

July 2 (Friday)

Went to meet most of the Motts folks for a panther hunt. After a good deal of trouble mustering about half a dozen of them and a neighbor's hounds, we started by moonlight for some trees on a prairie a few miles off. This was where a person the day before found the fresh remains of a calf which the panther had killed and buried in the grass for a future meal.

As soon as we came to the trees, we found the calf had been moved and more had been eaten from it and at the same moment the hounds started at full cry on some trail. From the direction it led we were afraid they were running on the heel scent but we could not call them off and so kept after them as hard as we could across a rough prairie.

We came to a dense jungle of thorny bushes with now and then a tree standing in the midst. Into this thicket the hounds ran him. By this time, we had little doubt that they were running him, hot on the scent. After making it a little too warm for his earthly comfort, the dogs treed him. The thing now was to get through the bushes to within a sure shot of the tree, which four of us started to do.

We had to crawl on our bellies at the expense of our clothes, pieces of which we were continually leaving behind. We came to within easy shot and poked our heads clear of the bushes to take aim. Before we could do so, we saw the panther spring down and lose himself in the heavy thicket.

We were standing almost immovably in the thorny mass, without being able to see more than a yard or two in any direction. The only way to get out was on our bellies which, snake-like, we proceeded to do. This mode of locomotion might have been pleasant enough in some situations, but not so much with a panther running about.

Before we reached the outside the dogs treed him again. One of the men on the outside fired a long shot and wounded him. We all fired at him, but found that we had to go into the thicket again to get a good shot at him. We went back in and when within 20 yards another man and I fired together, both balls taking effect and he came tumbling down.

We could hear from the cries of the dogs that a tooth-and-nail fight was being carried on and we scrambled to the scene of the action. Before we could get there, her combative organs were stilled in death. We found her to be a female and her cubs were likely not far off. She had been hit by four balls, one of which had only grazed the skin. We dragged her to the outside of the thicket after a while.

We put her on one of the horses and carried her to the first neighbors, where we skinned her. We drew straws for the skin, which was not my lot to win, and then went home.

July 3 (Saturday)

Went to Corpus with Thomas Wright.[26] I wanted to get some things (wine and sweet cakes) for a dance at the Motts.[27] I also bought some clothes, which I sadly needed. Colonel Kinney arrived in Corpus on Wednesday last and a few days previous a steamer, the Texas, paid a visit to the town.[28]

As we had planned, we struck into the prairie from Corpus to hunt for cattle on our way home. Several head of mine had strayed in that direction. The day was extremely hot and sultry, without the usual breeze. We found and

---

[26] Thomas Charles Wright (T. C.) came to Texas with his parents, Joseph and Seana Wright, in 1853. He later worked for Richard King and established his own ranch south of Orange Grove.

[27] In Noakes' diary, "The Motts" referred to Nuecestown. In general, the word referred to a grove or clump of trees that served as a landmark, an island of timber, in an otherwise open prairie. Some of these landmarks were named, such as Britton Motts, Chocolate Motts, and Grulla Motts.

[28] Henry Kinney, the founder of Corpus Christi, had been gone four years as he undertook what came to be a failed filibustering venture in the Mosquito region of Nicaragua. He was welcomed home with a ball in his honor on July 12, 1858. The Nueces Valley said the reception closed "as a matter of course with a joyful dance, in which the distinguished guest fought again his battles of conquest, appearing more than ever youthful, gay and gallant."

fetched home a cow and calf of Wright's but saw not a sign of anything belonging to me.

July 4 (Sunday)

I have felt unwell all day and am taking medicine.

July 5 (Monday)

I still feel badly. Have been jobbing around a little.

July 7 (Wednesday)

I went to a dance, which several of us had got up in the town. Feeling unwell, I came home again after about half an hour.

July 11 (Sunday)

The Valley paper[29] came out this week with an account of our panther hunt, which I sent to the editors for that purpose.

July 12 (Monday)

Preparing for the following day's trip.

July 13 (Tuesday)

Started early with two neighbors and a boy for a four-day cattle hunt. We had to ride until night without water, as the place where we had expected to stay at in the middle of the day was dry. At night we camped near a swamp where the mosquitoes were very bad.

July 14 (Wednesday)

In the saddle by sunrise. We were hunting among a large drove of cattle owned by Capt. Britton but found none we were after.[30] We crossed a creek and began hunting among the Encinal cattle we had found and penned 14 head of

---

[29] The Nueces Valley newspaper in Corpus Christi was established in 1851 by Benjamin F. Neal. By 1858, it was being published by James Barnard and Somers Kinney.

[30] Forbes Britton, a state senator, owned a ranch eight miles west of Corpus Christi. It was called "The Motts" and sometimes "Britton Motts." Ref. "When Corpus Christi Was Young: The Recollections of Anna Moore Schwien."

mine and one of the boy's [on the expedition].[31] We camped in some bushes.

July 15 (Thursday)

Same as yesterday. Still hunting cattle. At it again soon after daylight and by 10 o'clock had found several more. After we roped and counter-branded one of mine, which had been branded by mistake, we started for the next ranch, with 21 head of cattle. We reached the next ranch about 3 o'clock and the first thing selected a camping place and took something to eat. We were now on short allowance of grub, in consequence of one's coming with only sufficient food for two meals. We ate our allowance and then some of us saddled up again and took a hunt around the camp but found nothing.

At night we penned the cattle in the pen and turned in for the night. One of our party was an old man, an Irishman, our worthy magistrate. He had never been out at night before and we had fine fun with him. The sun during the day burned his nose so he made a paper plaster for it, and what with that, and the common inconvenience of camping out, which seemed nothing to us, the poor old fellow was sadly put out.

July 16 (Friday)

Started to hunt and drive our way home. Found two more head along the way and reached home about 4 o'clock, tired and hungry. When I went into the house, I found Kershaw away and not a thing in the house to eat or cook. I had to make myself contented with a melon which I took from the garden.

July 17 (Saturday)

Herding cattle all day.

---

[31] The Encinal Peninsula between Cayo del Oso and the Laguna Madre is where Flour Bluff is today.

July 18 (Sunday)

I am obliged to herd the cattle very closely or they will get away.

July 25 (Sunday)

For the past week I have done nothing but herd my cattle, penning them every night.

July 26 (Monday)

Went to a cattle gathering at Col. Parkinson's. As I was going down by the river, my horse stumbled and fell and we rolled over, but nothing was hurt. I found no cattle of mine there.

July 27 (Tuesday)

Same as before. Attending my cattle all day.

July 28, 29 (Wednesday, Thursday)

I did nothing but job around at home.

July 30 (Friday)

I was at home all day and in the afternoon, as I was going to the river to bathe, a couple of friends came along so we all went together. We were swimming about, the other two on the other side of the river, when I struck into some long stringy weeds which pulled me down. I could not get my head above water till I was near exhausted. The others thought I was diving for fun, as I could not call for help. I finally struggled to the shore. The water was about eight feet deep where I went under and, I believe, I would have drowned if I had been alone, since I would have been more frightened.

August 1 (Sunday)

Everything has been getting very dry for the past week or so.

August 2 (Monday)

I was at an election at the Motts.[32]

---

[32] It was held at the school house.

31

August 3 (Tuesday)
Went to Corpus. Sent a letter to Uncle Richard.
August 4, 5, 6 (Wednesday, Thursday, Friday)
Critters in my corn. Jobbing at home.
August 7 (Saturday)
Crossed the river and took a long hunting excursion on foot. The heat was great.
August 8 (Sunday)
Weather very hot with a few passing thundershowers.
August 9 (Monday)
Crossed the river in the boat and took my rifle for a hunt. I found plenty of tracks of panthers, turkeys and deer but the heat was so great that they had all retired to the thick cover. As I went through the swamp, I crossed the tracks of an alligator that must have been 17 or 18 feet long. I crept up on a buck and crippled him, but I did not follow up on account of the heat. I had been walking all day with only some saltwater to drink [from the river].
August 10 (Tuesday)
I was at home.
August 11 (Wednesday)
I rode out and killed a fine buck.
August 12 (Thursday)
I rode out among the cattle and cured the deer meat.
August 13, 14 (Friday and Saturday)
I did very little besides read and cook, the heat being very great. This is the hottest weather we have had this summer.
August 15 (Sunday)
Mr. Orchard saw a panther near here so we are in hopes of another hunt. I have been trying all week to shoot a large alligator which has taken up quarters at my watering place on the river. He has been too sharp for me so far.
August 16, 17 (Monday and Tuesday)
I was jobbing at home.

August 18 (Wednesday)

I was going to a stock association meeting, the first one held by the stock raisers in this country to organize themselves.[33] I could not find my horse until it was too late to go. I stayed at home. In the evening I shot an alligator in the river but with Kershaw being away with his boat I could not get him. In the morning when I was hunting for my horse, I killed two skunks.

August 19 (Thursday)

I was jobbing at home.

August 20 (Friday)

Towards evening one of the Wright boys and I went up the river to hunt turkeys, there being a nice moon for the fun. We had poor luck and only got one apiece.

August 21 (Saturday)

I went out to try and kill a deer but when I reached the place where I expected to find them, I found some hunters camped there. Consequently, the deer had run off. I struck off in another direction and came across a doe, which had been shot the previous day but had got away and died. I took her hide, but didn't fancy the meat. I unsaddled my horse and laid down in the shade. One of the hunters belonging to the camp I had struck in the morning came along and I went on with him. We did not go far before we killed a fawn which I packed on my saddle. A short time later we killed a doe and I came home.

August 22 (Sunday)

Went with a neighbor to a lake six miles off to watch for cattle as they came up to drink, but we found none of ours.

August 23 (Monday)

Was at home.

---

[33] The meeting Noakes missed, according to the Nueces Valley, was held at Santa Margarita on the Nueces River, at Miller's Ferry. Among the principal stock-raisers and ranchers who attended were Robert Love, H. Parkinson, Hamilton P. Bee, and W. S. Gregory.

August 24 (Tuesday)

I went to a dance at the Motts and stayed up till morning.

August 25 (Wednesday)

Went out and killed two fawns.

August 27 (Friday)

Went up the river with Reynolds and Orchard hunting cattle.

August 28 (Saturday)

Crossed the river to hunt for deer but did not get a shot.

August 29 (Sunday)

Weather fine.

August 30 (Monday)

Jobbing at home.

August 31 (Tuesday)[34]

Hunted the whole day in order to kill some game for the next day but had bad luck.

September 1 (Wednesday)

Hitched my steers [oxen] to my cart and drove into town to be loaded up for a picnic, which was to come off today. There were two carts and one wagon full that started together, the greater part having gone ahead on horseback. The place of the meeting was at a very beautiful spot miles up the river. At length it was reached in safety, finding about 40 horses tethered among the trees. About half of the riders were young ladies.

The spot by the river was one of those particularly beautiful places. The majestic trees skirting the river were intertwined with vines of wild grapes which, weaving among the long waving moss, hung in magnificent festoons from the branches. Beneath the trees the yucca and palmetto grew in great beauty and above this the rugged

---

[34] Noakes' calendar may have been out of date. Tuesday was the last day of August though he put it down as the first day of September.

face of high precipitous bluffs stood out in romantic forms, here and there overgrown by stunted shrubs.

Amid such scenes and with a sociable party, among which were some very pretty and attractive girls, and an abundance of good things to eat and drink, we could do no other but enjoy ourselves to the fullest extent. This we did. During the afternoon we amused ourselves dancing to the tune of a fiddle, singing songs, and playing various games till dusk. We took tea and then hitched up and drove to the Motts. We finished the day with a good dance in an empty store.

September 2 (Thursday)

Riding among my cattle and searching for a horse that belongs to Adams.

September 3 (Friday)

Jobbing at home.

September 4 (Saturday)

In the morning I wrote an account of the picnic to the editors of the Valley and in the afternoon went and tried, with no luck, to shoot some turkeys.

September 5 (Sunday)

Weather cool and pleasant.

September 12 (Sunday)

At the commencement of the week I made two or three attempts to start for Corpus but rain prevented me so at length I gave it up. I have employed myself jobbing about at home.

September 13 (Monday)

Working on my pig pound.

September 15 (Wednesday)

Fetched home my pie that I bought from George Reynolds.[35] I rode into the Motts to get some beef as a neighbor had killed a steer.

---

[35] A "pie" was a piebald horse with patches of white and black colors.

September 17 (Friday)

Went up to help Reynolds brand some cows. In the afternoon Reynolds, Mr. Orchard and I went up the river to get some turkeys when they came to roost. Mr. Orchard killed a couple and so did I.

September 18 (Saturday)

Worked all day at Mr. Orchard's making him some ox yokes.

September 19 (Sunday)

During the night I was very sick.

September 20 (Monday)

Still sick.

September 21 (Tuesday)

Sick all day. Could do nothing but lie on the cot.

September 22 (Wednesday)

Feeling very sick and queer. I borrowed some blue pills. I could hardly move and only with great difficulty could see to my cows and pigs.

September 23 (Thursday)

Same as yesterday.

September 24 (Friday)

I was still sick with a high fever. I could stay at home no longer, no one having come to see me for days. I got on the horse and rode up to Reynolds. I was there only a few minutes when I became considerably worse and started back home. Luckily a young man, Thomas Wright, one of my chums, was waiting to see me.

I got him to see to my horse, threw myself on my cot, and was soon shivering under a couple of blankets. I told the young man not to stay as I would soon be better. But the fever that followed seemed to take away my reason and when I came to myself it was near night. I had eaten nothing for several days and my nervous system had all but collapsed. After the fever went down, I was in a daze.

Before Wright left, I got him to shut the front door to keep the chickens from getting into the house.

I suffered delusions caused by brain fever. I found if I stayed alone any longer, I might lose my mind. I had the horrors on me. Everything was dirty and nasty and I was too ill to light a fire to warm the house or clean anything. I did not know how in the world to let anybody know my state and I could not remain alone any longer. As luck would have it, Mr. Orchard's daughter was out for a ride and came by the house. I was only too glad to send word to her father.

In the evening Mr. Orchard, his son, and Mr. Reynolds came to see me. Before leaving, Reynolds made me agree to shut up the old place the next morning and come stay with him until I got better. John Orchard, the son, stayed with me that night and saw to my cattle.

September 25 (Saturday)

Went up to Reynolds' to stay. Still very sick.

September 26 (Sunday)

Had another bout of chills and fever in the middle of the day.

September 27 (Monday)

Mrs. Reynolds and her child are very sick today, so much so that she cannot do anything. Mrs. Orchard came to help her. Up to the present, I haven't eaten anything besides a little bread. The weather is very unhealthy for this country. It may be owing to the comet, which is now visible at night in the northwest.[36]

At my request a Dr. McKelvey called to see me. He is an old gentleman, a medical man who has taken to stock-raising and owns a ranch four miles off. He does not practice his profession here but is kind and generous in giving advice gratis to his neighbors. He told me I was

---

[36] Donati's Comet was visible in the northern hemisphere between September 1858 and March 1859.

suffering from a very violent bilious attack attended with fever and gave me 15 grams of calomel.

September 28 (Tuesday)

The first thing I took a strong dose of castor oil and was very sick all day.

September 29 (Wednesday)

Took three doses of quinine before the chill came on, which was about 12 o'clock.

September 30 (Thursday)

Came home, as I was able to do for myself.

October 1 (Friday)

Did little jobs indoors. Today I saw the first geese and ducks pass over, indicating that cold weather is not far off.

October 2 (Saturday)

No return of fever since Wednesday. Today I have diarrhea, which makes me weak.

October 3 (Sunday)

Dined at George Reynolds' for a change.

October 4, 5 (Monday and Tuesday)

Feeling better and jobbing around a little.

October 6 (Wednesday)

Went to the river to get some water to cook with. Came down with chills and fever, but by evening I was better.

October 7 (Thursday)

Stayed indoors all day and nursed the chill.

October 8 (Friday)

Hoed some in the field. Came down with another chill and fever. Felt awfully wretched. I had not seen a soul since yesterday and no one came near me. When the fever was on me, I would give anything for somebody to be near me. The day seemed to never end and yet I dreaded the night. Of all the miseries endured in a wild country, the worst is being ill and alone. If any of my neighbors knew that I required assistance, they would be with me, but sometimes I can get along alone. But when I am taken so much worse, I have no means of letting my neighbors know and so have to stick it out.

I have to see to my stock, although I am hardly able to crawl. Everybody you see has a different remedy and you don't know what to do. But whatever it is you ought to have, you cannot get it for love or money.

October 9 (Saturday)

I have fallen off to nothing but skin and bones. Kershaw and a man named Neal came this morning and will stay all day. I am glad to have company. I took about 25 grams of calomel.

October 10 (Sunday

Saturday night I took as near as I could guess 25 grams of calomel and early Sunday, I took a large dose of castor oil. The effect of so much medicine of course made me very ill. The chill and fever came on about nine a.m. and lasted two or three hours. About the middle of the day Dr. McKelvey called to see me and gave directions on how to proceed with myself.

October 11 (Monday)

I took three doses of quinine, which has broken the chill and which up to the present time has not returned. My neighbors during the past week have been exceedingly kind, finding that I could not bake or get anything from Corpus, they have sent me bread and little things, which have been very acceptable. My near neighbors seem to be tired of me so it's my farthest neighbors who are most kind now.

October 15, 16 (Friday and Saturday)

I have had meat and was pretty fortunate in getting it. On Wednesday a neighbor left me a duck and on Friday I killed a goose that settled within gunshot of the house. On Saturday I killed three more from a gang that came too close to the house. I gave them all away since the meat is not exactly suited to my present condition.

October 17 (Sunday)

This morning we had a slight shower — barely enough to settle the dust. I hope more may follow as the country is sadly in need of rain, everything being dried up. The river now, after the southeast wind has been blowing strong all day, is quite brackish.[37]

I feel a great deal better in health today. All I require is something to strengthen me. It takes me pretty well a week to get medicine or anything from town.

October 18 (Monday)

Feel about the same.

October 19 (Tuesday)

Several people took shelter on my place.

October 20 (Wednesday)

I took a stroll in the Motts to see some of my neighbors.

October 21 (Thursday)

After nine days, I have another chill and violent fever.

October 22 (Friday)

Taking more quinine.

October 23 (Saturday)

I made a trap of my cast net to catch the coons and critters in the field and sometimes I get two or three a day. I had a good patch of watermelons which were worth several dollars in Corpus. As I was too ill to go, I had agreed with John Williams to take them, but when he went to get them, they were all destroyed, the coons or something having cleared them all out. I walked to the Wrights to get a book to read. I am tired of being alone and have read everything I have in the house. John Orchard got me a keg of water from the river but it was very salty.

October 24 (Sunday)

I am very bilious. No more entries until Saturday, October 30.

---

[37] When the river was low, the current weak, and the wind blowing inland, bay tides pushed saltwater up to the Motts and beyond.

October 30 (Saturday)

I have been gradually improving but I dare not go into the river or get my feet wet in the dew. I believe the improvement is due to an elixir, a concoction of whisky, rhubarb, chamomile, calomel, with a little quinine added. I take another elixir several times a day to strengthen me and give me an appetite.

The river is rising and we shall have fresh water again.

October 31 (Sunday)

After writing up my diary yesterday, I had another chill. Dr. McKelvey called to see me and prescribed quinine and blue mass pills in case of another chill.[38] I got so lonely later that I walked to the Motts to have a chat.

November 1 (Monday)

During the night it blew up a most horrendous norther accompanied with rain and thunder. I was lying on my cot with high perspiration and a few minutes later I was shivering under everything I could pile on me. This morning, having a calf strayed off, I went in search of it but the wind chilled me so that I was glad to get home. I had another chill and although I was sitting close over a good fire, I could not get warm till the fever came on me. As soon as the fever came on, I was clearly out of my head. I took a quinine pill and a blue mass pill every two hours.

November 7 (Sunday)

I had to sit over the fire all night. I could not keep warm in bed. All week, except for Friday when I went to visit the Wades, I ate only simple things, such as mush, rice, and beef tea.

November 15 (Monday)

I started for a stroll to Orchard's and as I was going out of the house, I saw a steer eating some seed I had in a

---

[38] Medical definition describes blue mass pills as mercury-based medicine common from the 17th to 19th centuries.

hamper. I went to grab part of a broken ax handle to throw at it and in the process, I got a long splinter in my hand. When I tried to pull it out, I broke it off and left half an inch in my hand. I'm afraid I will have a bad hand as it will not heal until the splinter is out. And I cannot get at it by any means. It is among the tendons of my fingers, which makes them stiff and painful to move.

November 16 (Tuesday)

Remained in the house till about three when I took a walk to Wright's for a short chat, getting back in time to water my cows and pigs. This evening I feel much better, having eaten a small joint of mutton which Adams kindly brought me.

November 17 (Wednesday)

Last night I took another dose of blue mass and quinine and worked it off early this morning. This was to break the fever in case it would come on me, today being the ninth day since the last time I had it, and it has served me well twice before. My hand is no worse and is not quite so painful today. I have been treating it with (illegible) to keep the inflammation down.

November 22 (Monday)

Since Wednesday the weather has been warm. I have had no return of the fever. Yesterday I felt much better and went across the river and got enough moss to stuff a mattress, of which I was in need.[39] I have been working around the house, getting ready to kill a beef as soon as my health permits. It is cold and miserable. I am thin as a skeleton.

November 23 (Tuesday)

Last night a man come along about dark looking for accommodation. I learned that he was sent here by a

---

[39] Spanish moss was prized for use as a mattress-filler because it was believed to repel bugs. The Mercer Diaries of Port Aransas also mention trips made to gather moss to stuff mattresses.

neighbor, although they knew that I have been so sick that I could not take care of myself. I have nothing in the house to eat for a person in health and no warm bedding for a visitor. This is not the first time I have had strangers imposed on me by some of my neighbors.

November 24 (Wednesday)

Last evening, I attended a meeting in the town held to devise some means of making proper and safe watering places at convenient spots on the Nueces River. The attention of stock-raisers has been called to the project from the fact that too many cattle are being bogged down by reason of the bad state of the watering holes along the river. Each agreed to help make two good places, one of which being on my land. I had worked too hard and this brought on a chill. It was on me before I started for the town, but I had to go. The fever became so bad in my head that I was obliged to stay the night at Mr. Wade's.

November 25 (Thursday)

Don't feel so well today.

November 26 (Friday)

Same as yesterday.

November 27 (Saturday)

Took a walk with my gun, killed a goose and partridge and saw a rattlesnake.

November 28 (Sunday)

Soon after breakfast Kershaw came along, bringing a man with him. They stayed all day and cleaned me out of what little grub I had in the house.

November 29 (Monday)

Kershaw and his mate still here. Finding there was no more grub to get out of me, they fetched some of their own from the boat, which they cooked here. They left towards evening. Kershaw and I dissolved our partnership months ago. I kept the field on condition that I help him fence another field of the same size on his land whenever he settles here. So far as his living with me, he had all the benefit but treated me shabbily in the end. He is now living with some people on the other side of Nueces Bay, who I think will soon grow tired of him.

November 30 (Tuesday)

Jobbing about all day and caught a large catfish.

December 1 (Wednesday)

Caught two large catfish and spent the day at Wright's.

December 2 (Thursday)

Caught three more catfish, which I am salting and going to dry. At night there was a dance at the Motts. I tried to dance the fever out of me. I stayed until I was tired and came home feeling no worse.

December 3 (Friday)

Caught two more fish and have been looking for my horse to hunt my cattle. Found my horse sick. He cannot live another day. If I can get away anywhere, I will be off, being no good at home — out of grub, out of money, out of health, my horse dead, my steers vanished, no one knows where. I will let my cattle drift and be off, as I am no good at home.

Martial law has been declared in Corpus Christi
and male inhabitants organized into a company.
They have a captain, lieutenant, and one
cannon. They keep a number of men on patrol
every night. I thought that as everybody
seemed so frightened there must be cause for
alarm. I started for the Motts as soon as I could.
At the Motts, after a good deal of joking, we
decided there was no necessity for us to do
anything but keep our guns in order.

—*Nov. 9, 1859*

BEFORE THE WAR

1859

January 5 (Wednesday)

I have been away since Dec. 3. Went to Corpus. The
chills again settled on me. The day was bitterly cold when I
started. I went down in Reynolds' wagon and took up
quarters at Mr. Almond's.[40] I stayed a week at Almond's
then went to Adams, where I still am at present, paying him
$10 a month. The change had the desired effect; my
strength has returned and as I felt anxious to see about
things at home, I came up yesterday to fetch my steers and

---

[40] Joseph Almond, a native of England, came to Corpus Christi in 1852, at the
same time as the Wades and other English settlers. He had a home in town
before he became a sheep-raiser and later cattle rancher. Almond also kept a
diary, which was much like that of Noakes' diary, as it was a plain record of
work and daily activities.

45

cart to bring home flour and things for housekeeping. I propose to establish myself in my lonely home, prepare my field for plowing, and see if I can get a horse to hunt my cattle.

I borrowed a horse from Adams and came home, intending to get my steers and start back early. I found one steer and put him in the pen. I learned from the neighbors that the other steer died about two hours before, so my plans were defeated. I went to my old house to see what had become of my things. My chickens had all been killed, the heifer calf I raised by hand had drowned in the river, and poor Peter, my dog, had been killed by someone in the Motts (as I learned this evening). But my house and property were all right, so I suppose I must not grumble.

January 31 (Monday)

I reached home this evening in the rain [after another stay in Corpus Christi]. I again found my house and its contents all right, which speaks a great deal for the honesty of the neighbors, as I left everything I own to the mercy of the public, as everybody knew. But thank goodness I have made no enemies yet and my things were there as I left them.

Adams will let me have a yoke of steers and his son until I can plow my field. Adams and a man named Charles Holdsworth rented my house in town for three months for ten dollars.[41] Part of this money, with the hide of a cow, procured for me the most necessary articles for housekeeping to bring home. I did not sell my lathe [to buy a horse]; I would not let it go. I intend to trade my six-shooter for a horse instead. I don't have the means to buy another work steer so must do the best that I can without one. I have now lost all my best milking cows and everything else I set any value on.

---

[41] Charles Holdsworth, 43, originally from England, was boarding with the Robert Adams family in Corpus Christi before he rented Noakes' house in town. Ref. 1860 Census.

February 1 (Tuesday)

I went everywhere to borrow a plow to use next week and finally succeeded. In the afternoon I worked in the field and in the evening, I cooked some rice and roasted coffee.

February 2 (Wednesday)

Cleaned my clock and jobbed in the house. Took down an old fence between my fields and hauled it away with my cart. Piled up corn stalks to burn. I brought home another puppy, which I named Nipper. He is a Scotch terrier breed, just weaned.

February 3 (Thursday)

Brought home some firewood and a plow from McKenzie's.[42]

February 4 (Friday)

Last night I woke with a choking sensation in my windpipe. I jumped out of bed and as I soon as I got a light on saw that it was blood coming from the lungs. I thought that a blood vessel had ruptured in the lungs. I was afraid to lie in bed any longer so I dressed and made a fire, spilling blood very fast all the while. By keeping still, it soon stopped and I got a little sleep towards morning.

After breakfast I fetched up the steers to pick up a little dead firewood along the river but the steers started running with the cart and as soon as I commenced running the blood started to pour from my lungs so fast as nearly to choke me. I had to let the steers run, which they continued to do along the river until they collided with two trees, the cart jammed between them and the steers compelled to stop.

I could not get the cart out, with blood still coming from my mouth. I unyoked the steers where they stood so I could

---

[42] William McKenzie of Nuecestown, a farmer and stock-raiser, was from England and his wife Jane was from Ireland. They had five children. Ref. 1860 census.

get back to my house. I was feeling faint and afraid it would cause my death.

February 5 (Saturday)

Since yesterday I have stayed very quiet, avoiding exertion, and up to this morning have had no return of the bleeding.

February 12 (Saturday)

During the past week I have avoided all exertion. Adams and son came from Corpus to plow my field but I had to alter my plans according to my health and they returned home Tuesday. I have been afraid this past week and have stayed among my neighbors mostly at night. Have had no return of bleeding, and hope with proper care not to be bothered with it. I received a bottle of medicine from Corpus, which was not what I had sent for, so I returned it. I received a letter from Emily yesterday and returned answer today.

February 19 (Saturday)

One week later. I worked around at odd jobs that did not require great exertion. Spent a few nights at Wade's, but now sleeping at home. Have not succeeded in getting a horse. The last part of the week I have been gardening, planting shallots, watermelon, tomato, mushmelon [cantaloupe]. I hope I am going to get well soon. I want to commence plowing on Wednesday.

February 20 (Sunday)

Rained and cold. Took a walk into town (the Motts).

February 21 (Monday)

Dug a little in the garden and planted some beans. Worked on the roof of the house. Tried to get a cow and calf of mine from Reynolds' place but they ran away. A misty cold rain.

February 22 (Tuesday)

Adams' son arrived from Corpus with the steers.

February 23 (Wednesday)

Commenced plowing.

February 27 (Sunday)

Have done more than half the field since Wednesday. I can now do a pretty good day's work.

February 28 (Monday)

Rained hard all day and night Sunday. Too wet for plowing so we jobbed around, grubbing out roots in the field, sticking beans, and fetching firewood.

March 1 (Tuesday)

Finished plowing the top part of my field and planted it in corn.

March 2 (Wednesday)

Plowing. Went to Orchard's to get some meat, he having killed a cow.[43]

March 4 (Friday)

Finished plowing and planted some corn.

March 6 (Sunday)

Yesterday I finished plowing and planting. The wind was so strong I thought the old house would blow down. Almost a hurricane.

March 7 (Monday)

I planted some seeds, as before, and added a buffer of gourds around the fence. My mare got out during the night. Adams' son took the steers back to Corpus.

March 8 (Tuesday)

Caught my mare. A cattle hunt started from here but on account of my health I was afraid of the exposure and did not join them.

---

[43] There was no butcher at the Motts and no supermarket where they could pick up a rump roast or beefsteak wrapped in cellophane. Their meat supply came on the hoof and when neighbors killed a cow, pig or mutton it was customary to share out the fresh meat.

March 13 (Sunday)

I have been doing a little of everything. My mare broke away and I have been unable to get her. I planted a few flower seeds and yesterday I fetched up a cow on foot. The cattle hunters returned, bringing many cattle but only two head of mine.

March 20 (Sunday)

The greater part of last week was spent on my new mare. She broke away one night and it took me most of the following day to get her again. She has destroyed four or five dollars' worth of rope. The cattle hunters brought me home a heifer that I had not seen in more than two years. Received a letter from Edmond the other day.[44]

March 21 (Monday)

Jobbed at home.

March 22 (Tuesday)

Cattle hunting. Nearly everybody in the Motts went. We rounded up cattle on Blucher's Prairie and cut ours out.[45]

March 23 (Wednesday)

Cattle hunting again. The Motts boys driving cattle from Oso Creek and the Corpus gang driving from Tule Lake.[46] Met at the large water hole on Blucher's Prairie where the Corpus boys cut out their cattle and we took the balance to the Motts.

March 24 (Thursday)

At home most of the day. Reynolds killed a beef in the morning and I fetched some cuts home.

---

[44] Edmond Noakes was Thomas' brother, the second oldest. He moved to the United States in the mid-1850s and lived for a time in Kansas and at Mobile, Ala.

[45] Blucher's Prairie was described by Charles Blucher as land his father Felix Blucher owned, which extended from Turkey Creek below Nuecestown to the flats on the south side of Nueces Bay.

[46] A salt lake west of Corpus Christi.

March 25 (Friday)

I ran in a cow and calf and fetched home a load of firewood.

March 26 (Saturday)

Rainy. Jobbing indoors.

March 27 (Sunday)

Cooking and getting ready for camping out. A man brought a horse to me, which I bought, trading him my six-shooter with five dollars to boot. It is a gray horse not thoroughly broke.

March 28 (Monday)

Started with 20 others on a week's cattle hunt, intending to search a kind of peninsula we thought contained a good many stray cattle. Rode all day and camped after dark, not being able to find water before. We came upon a bunch of mustangs but did not run them. The water where we camped was as muddy as cream.

March 29 (Tuesday)

Reached the peninsula, drove all the cattle up, and cut out the strays, which were very few belonging to our party. Drank muddy water all day and camped at a mud hole that night. I slept with my head near some bushes with my saddle for a pillow. Just as I laid down, a rattlesnake started rattling close to my head and I soon rid myself of such an unwelcome neighbor with a few strokes of my whip.

March 30 (Wednesday)

Hunted all day. Camped near the pen of the Encinal Ranch. Being out of grub, we killed an unbranded yearling to cook.

March 31 (Thursday)

Rounded up all the cattle at the ranch and all around for about 10 miles and cut out our cattle and drove them about five miles to another ranch. We penned them and camped for the night.

April 1 (Friday)

Hunted up the creek till we were within seven miles of home, where we rounded up and cut out our cattle. All but eight went home. We camped at a place owned by men named Ball and Terry. They cooked a large pot of mush and gave us as much butter and milk as we could eat.

April 2 (Saturday)

After another turn at the mush and milk, I saddled up and rode to an Irishman's a short distance off and traded him a three-year-old steer for nine hogs.[47] I drove them home, reaching my place a little after the middle of the day. I am going to try to raise hogs on the other side of the Nueces River, where they can do no one any damage. I ear-marked these and Reynolds and Hennard helped me take them over the river. Found a heifer dead in my pen when I got home.

April 3 (Sunday)

Went over the river and fed the hogs. Towards evening I penned a good many head of cattle.

April 4 (Monday)

Killed a beef, Reynolds and Hinnant helping me.[48] We put four more hogs across the river.

April 5 (Tuesday)

Salted down the remainder of the beef, most of it having gone to pay my debts. Fed my hogs. I then rode to a stock gathering six miles off, but found nothing of mine. I feel unwell today and have been spitting up blood.

April 6, 7 (Wednesday and Thursday)

Driving rain for two days. Jobbing around.

April 8 (Friday)

Rode out on my new horse. Saw some steers Reynolds had lost. Thinned out some corn.

---

[47] In a later entry he was identified as William Cody.

[48] John Hinnant and wife Nancy Hudson Miller Hinnant settled at Nuecestown about 1857, after they had moved from Gonzales County. They came originally from North Carolina. The Hinnant family later moved to the Lagarto area and established Los Picachos Ranch.

April 9 (Saturday)

Rode to Corpus with Reynolds and Hennard. Nothing to buy since I had no money and could get none. Rented my house to [Charles] Holdsworth for $4 a month from April 1. Country needs more rain. Everything is looking bad and crops may fail.

April 10 (Sunday)

Wind blew all day. For the past week I have been spitting up blood and do not feel well.

April 17 (Sunday)

One week later. For a week the wind has been blowing. Things are dying for want of rain and the river is very brackish. This morning I went out with Hennard and a man named Shaw to see to the hogs.[49] I took my gun and Hennard took three hounds. One of my sows and two of Hennard's were missing. I shot a large alligator and wounded another. We struck the fresh tracks of a panther which no doubt accounts for the missing hogs. It was too dry to hunt him today but I intend to go over with the hounds tomorrow.

April 18 (Monday)

Went to Tule Lake to get a cow. Did not find her.

April 19 (Tuesday)

Went cattle hunting with Mr. Wright along the Oso Creek.[50] Rode all day and towards night came across a cow with a young calf at Tule Lake. The cow got away from me in the brush, my horse being too timid to run her. I came home with nothing.

April 20 (Wednesday)

I was told some cattle hunters from Banquete Creek were going to round up at Tule Lake today and drive the cattle

---

[49] Charles Shaw, born at Saddleworth, England, 1824; died at Nuecestown, 1878.

[50] The Oso Creek flows from north Nueces County 28 miles to the southeast, skirting the outlying area of Corpus Christi, before emptying into Corpus Christi Bay. One of Henry Kinney's four original ranches was on the Oso.

by the Motts, so I thought it would be a good opportunity to get home a wild cow of mine. [51] I went out as soon as I could, found this cow and drove her into the herd. While I was attending to another cow and calf, the wild one broke from the herd and got away. But I fetched the other one home.

April 21 (Thursday)

Went to Tule Lake again to hunt for the wild cow but could not find her.

April 22 (Friday)

Hunted cattle in the morning. In the evening I fetched two boatloads of firewood from the other side of the river.

April 23 (Saturday)

Got my steer and one of Reynolds' and fetched home a load of firewood which I brought from the other side of the river the day before.

April 24 (Sunday)

We need rain.

April 25 (Monday)

Cattle hunting all day at Tule Lake. Found three cows.

April 26 (Tuesday)

Cattle hunting near Corpus. Found nothing.

April 27 (Wednesday)

The Banquete boys were here and we drove up all the cattle for some miles around to cut out our own and drive home.

April 28 (Thursday)

Got my steers and cart and fetched two loads of firewood for Reynolds, in return for some that he brought me when I was ill.

April 29 (Friday)

Did not feel well in the morning so did very little. Rode out and brought in my mare.

---

[51] Banquete Creek joins Agua Dulce Creek a mile southeast of the town of Banquete, where the combined streams form Petronila Creek.

April 30 (Saturday)

Went to Corpus to get some money from the Dredge Company but did not get it. Found a letter from mother at the Post Office. Reached home and went to the Motts in the evening.

May 1 (Sunday)

Had a storm last night at the Motts. The beautiful spring bird which visits us at this time of season has arrived and may be seen everywhere in great numbers. This morning I went for a ride with two lady acquaintances named McGregor.[52]

May 2 (Monday)

Plowing corn all day.

May 3 (Tuesday)

Had a rain and thunderstorm.

May 4 (Wednesday)

Weather fair, but windy.

May 5 (Thursday)

Plowing my corn. Altered a saddle for Mr. Wright in the morning.

May 6 (Friday)

More rain. We have had plenty of rain now, enough to last through this season and no doubt we will have a plentiful harvest. Today I have been making some water tanks for George Reynolds at his house, my labor going towards a working debt of a year's standing.

May 7 (Saturday)

Weather looks very much like it will rain. Working at Reynolds' on the same job.

---

[52] Daughters of John Steward McGregor and his wife Mary Ann, who settled at the Motts in 1852. They later moved to the Oso community, 12 miles southwest of Corpus Christi.

May 8 (Sunday)

Big storm last night. Today the wind is light and the sun very hot. Last year I took a journal and two papers so that I would know what was going on in the world. But my losses have been so great that I cannot pay for them. Now I am quite without news and ignorant of what is taking place in the world. I borrow books now and then as I cannot be without reading material.

May 15 (Sunday)

I have worked all week at Reynolds' except for Friday when I worked a day in my field hoeing corn. The vegetables are beginning to come in. Last night when I came home, I found my gate open and the cows and calves out and gone. The first thing I had to do this morning was to get them home again, which I did.

May 16 (Monday)

Worked at Reynolds' on the water tanks.

May 17 (Tuesday)

Worked part of the day at Reynolds' and the balance at home.

May 18 (Wednesday)

I made a cheese for Mr. Orchard.

May 19 (Thursday)

I was at home hoeing in the field and cooking.

May 21 (Saturday)

Went for a day's cattle hunt with several men, but did not find the cow and calf I was looking for. Rode for the most part of the day and my horse gave out about seven miles from home. Mr. Hennard's boy was along so I shifted my saddle to his horse then I rode behind George Reynolds on his horse. We tried to drive my horse with the cattle but could not get him to move along so we yoked him to an old steer in the herd and he pulled him along till he dropped. I tied him to a small bush next to where he laid and left him. Got home about dark.

May 22 (Sunday)

Very hot. No breeze. Borrowed a horse from Hinnant and went out and fetched mine home.

May 29 (Sunday)

During the past week it has been hot and dry. The corn is in tassel and needs rain. This morning Hennard and I went down the river in the boat, trying to find our hogs, which were missing. We could not find them.[53]

May 30 (Monday)

Jobbing around the house.

May 31 (Tuesday)

Saddled my mare and went to get my horse. As soon as he saw me coming to get him, he started running. I chased after him the whole day until I had fairly broke down my mare. I was after him from 8 o'clock until the evening. I finally had to give him up. I never expect to see him again. I am without a horse.

June 1 (Wednesday)

Working at home all day.

June 2 (Thursday)

Weather hot.

June 3 (Friday)

The corn in the field has burned up. The crop is a complete failure. Worked at home, then went hunting and fishing.

June 4 (Saturday)

Went to Tule Lake with several men to hunt what cattle we could find. Could not find my mare so I went on a mare

---

[53] Noakes mentioned a neighbor named Hennard several times but the census for 1860 and 1870 show no such name. Joseph Almond in his diary mentioned Hennard and placed him near Lagarto by 1873. After the death of John Ludewig, Mrs. Ludewig advertised her cattle brand in the Nueces Valley and said her only authorized agent was Mr. T. Hennard. No other references could be found.

of [John] Heward's.[54] I fetched home two young cows with calves and several head of mine, one of which was a calf I thought had been lost. I earmarked and branded it soon as I got home, with Reynolds helping me. I then helped him do some branding.

June 5 (Sunday)

Weather hot.

June 6 (Monday)

Very hot and dry. I spent the better part of the day chasing my mare.

June 7 (Tuesday)

Went to a picnic we got up in the Motts. There was a good attendance and we had a very nice day. We held it at a ferry crossing a few miles up the river.[55] We went rowing in the river, danced some, and ate a great deal. We started for home at sundown. There were two wagons, a buggy and about 40 horses. Most of the young ladies and young men were on horseback. Everything passed off with great fun and glee.

June 8 (Wednesday)

Loafing around and getting over the last night's effects.

June 9, 10 (Thursday and Friday)

On the first day I was jobbing about at home. On Friday I started early with Reynolds on a boat down the river to hunt my hogs, catch fish, and shoot alligators. Found the hogs, but my best sow was dead. Shot an alligator but did not get him. Nor could we get any fish. Sometimes the river swarms with fish and at other times they are scarce. About three p.m., after looking after things at home, I sailed up to the town and got two young ladies to accompany me on a sail up the river.

---

[54] John Heward and wife Nancy had five children. They came from North Carolina before settling at Nuecestown. Ref. 1860 Census.
[55] Miller's Ferry, operated by Samuel Reed Miller, was at Santa Margarita, an ancient crossing place on the Nueces River, also known as the De Leon Crossing, about eight miles upstream from the Motts.

June 11 (Saturday)

Went to Corpus lake.[56] I met Reynolds, Heward and two or three others who had gone down the day before to watch the lake for stray cattle. They had two heifers with calves of mine in the herd. Reached home at 4 p.m. When I arrived at the pen, lo and behold, my runaway horse had been found and brought home. I had offered a reward to anyone who found him. Later I went for a sail up the river with two young ladies and one of their brothers. We amused ourselves swimming and fishing. I reached home about 12. It was a beautiful moonlit night.

June 12 (Sunday)

Everything is parching for want of rain. It poured down so close we could almost hear it, but we got none. My little dog died the other day of distemper. I hated for Nipper to die as I was much attached to him. Everything I value seems to die. I look upon it as a thing to be expected.

June 13 (Monday)

Killed one of the pigs. Hennard helped me. It commenced raining just as we had scalded him. We had a real shower. In the evening I fetched home a cow and a calf.

June 14 (Tuesday)

Most of the morning was spent curing my pig, at least what little was left, as it took nearly all of it to share out with my neighbors. In the evening I went for a sail up the river with the two young ladies.

June 15 (Wednesday)

Jobbing at home all day.

June 16 (Thursday)

Planting peas in the field.

---

[56] Noakes was referring to the Salt Lake located a mile west of town. The lake disappeared in a drought and the area around it became known as the salt flats.

June 17 (Friday)

At night I have been boating on the river, which has given me a bad cold.

June 18 (Saturday)

I was at Mr. Orchard's framing a gateway and doing other little jobs.

June 19 (Sunday)

Feeling unwell since yesterday. Last night I took some pills which made me feel sick today.

June 20 (Monday)

Feel better today, yet have a bad cold. At home in the evening.

June 21 (Tuesday)

Hunted up two beeves to try and sell to a man named Collins who has come from a way east to buy cattle. My neighbors rounded up cattle for sale and by night we had several head penned.

June 22 (Wednesday)

Drove the cattle about six miles to a ranch where Collins was staying. He would only buy one of mine. The others were not fat enough.

June 23 (Thursday)

At home.

June 24 (Friday)

Took a sail down the river to fish, shoot alligators, and hunt my hogs. I shot one alligator but did not get him. I caught no fish and only saw one sow, so I came back as nearly as I went.

June 25 (Saturday)

Branding and marking calves. In the evening I took a ride around as usual to see to my cattle and to keep my horse in riding order. I am obliged to ride him every day; he is quite wild and very hard to mount if left alone a day or two.

June 26 (Sunday)

Had a good rain today.

June 27 (Monday)

Shot two alligators in the river to skin.

June 28 (Tuesday)

In the morning I loaded one of the alligators, the smallest is about eight feet long, and commenced skinning it but could not finish before it got dark.

June 29 (Wednesday)

Very wet all day. The rain started early.

June 30 (Thursday)

Planted some beans and peas in the field.

July 1 (Friday)

Felt unwell since yesterday, feeling bilious and feverish, and feared I might get the old complaint again. I started for town, getting John Orchard to see to my things. I took a strong dose of calomel and slept at Holdsworth's in my own house.

July 2 (Saturday)

Spent the evening with John Curr.

July 3 (Sunday)

The weather is very unhealthy and I am afraid it will cause a good deal of sickness. Corpus is all alive about a railway which is being projected. I don't suppose it will ever be commenced; it is supposed to run to Mexico. Wrote a letter to mother and received a Sussex Express newspaper.

July 4 (Monday)

I was going to a ball at San Patricio, 15 miles up the river, but was prevented by the rain.

July 5 (Tuesday)

Still felt unwell. Turned out all my calves and sold my pig in order that I might get away from home for a change.

July 6 (Wednesday)

Captain King is the proprietor of a large ranch 40 miles from here.[57] He has repeatedly sent word to Heward, my next neighbor, that the panthers were killing his colts and he would be glad if Heward would come with his hounds and kill them. Heward wanted me to go with him, which I was only too glad to go. I felt sick at the time but I knew it would do me good.

Heward had lent several of his dogs and we were unfortunate about getting them back. Instead of starting with 11 dogs, as we had expected, we only had three. We rode nearly all day and camped on the San Fernando Creek, about five miles from the Santa Gertrudis Ranch.

We saddled up a little before dawn and tried the creek timber with the dogs. I shot a tiger cat [bobcat] and then we rode for the ranch. Heward had killed one [tiger cat] the day before as we were coming out. We took our breakfast at a water hole about a mile from the ranch. As we reached the ranch, a heavy shower commenced. We made arrangements with Captain King about the hunting, then rode about a mile to another ranch owned by Major Chapman but managed by a man named Bryden.[58] I knew him very well. Here we met George Reynolds, who had missed us the day before. We took dinner with Bryden.

After a long shower, we mounted our horses and rode to King Ranch where we got an extra supply of provisions and rode about five miles down the creek to the scene of operations. There stood a small lumber shanty built for the

---

[57] Richard King, who, with Mifflin Kenedy, ran a steamboat line on the Rio Grande, founded King Ranch on Santa Gertrudis Creek in 1853. It was the beginning of the legendary ranch and famous cattle dynasty.
[58] Maj. William Chapman had a sheep operation on Santa Gertrudis Creek. He died in 1859. James Bryden handled Chapman's sheep on shares. He worked for Helen Chapman after her husband's death. Bryden was a ranch foreman and trail boss for King Ranch. He later bought the Diezmero Ranch on the Nueces River, formerly owned by James Durst.

Mexican vaqueros that herded the horses. Near this shanty, beneath a tree, we made camp and took our supper.

About two hours after sundown we started with an old Mexican as a guide to hunt in some thickets. We soon treed a tiger cat, which I shot. Reynolds had no gun and Heward only had a revolver, so the killing devolved on me as I had my rifle. We rode until about one o'clock in the morning, when we regained our camp and took a little sleep. When day dawned, we started again but killed nothing that morning.

July 7 (Thursday)

Same as yesterday.

July 8 (Friday)

During the day a Mexican brought word that a colt had been killed the previous night by a panther. We found the tracks of the panther and ascertained the thicket where she had gone. This climate being too hot for dogs to hunt in the daytime, we have to hunt on moonlit nights. That night we started for the thicket which we reached just as it was getting dark. The moon was not more than half full.

We had no sooner than entered the wood than the dogs started at full cry on some trail. In a very short time, we heard that they had treed their game. We now forced our horses through the almost impenetrable brush until we were close enough to see a fine panther on a low stump, which the dogs were barking at.

I dismounted and handed the reins of my horse to someone to hold and with my rifle crawled through the bushes. It was so dark I had to get very close to the panther to see him distinctly enough to take aim. I was within six or seven yards of him before he saw me, being so much engaged with the dogs.

The moment he caught sight of me he threw back his ears and exhibited a fine set of teeth, but his time was come, for as he turned upon me I gave him my ball [bullet] full in the chest, which dropped him dead and doubtless save the life of some of the dogs. We put him on one of the horses and as soon as we got out of the thicket we camped, skinned and cut up the panther, and roasted the meat for the dogs.

July 9 (Saturday)

We were moving before dawn and hunted the dogs through the thicket but only killed a tiger cat before it became too hot to continue. There was plenty of smaller game in the cover: wild hogs, deer and turkey, but we were not in pursuit of them. We rode back to camp and in the evening, we rode to another thicket on the other side of Santa Gertrudis Creek.[59] The dogs got among a scattered gang of hogs which ended our chances of getting another panther that night. We camped down.

July 10 (Sunday)

We killed another cat and returned to camp, deciding to leave these covers till the weather gets cooler and the dogs could hunt better. At present they are too far from fresh water, and if the dogs become overheated, we have to pack them to water on our horses or they will die.

Towards evening we saddled up to go to Captain King's ranch. On our way we encountered a regular hurricane, which came up like a norther. The previous part of the day had been exceedingly hot, without a breath of air. When we started for the ranch, nothing could be seen indicating an approaching storm except a dark cloud rising above the northern horizon, but before we had ridden three quarters of an hour the storm reached us. Dense black clouds came sweeping up toward us, accompanied by thunder and rain, but as yet not a breath stirred. At length clouds of dust swept down on us on the prairie. The ranch cattle threw up

---

[59] The Santa Gertrudis Creek flows through Duval, Jim Wells and Kleberg counties before it disgorges into Baffin Bay. It was named for the Santa Gertrudis land grant, which became the genesis of King Ranch. The Texas Rangers long kept a campsite on the Santa Gertrudis, about half a mile from where Richard King built his ranch house.

their heads and tails and scampered as fast as their legs could carry them.

The storm reached us with a fury and for a moment I had to hold hard to my saddle horn to stay on my horse. It blew for a quarter of an hour but did not rain a great deal. Then everything became as calm as ever.

We reached the ranch, where we stayed all night. Captain King made us a present of a mare apiece for having killed the panther, and treated us very handsomely. Heward and Reynolds decided to return home the next morning.

July 11 (Monday)

At dawn Heward and Reynolds started for home, taking the mares with them. I had not yet had my fill of hunting so stayed with the determination to kill another panther, if one were to be found. I took the dogs that morning and hunted a wood without result. I waited till night and hunted till morning but with no success. I killed a tiger cat, but no panther.

July 13 (Wednesday)

Went to the ranch to get meat for the dogs. They killed a sheep for me. I hunted until night, and killed another tiger cat.

July 14 (Thursday)

Finding that I would get no panther, I started for home a little after nine in the evening, so as to ride all night, owing to the intense heat. As I rode along over the prairie, a gang of mustangs continued to charge around me, snorting like steam engines, and keeping along with me for some time. I unsaddled a little before daybreak at a creek and took a short nap. By sunrise I was back in the saddle.

July 15 (Friday)

Reached home about 6 p.m. My house was all right but I found all my stock in a bad plight.

July 16 (Saturday)

The first thing I had to do was to see to my cows and calves and doing what I could. The Nueces River is so salty that neighbors are digging a well and I have been assisting at that most of the day.

July 17 (Sunday)

Sent a letter to Capt. King relative to my going there to work on a new house the captain is building. Rode my new mare to dine at George Reynolds' home.

July 18 (Monday)

Jobbing about the house.

July 19 (Tuesday)

Same as yesterday.

July 20 (Wednesday)

Heward and I went fishing and caught some mullets.

July 21 (Thursday)

Went down the river to hunt my hogs, but could not find them.

July 22 (Friday)

Went alligator shooting early in the morning. I do not know how many I killed in consequence of their trick of sinking to the bottom when shot. Later I went fishing with Heward and Reynolds. Caught some.

July 23 (Saturday)

Dined at Orchard's. When I returned home, Thomas Wright rode up to say that a man named Parrish was dead and somebody was wanted to make a coffin. I did not have the boards to make it but agreed to come up to the town and assist anybody who would make it. One thing or another hindered us from commencing it so we put it off until morning.

July 24 (Sunday)

Slept at Wade's and at daylight he and I began the coffin, finishing it about 9 a.m. I then rode Wade's horse home to change my clothes for the funeral, as everybody in the place went to funerals. I dressed and remounted the horse. I was no sooner in the saddle than the horse began to pitch and buck in a most furious manner. I stuck to her till the saddle went and then came down on my head. It did not hurt me but I had had enough of it so I picked up the saddle, caught and tied the horse, and walked to the funeral.

The other day a neighbor's wife was bit by a rattlesnake on the back of her hand.[60] The proper remedies were applied immediately and she recovered. I have run several very near chances of being bit during the week but have escaped so far. One day I trod on a rattlesnake and one evening I fell on a moccasin snake, but it being coiled up, my hand rested on its head which prevented me from being bit.

July 31 (Sunday)

Yesterday I went to Corpus, where I found a letter from Edmond.

August 1 (Monday)

I spent the day in town acting as clerk in an election. It was the state election. We had a good many Mexicans in to vote and to make more certain of the legalities of their votes, we swore most of them, but not having such a thing as a Bible at hand we swore them on a law book. Some will swear to anything. One man swore that he had lived in Corpus 25 years, although everybody knows that at that date [about 1834] Corpus was unknown.

The young fellows got up horse-racing. When there was to be a particular race, we would stop business and have a recess, judges, clerks and all would go out to watch the race. One of the judges told me he thought the country was improving since generally in the past by the time the voting was over the judges and the clerks would all be so drunk that they had to wait until the next day to count the votes. But this time, he said, we are all quite sober.

---

[60] Ann Gibbs, the wife of William Gibbs. 1860 Census shows he was from England and she was from Wales.

August 2 (Tuesday)

Riding around.

August 3 (Wednesday)

In the evening went sailing on the river with some girls.

August 4 (Thursday)

Just jobbing around. Learned that all my hogs got out and swam the river and went back to the man I bought them from. He shot some of them because they were rooting up his crops. I haven't any means of getting them home so I guess they are lost to me. This, like every other speculation I have made in this country, has turned out a failure.

August 5 (Friday)

I was riding around.

August 6 (Saturday)

Jobbing around the house.

August 7 (Sunday)

Went to church.

August 8 (Monday)

Getting ready for camping out. A large party of cattle hunters intend to start tomorrow.

August 9 (Tuesday)

Started on the cattle hunt. Rode to Gregory's Ranch.[61]

August 11 (Thursday)

We rode around, hunting for cattle.

August 12 (Friday)

We spent several days in the hottest weather with a large company of cattle hunters. The place where we camped was a barren waste of sand which the winds have driven up into little hills like snow drifts. Not a tree to be seen and winding about among the sand hills are little salt lakes or

---

[61] Noakes and the cattle hunters from the Motts visited the ranch of William S. Gregory the year before, in April. The ranch was 15 miles south of Corpus Christi on the historic Laureles tract.

lagoons whose waters in a dry time evaporate and leave a coating of salt.[62]

No one can imagine what a hardship it is cattle hunting in such a country, unless he has experienced it. The only place where we could get water was to dig a hole for each of us with our knives to procure water for our supper.

This cattle hunt rounded up several thousand head in the herd we had up. We cut our more than 500 head belonging to our party. We penned our cattle.

August 13 (Saturday)

The cattle broke out of the pen. We penned them again on a ranch owned by Capt. Fullerton.[63]

August 14 (Sunday)

When we got to Fullerton's ranch, we found some half-grown pigs running about. We soon ran one down, killed, cooked, and ate it in a short time. We sent word to Fullerton that we had done so as we did not want to exactly steal it.

August 15 (Monday)

Took our breakfast and rode to the pen, where we found that more than half the cattle had broken out during the night and were gone. We drove our cattle about 10 miles up the Oso Creek and penned them at Bee's Ranch for the night.

August 16 (Tuesday)

Back home. Went up to Reynolds' place to put a new tongue in his wagon but was too sick to work.

---

[62] A good place to camp would have provided the three essentials, wood, water, and grass.

[63] Samuel W. Fullerton, a former ship captain, owned the Encinal Ranch in a partnership with Joseph Howell. Fullerton lived in town, not on the ranch. He was the executor of the Schatzel estate and inherited Schatzel's "Mansion House" on South Broadway. His daughter Rachel married Perry Doddridge. Doddridge later owned the Encinal Ranch. The ranch was located near today's Flour Bluff and the Laguna Madre.

August 17 (Wednesday)
Still too sick to do anything.
August 18 (Thursday)
I did little or nothing all day.
August 19 (Friday)
Sharpened a saw for John Williams.[64]
August 20 (Saturday)
I still have a pain in my chest.
August 21 (Sunday)
Went to church and stayed at Wright's till evening.
August 22 (Monday)
Last night I was very much troubled with my chest. I am under the impression that I am in a consumptive state and I am afraid that my constitution is not strong enough to withstand the hard life I am leading.
August 23 (Tuesday)
Did very little.
August 24 (Wednesday)
Felt better but did no work.
August 25 (Thursday)
Took my cart and steers and drove about five miles down the Oso Creek to try and bring home some of my hogs which swam the river and went down there. I camped at the place of an Irishman named [William] Cody from whom I bought the hogs.
August 26 (Friday)
With the help of Cody I caught the two sows. In the evening I commenced gathering corn.
August 27 (Saturday)
Had to take my horse five miles to water, the river water being too salty to drink.

---

[64] John Williams, a bachelor carpenter from North Carolina, was considered one of Noakes' closest friends at the Motts.

August 28 (Sunday)

I called to see a person named Gibbs whose wife was bitten by a rattlesnake a month ago. Mr. Gibbs took me to the house. Her hand was horrid looking. Nearly all the flesh from the back of it was rotted away. No doubt she would have lost her life from the bite if they had failed to use the proper remedies.

The moment she was bitten they stopped the circulation by tying a tourniquet about the wrist, then cut the places where the fangs entered to make them bleed freely, rubbed saltpeter in the wounds, and to counteract the poison in her system they gave her three pints of whisky.

August 29 (Monday)

I got up three hours before daylight to send John Orchard off with a cartload of watermelons for Corpus. While seeing about the melons, my attention was attracted by long rays of light shooting up from the north, which I concluded to be the northern lights. I was surprised, as I did not think they were visible from these latitudes.

August 30 (Tuesday)

I stayed busy getting in my corn.

August 31 (Wednesday)

Hunting horses.

September 1 (Thursday)

Found and roped my mare and then went shelling corn.

September 2 (Friday)

Shelling corn.

September 3 (Saturday)

Jobbing around the house.

September 4 (Sunday)

The cattle are suffering for lack of water. The river is too salty from the bay. Helped Hennard with his cattle. We had a heavy rain.

September 5 (Monday)

Rain and thunderstorm.

September 6 (Tuesday)

Thunder and rain. Rode around with Hennard's dogs but found nothing.

September 7 (Wednesday)

Shelling corn and rode around among my cattle.

September 8 (Thursday)

George Reynolds called early. We agreed to start for Santa Gertrudis Creek about 45 miles from here, where we heard our horses were. It took me till noon to get my mare to go on. Ate at Reynolds and then we started. We reached James Bryden's ranch, where we were kindly invited to make that our stopping place.

September 9 (Friday)

After breakfast we rode to Capt. King's ranch two miles away to get our horses. I caught mine as soon as we got there. We had to wait all day before Reynolds could get his. Then we rode back to Bryden's where we stayed the night.

September 10 (Saturday)

Heavy thunderstorm and a good deal of rain. We were waiting for Bryden, who was away. Reynolds wanted to trade with him for a horse. We waited for him all day and stayed the night.

September 11 (Sunday)

Started early for home. When we were about halfway there, heavy thundershowers passed over us and it rained hard. We covered ourselves with our blankets and did not get very wet. Reached home about sundown.

September 12 (Monday)

Planted shallots. The river is running fresh again. Found a heifer dead in the chaparral.

September 13, 14, 15 (Tuesday, Wednesday, Thursday)

Jobbing about. Planted onions. Weather exceedingly hot.

September 16 (Friday)

Took the rest of my corn to the store.[65] I borrowed an augur so I can bore for a well.

September 17 (Saturday)

Bored the first thing. When I reached down about 14 feet I came to good water. So now I know I can get good water by digging for it. When I first came here, I was told by everybody that if you dug a well you would only find saltwater. But recently people have begun to use augurs to bore for water and the result is that everybody is getting good well water from where they thought it would be too salty and brackish. After dinner I planted shallots and jobbed around.

September 18 (Sunday

I am taking care of myself. It was about this time a year ago when I came down with the ague. For the last two weeks before breakfast I take a tonic made of chamomile leaves and red pepper steeped in whisky. I believe it is doing me a lot of good.

September 19 (Monday)

I fixed a pump for Reynolds and put it in his cistern. Then rode down the Oso and hunted for cows with Reynolds.

September 24, 25 (Saturday and Sunday)

Since Tuesday morning I have been in Corpus. I went to take down my stable which I intend to bring up here. I have pulled it down and Reynolds will haul it home for me. Came home today. In Corpus I heard a report that Indians were menacing the outside settlements and intended to carry everything before them. They can come into Corpus if they like as there are no troops to protect this part of the

---

[65] Robert Adams in his memoirs said at that time there was only one small store at the Motts, which was owned by Herman Vetters, whose wife was the sister of William McGregor. Vetters' store also served as the post office for the Motts.

country. I was galloping my horse today when he stumbled and I yanked my back. I can hardly move.

September 26 (Monday)

Hauled home a load of wood.

September 27 (Tuesday)

Went to Corpus with George Reynolds and his wagon. Mr. Orchard with his cart fetched home my stable and some new lumber to floor it. Received a letter from William and Fannie.

September 28 (Wednesday)

Jobbing around with the lumber and my corn.

September 29 (Thursday)

Went to Corpus to put a roof on a shed for Adams for the use of his steers last spring to plow my field. After dinner I went into town to select the lumber.

September 30 (Friday)

Worked all day on Adams' shed.

October 1 (Saturday)

Worked all day on the shed.

October 5 (Wednesday)

Began building my shed. I went up to town to mail my letter to William. A young fellow named McGregor walked home with me and stayed all night.

November 6 (Sunday)

Strolled up to Reynolds after finishing my shed. I heard that a strong body of Mexicans headed by a man named Cortina had taken Brownsville on the Rio Grande and intended to invade the whole country.

November 7 (Monday)

I went up to see Reynolds again. After supper, I found them very much scared by the reports in circulation about the Mexicans. A printed circular confirmed the reports that Cortina was at the head of 900 men, had taken Brownsville, and was now on his way to Corpus, swearing vengeance against every white man and declaring his intention to sweep the whole country, from the Rio Grande to the Nueces and from there to the Colorado River. The circular had been put at the door of the store in the Motts. All of us were warned to prepare for the worst. I put my double-barreled gun close to my bed that night.

November 8 (Tuesday)

I heard that men were organizing themselves into a company for defense of the Motts. I went up as I wished to be among them. We heard that the Mexican invaders were only 50 miles from Corpus.

November 9 (Wednesday)

Went to Corpus to see the principal man of the dredge boat company to get some of the money they owe me, but I was unsuccessful, of course. I found everyone in Corpus frightened out of their wits about Cortina's Mexicans and looking for them every hour. The last reports received in Corpus stated that Cortina's army had increased to a thousand men, that they had several cannons and that priests in Mexico were paying them.

Martial law has been declared in Corpus Christi and male inhabitants organized into a company. They have a captain, lieutenant, and one cannon. They keep a certain number of men on patrol every night. I thought that as everybody seemed so frightened there must be just cause for alarm. I started for the Motts as soon as I could. At the Motts, after a good deal of joking and talking about cattle hunts, we decided there was no necessity for us to do anything but keep our guns in order.[66]

---

[66] The Ranchero newspaper in Corpus Christi carried frightful accounts of Gen. Juan Nepomoceno Cortina's raids and activities on the border in its editions during October and November 1859. The distilled reports from the Brownsville Flag said Cortina's men were threatening Brownsville, that Cortina had captured the mail and made the mail riders prisoners, that Brownsville was barricading its streets and preparing for an attack, that Cortina attacked Rio

December 25 (Sunday)

I believe another fight took place a few days since between Cortina and the Americans, but I don't know the particulars.

December 31 (Sunday)

I worked all day on some alterations they were making at the meeting house at the Motts, putting in fresh window panes. Most of the people around here lent a hand.

Grande City. Nueces County Sheriff Mat Nolan returned from the border with a report that Cortina sent an advance force of 60 or more men up the road from Brownsville toward King Ranch at Santa Gertrudis. The Committee of Public Safety in Corpus Christi headed by Henry Gilpin held meetings and issued proclamations. Citizens were organized into a militia unit called the Corpus Christi Guards and patrols on horseback and foot made the rounds during the night hours.

If we do not get rain soon, the cattle must die. It is pitiable to see them, with no grass and no water, hundreds bogged in the river trying to drink. All the vegetation is burned up and many places present nothing but dry sand hills. The whole country has a most desolate appearance.

—July 8, 1860

BEFORE THE WAR
1860

January 3 (Tuesday)
Went to a dance last night at the Motts got up by the young folks and spent a pleasant evening.

February 2 (Thursday)
Orchard was moving the schoolhouse today.

March 4 (Sunday)
Affairs on the Rio Grande do not affect us much here, other than the shortage of horses. The animals are very dear. The Rangers are continually having skirmishes with Cortina's men and from the manner at which they are working I have no doubt that it will lead to war with Mexico.

March 16 (Wednesday)
Went to a party yesterday they got up in the Motts in order to regulate the working of a small circulating library which was recently purchased by subscription. They had no

dancing but passed the time with various amusements. All the feminine population of the Motts, I believe, were there as well as that portion of the masculine which had stayed home from cattle hunting.

* * *

A missing portion of Noakes' journal extended from March 17 through May 16. —M. G.

* * *

May 17 (Thursday)

We have a great accession to the Motts in the person of Mr. Taylor.[67] He has been here for some months and is a schoolteacher by profession. He has opened a school at the Motts which is attended by all the young men and women of the community. Most of them, coming here while quite young, have had no chance to acquire an education.

Now, feeling their lack of an education, they are glad to take advantage of the opportunity and have started to school. The parents of these young people are for the most part well-educated and it is to their regret that their children have been deprived of this comfort in this new waste of land where so much can be done in the future. I do believe that Mr. Taylor will achieve a perfect reformation in the Motts as to manners and scholarship among the young people.

May 20 (Sunday)

After supper Reynolds and Adams came along. I saddled up and rode to Reynolds to see Elizabeth Adams and Mrs.

---

[67] Henry (also called Horace) Taylor was a schoolteacher from Ohio. He served as postmaster at Corpus Christi after the Civil War. Another man named Taylor lived at the Motts; he was Edward ("Ned") Taylor, George Reynolds' uncle. The 1860 Census shows he came from England, that he was 57, and was not married. Robert Adams, who went to the Motts school, said the teacher "was a large man who lived with his mother; after her death he married."

Couling. Elizabeth was up from Corpus on a visit. We went to church together that evening.[68]

May 21 (Monday)

I was gadding about all day with Elizabeth, Mrs. Couling and Mrs. Reynolds. We dined at Mr. Orchard's and in the evening went for a ride. Elizabeth got thrown but did not hurt herself. We spent a pleasant evening at the Reynolds.

June 3 (Sunday)

Busy about the house in the morning. John Orchard and his sister were dipped in the river in the afternoon in accordance with the rites of the religious sect to which they belong. Everybody went to the service at the river.

June 6 (Wednesday)

Went to Corpus yesterday to see Dean Howard again about my dredge boat. I was told that he had a bond sale and went away the night before. The city of Corpus Christi had issued five hundred thousand dollars in bonds to finance the dredging of the channel and the opening of the mudflats to Aransas Pass channel. [Somers] Kinney sold out to Howard and some other New Yorkers who have agreed to sell the bonds at 12½ percent.[69] The company was given all rights and privileges and powers to collect tolls from ships and incoming boats and protection from the city for the execution of same. In spite of such favors, Howard has refused to pay me for my labor and what he

---

[68] Noakes courted Elizabeth Adams but she ended up marrying Thomas Charles ("T. C.") Wright, son of Joseph and Seana Wright. There was no church in Nuecestown but religious services were conducted on alternate Sundays at the schoolhouse. Several preachers lived nearby or within riding distance, including Rev. Stephen Orchard and Rev. J. P. Perham. Ref. Joseph Almond Diary.

[69] Somers Kinney, a cousin of Henry Kinney, founder of Corpus Christi, came to Texas in 1852. He was awarded a contract in 1854 to dredge a channel through the mudflats blocking Corpus Christi Bay. The contract was withdrawn in 1856 due to lack of progress. Somers Kinney was later associated with the Nueces Valley newspaper and the Brownsville Flag. He died in Houston in 1870.

owes me on my boat. I will get nothing, and must take the loss, so might as well stop trying.

June 15 (Friday)

Went to Mr. Taylor's the first thing this morning to make him a blackboard for his school.

June 16 (Saturday)

Took me till noon to finish the blackboard.

June 17 (Sunday)

Went to the Motts to a meeting in the morning. This evening I went to another baptizing in the river, when many more people were dipped.

June 20 (Wednesday)

Bored another well and reached water at 24 feet. It was necessary for my stock.

June 24 (Sunday)

Felt so lonesome today. Feel as though I am all alone with no one to care for me although I get fine letters from home. I can visualize the home and land of my birth with its culture and beauty of natural surroundings. But I have been ill so long that I miss someone to care for me, especially when I am very ill. How I envy the birds flying around this quiet Sabbath. They have no regrets for the past, no cares for the present, no fears for the future.

July 1 (Sunday)

There has been a comet visible for the last few nights in the northwest.

July 4 (Wednesday)

Rode down to Corpus with the teacher, H. Taylor, to see what was going on in town. The schools in Corpus met at the courthouse for examination, after which good refreshments were served then they went home.[70] The

---

[70] An account of the events at the courthouse was printed as a letter to the editor of the Ranchero and signed "Spero," which probably was Noakes. He had previously written accounts for the paper of a panther hunt and a picnic at the

Motts celebrated the Fourth with a dance and a barbecue, but I did not go.

July 8 (Sunday)

Rode down to Corpus and spent the day at Adams' place, going to meeting [church] with Elizabeth, both morning and evening. If we do not get rain soon, the cattle must die. It is pitiable to see them, with no grass and no water, hundreds being bogged in the river trying to drink. All vegetation is burned up and, in many places, presents nothing but dry sand hills. The whole country has a most desolate appearance.

July 14 (Saturday)

Last night we had no rain. The day up till three o'clock was excessively close and still, not the slightest breeze blowing. Just at that time a tremendous wind began to blow, and became a regular tornado. I never remember seeing anything so awful. The air was perfectly darkened and you could not see anything around you but dust and flying rubbish and the roar of the wind was heightened by the crack of the thunder, which proceeded from a black funnel-shaped cloud overhead. Altogether it was enough to scare the bravest, with the lightning flashing in rapid succession around the house. I was afraid the house and everything would be blown away. The rain that followed was no more than enough to dampen the dust.

July 20 (Friday)

I have been working all day on a guitar belonging to some lady neighbors of mine named Ludewig. They are Germans. I promised to repair it for them.

Motts. The letter describes the students' competition in the "Sabbath School Celebration on the Fourth" and points out that the academic and talent exercises were opened by Rev. S. C. Orchard of Nuecestown (Noakes' neighbor) and an introductory address was made by Mr. H. Taylor of Nuecestown (Noakes' friend.) More than 250 children participated in the event; they were organized by religious affiliation since there were no public schools at the time.

July 21 (Saturday)

In the morning I was gluing the guitar and reading. In the evening I rode out and killed a fawn for fresh meat.

July 23 (Monday)

I finished the guitar and took it to the Ludewigs. It was my first visit.

July 26 (Thursday)

The cattle will commence dying pretty soon. Many are so weak and poor that they can barely walk. Ruin stares us in the face. There is not a blade of grass and no water. Even the snakes seem affected by the drought. The last few days I have seen nothing, it seemed, but snakeskin shriveled up. The deer are so starved that they walk about in the town and are bold because they want water and food.

August 3 (Friday)

No sign of rain. I rode up the river with George Reynolds and William Wright to get a great many of the bogged cattle. We pulled out eight head of cattle, a yoke of steers, and one horse, until we were so tired that we went home. I started a new well and Mr. Orchard is helping me. He hauled the lumber from Corpus to curb the well. He brought me my greatest delight, the Illustrated London News, all the world's news.

August 4 (Saturday)

Worked on my well and hunted [John] Ludewig's horses. Well-digging is hard work. I have to get down in the well to fill the bucket then climb up again to empty it. For that reason, I cannot get down below three or four feet a day. Things have got to be as much like famine as I hope I shall ever see.

August 8 (Wednesday)

No rain yet. I worked at the well all day assisted by Mr. Ludewig. We succeeded in getting good water at 18 feet. I have not had a better streak of luck since I have been in the country than in getting good water where I have. The well will be worth a great deal to me.

August 15 (Wednesday)

Nolan, the young officer that was shot in Corpus the other day by Warren, is dead.[71]

August 31 (Friday)

It has been raining for most of this month and the river has risen and overflowed all the bottoms. I have dug a ditch from my yard to the river to drain the water from my premises around the house. Today, an examination took place at Mr. [Henry] Taylor's school in the Motts and I was there helping him all day. In the evening we had a dance. The mosquitoes almost broke up the dance.

September 8 (Saturday)

Went to Corpus with Henry Taylor and rented my house to a widow woman and her two daughters for three dollars a month.

September 9 (Sunday)

We had a heavy thundershower and the water covered the marsh in front of my place. I must continue to dig the ditch to the river to drain it.

September 15 (Saturday)

Rain and more rain every day. This is how I spend my day: Get up at sunrise and go down to the old hut (I sleep in the shed I built) and light a fire, and while I am about it I smoke a pipe and put the coffee pot on. Next, I wash and go to the pen and bring out my horse and stake him. I milk

---

[71] On Saturday, Aug. 4, 1860, John Warren, a butcher, in a drunken rage stabbed James Barnard, owner of the La Retama Saloon on Chaparral Street. Sheriff Mat Nolan and his brother Tom, a deputy sheriff, found Warren at Richardson's store next to Ziegler's Hall. During a scuffle, Warren shot Tom Nolan at point-blank range. Sheriff Nolan and other men in the town chased down Warren and shot him to death. Tom Nolan died 11 days later on Aug. 15 and was buried in Old Bayview Cemetery. The events were described in detail in the Ranchero. See Appendix 3.

and go to the hut for breakfast, as my coffee by this time boils. After breakfast I turn the calves in and the cows out, take water to the calf pen, and if anything requires doing there I do it. I wash up the crockery ware in the house and dirty dishes, if I have any.

I then consider my household duties done for the morning and set about doing my out-of-door work till about 11, when I again light a fire and get dinner, which takes till nearly 1 o'clock. I read for an hour and then to work again. At 5 I make a fire for supper and another one in the pen to smoke off the mosquitoes from the calves, get up the cows and take what milk I require, bake bread, and get my supper, and after taking my horses into the pen and turning my calves out, so the horses can get the benefit of the smoke, and after doing a thousand and one other odd jobs, I consider my work at home done for the day, as the sun has completely disappeared in the west and it is now quite dark. If I need anything I go to the store and get it. If not needing anything, I go and have a talk with a neighbor or stay at home and read until 10, when I go to sleep.

September 19 (Wednesday)

We rounded up at Flour Bluff and from there crossed the lagoon.[72] It was belly-deep on the horses and half a mile wide. We drove the herd toward Comanche Camp and reached there three hours before sundown. We killed a yearling for food. The mosquitoes were very bad.

September 20 (Thursday)

We rode around, found no cattle, and after dinner were joined by six hands from Corpus who had been in search for two days. We drove the cattle to Gregory Ranch and camped.

---

[72] Laguna Madre (mother lagoon) is 120 miles long and from two to six miles wide separating Padre Island from the mainland.

September 21 (Friday)
We rounded up our herd and camped. We had fun singing and spree-in most of the night. Killed another yearling and ate it up by morning.

September 22 (Saturday)
We rounded up and drove to West Oso and from there drove home. I got two head.

September 23 (Sunday)
I went out and caught my horse and took a bath in the river and went to the Motts.

September 24 (Monday)
I was at home all day.

September 25 — 28 (Tuesday — Friday)
Cattle hunting up the Agua Dulce Creek as far as Banquete Creek.

September 29 (Saturday)
Weather most of the time showers. There were 14 of us hunting.

September 30 (Sunday)
Very hot. I stayed home.

October 1 (Monday)
Jobbing about the house.

October 2 (Tuesday)
I drew a plan for Mr. [James] Hobbs' house and took it to him.[73] It was drawn on the lines of an English cottage but of course it would have to be cheaply built.

October 3 (Wednesday)
Last night I had a violent fever and took a dose of medicine this morning consisting of calomel and salt.

---

[73] James Hobbs lived near Nuecestown and operated a gristmill. Hobbs, wife Sarah and six children arrived in Texas in 1852 from Derbyshire, England. Sarah Hobbs died in the yellow fever outbreak in 1854. The oldest son, William, married Harriet Wright and established the Hobbs Ranch near Lagarto in 1886.

October 4 (Thursday)

Last night we rode till midnight. Penned all the cattle from around the Motts. I came home and went to bed. The first thing this morning I saddled up and went to the Motts to help with the cattle. When I reached the store, my fever was so bad I had to lie down. I stayed there till noon, when the cattle hunt was over. I came home feeling very ill. When I reached home a person called with a letter from a person named Moses saying that the horse, I lost last April was at his ranch and he wanted me to take him away.[74]

October 5 (Friday)

Ned Taylor and I rode to Banquete Creek and skinned a calf that died during the night.

October 6 (Saturday)

I rode to Corpus and stopped [stayed] at Adams. Sold my horse cart to Cannon.[75]

October 7 (Sunday)

I settled with Cannon about the cart, dined at Almond's, and after seeing Adams again I returned home.

October 8 (Monday)

At home most of the day.

October 9 (Tuesday)

Geese and sandhill cranes are flying over this week. The up-country people came down to the Motts and we helped them round up their cattle.

October 10 (Wednesday)

Jobbing at home all day.

October 11 (Thursday)

Started to Corpus and about halfway there it started to pour. For three hours I took shelter in a new house

---

[74] Probably J. Williamson Moses who owned a ranch and store at Banquete. Noakes didn't say whether he reclaimed the horse. The owner of a stray animal, on proof of ownership, would be liable to pay a claim for damages.

[75] John Cannon, who later served as constable, lived in a small cottage at Mesquite and Starr, on the corner where Taylor Brothers' Jewelry Store was later built.

belonging to Mr. Byler. After the rain I rode on to Adams and stayed the night.

October 12 (Friday)

I went into the city and did my business and took dinner at Adams and returned home.

October 13 (Saturday)

I was busy at home all day.

October 14 (Sunday)

I passed the day after breakfast like I do every Sunday, alone.

October 15 (Monday)

About a dozen of us started our last cattle hunt this fall, taking the route by Corpus. We spent the first night at Corpus Lake [Salt Lake, a mile west of town].

October 16 (Tuesday)

Weather cool of a night but hot in the day. We rode to Rincon [North Beach] below Corpus and rounded up the cattle there. We hunted the prairie at the back of the town and took our cattle back to the [Salt] Lake to pen them and get our dinners. We started for the Encinal Ranch about nine miles away. We had barely reached halfway when my horse gave out and I had to camp alone.

October 17 (Wednesday)

Last night cold. I caught up with the rest of the crowd again and we rounded up Fullerton's cattle, cut out our strays and penned them, killed a yearling, and camped for the night.

October 18 (Thursday)

Weather still cool. We drove to McLaughlin's [Oso Ranch] and made another roundup and from there to Britton's Ranch when my horse again gave out and I was obliged to stay behind. I made a fire and got some dinner and while occupied with that I determined, after my horse was rested awhile, to make for home and if I could reach there that night, I would get another horse and go straight

87

back. I had twelve miles to go but I could not get my horse more than halfway, so I had to turn down in the middle of the prairie without water.

October 19 (Friday)

Reached home at 8 a.m. and hunted in vain for my horses. I had a steer lying dead so I skinned it and started horse hunting again. I caught my black horse two hours before sundown. By that time, the boys were back with the herd, which we put in another pen.

October 20 (Saturday)

We met at Orchard's pen at seven o'clock and cut out our cows with calves and took them home. I found three cows with unmarked calves. The rest of the day was taken up in seeing to my horses.

October 21 (Sunday)

Nights are cool and frosty. Today was spent in doing little jobs that were neglected during my absence.

October 22 — 27 (Monday — Saturday)

The week passed doing work at home.

October 28 (Sunday)

The weather this past week has been warm and some days windy. This morning looks very bad from the east, like a squall.

October 29 (Monday)

I have been employed about my horses, having yoked my dun to my black. Consequently, I have to hunt them up every day. And as I have ridden my colt, it necessarily has taken more time to do so. Between which I have been covering another whip handle and making the whip. I expect the next norther to be bad as the geese have been arriving the last few days. Yesterday I gave a day to the schoolhouse and fixed up the chimney.

October 30, 31 (Tuesday, Wednesday)

Weather fine and warm. I was battening up my shed to keep warm. Two hours after daylight a cold wet norther came roaring in, but the rain amounted to nothing. I finished the whip I was making.

November 1 (Thursday)
I went to the Wrights and did some little jobs for them. After dinner I rode around on my colt.

November 2 (Friday)
I cut the wood and commenced work on some wooden stirrups I want to make. Those I ride with are falling to pieces. Toward night I rode the colt out.

November 3 (Saturday)
I rode till noon, looking in vain for Orchard's and my mares. He wanted me to pen them. I then worked on the stirrups.

November 4 (Sunday)
I saw the mares come in to water so I saddled up and got them. The rest of the day, till 2 p.m., I spent cleaning up and cooking.

November 5 (Monday)
I finished the stirrups and did other jobs.

November 6 (Tuesday)
Worked on the fish net.

November 7 (Wednesday)
Rode up the river at the request of Mrs. Thurman to hunt a beef for them to kill as they were out of meat. Mr. Thurman was away on a cattle hunt. I found a steer, drove it home, killed and quartered it for them, and brought home as much as I wanted for my own use.

November 8 (Thursday)
Weather cold and wet. I have been working on my fish net.

November 9 (Friday)
Weather fine, the norther done for. I worked at my net and rode around on the colt.

November 10 (Saturday)

Rode out and fetched in my work horses and after dinner hunted and brought home the mares, bringing the colt and the horse out with them.

November 11 (Sunday)

I have passed the day as I usually do on Sunday, alone.

November 12 (Monday)

Rode down to Corpus to get some money from Cannon which he owes me for my cart, but could not get a cent so had to return home without it — empty saddlebags.

November 13 — 17 (Tuesday — Saturday)

Worked at home, jobbing around.

November 18 (Sunday)

Since Monday I occupied my time as usual at home. On Wednesday a little past sunrise a norther came, with rain and thunder, and we had a good shower.

November 19 (Monday)

Went cattle hunting with Shumate on the prairie back of the Motts.

November 20 (Tuesday)

At sunrise we had a driving mist which changed into a norther. I had got my horse ready to start for Corpus tomorrow when my wild ones, loose in the field, jumped the bar rails and cleared them. My black horse, also in the field, broke through the fence. I borrowed a horse to hunt him but did not find him by dark.

November 21 (Wednesday)

I borrowed a horse from Reynolds and by noon had my black horse home to hunt the dun horse with. I hunted for him till night without success.

November 22 — 24 (Thursday — Saturday)

The norther was nearly spent on Thursday night when it blew up again and was very cold. Saturday morning, we had a frost and there was ice on the water in my well bucket. These three days have been spent searching for my horse in the woods at the back of the Motts where I traced him by his rope trail, but as yet I have not caught him. I believe it will be a long time before I do. I may as well hunt for deer in that thicket as for a horse as wild as he is. Received a letter from Emily.[76]

November 25 (Sunday)

I fetched my mares and caught my roan horse. My black one has had enough of it for now.

November 26 (Monday)

Went to Corpus to get some money, stayed the whole day but could not get a cent and returned home with empty saddlebags. I went and saw a member of the dredge boat company to see if there was any chance in the world to get any of what they owe me. I found that my only chance is to sue them. By way of consolation I found that I was about to be sued by another company for $25 for signing my name to a subscription list for the benefit of the company I worked for and who has never paid me.

November 27 (Tuesday)

A cold norther came up about 8 o'clock as I was starting out with Reynolds and his wagon to fetch a load of firewood. In the evening I went to hunt my horse.

November 28 (Wednesday)

I was hunting my horses for no purpose.

November 29 (Thursday)

This was Thanksgiving Day. I was fishing all day with the Misses Ludewig and spent the evening there. When I came home at night, I found my runaway horse in the field. Mr. Wright found and caught him and brought him home during the day.

November 30 (Friday)

Was at home till dinner, after which I found a cow of Ned Taylor's with a young calf and drove her up.

---

[76] His sister in England.

December 1 (Saturday)

I was washing in the morning. In the evening I rode my runaway horse around. I posted a letter to Emily today.

December 2 (Sunday)

In the evening I saddled up my wild dun horse and rode him off very well, but after getting a little past John Hinnant's he commenced to pitch and threw me, but I didn't get hurt.

December 3 (Monday)

I looked for my horse.

December 4 (Tuesday)

I caught up my black horse to hunt up the missing part of my saddle. I found one stirrup and the reins today. Mr. [Donald] McIntyre came for dinner.[77]

December 5 (Wednesday)

I went down the river cattle hunting.

December 6 (Thursday)

I rode my wild horse all day to gentle him. A large rattlesnake struck at his leg as we were passing a hole, but hit him on his hoof. I killed the snake for his fat.

December 7 (Friday)

After dinner I rode out cattle hunting with the Misses Ludewig and remained at their house all evening. They play the guitar and sing very nicely and I spend many pleasant evenings in their company. They have made me quite a vocalist. In all my travels I never saw two sisters of such opposite dispositions as the Misses Ludewig. They are German by birth, living with their parents on a ranch a mile from here. There's a son who is in business in Austin. Mr. Ludewig, I believe, has been a merchant and is quite unaccustomed to country life. The management of cattle and the work he should do is subsequently done by his youngest daughter, Mary, who is a model Amazon, an

---

[77] Donald McIntyre and his wife Mary were from Scotland. They had four children at the time of the 1860 census.

excellent rider, can herd a cow as good as any of us, fond of nature and perfectly original, although not very good looking. She is a girl of good sense and taste and has a very sweet voice and temper. Her sister Ellen is quite her opposite in most respects, being of an exceedingly quiet and timid disposition and only fitted for indoor pursuits. She is better looking than her sister.[78]

December 8 (Saturday)

I was fishing all day with the Misses Ludewig and spent the evening at their home.

December 9 (Sunday)

I was at home most of the day.

December 10 (Monday)

I was cutting posts in the chaparral.

December 12 (Wednesday)

I was cattle hunting with the Misses Ludewig.

December 13 (Thursday)

I was cutting posts again.

December 14 (Friday)

I was fishing all day with the Misses Ludewig and spent the evening dancing and singing.

December 15 (Saturday)

I was at home all day.

December 16 (Sunday)

Weather inclined to rain.

December 17 (Monday)

I rode down to Corpus with the Misses Ludewig, tried to collect some money but couldn't.

December 18, 19 (Tuesday and Wednesday)

I was home doing various jobs.

---

[78] The 1860 Census shows John Ludewig and his wife were both 49, Ellen was 22, and Mary (Marie) was 18. The census taker put down the wife's name as Teraser but it was probably Theresa. Easily half the names of Nueces County residents in that census were misspelled.

December 20 (Thursday)

I went to Corpus to get some money but couldn't succeed and returned home.

December 21 (Friday)

I was riding all day. In the evening I drove up a beef to kill the next day.

December 22 (Saturday)

I killed the beef and was busy all day.

December 23 (Sunday)

I have been busy attending to the meat from the beef I killed yesterday.

December 24 (Monday)

I was working at home most of the day. At night I rode to Atkins' place for a dance.[79]

December 25 (Tuesday)

Christmas Day. I spent the day at Mr. Ludewig's with my fiancé.

December 26, 27 (Wednesday and Thursday)

I was at home.

December 28 (Friday)

Out hunting my horse. Ground wet.

December 29 (Saturday)

Stayed all night at Ludewig's. It was the coldest day we have had this winter. During the day I sat over the fire and read. Hinnant and Atkins took dinner with me.

December 30 (Sunday)

Ground covered with snow and pretty deep. Turned out all my calves. A young man, a stranger here named Cox, danced with us at Atkins the other night. After that he went to Corpus and got into a gambling row and was shot dead.

---

[79] Noakes refers to Atkins several times but neither the 1860 or 1870 census show an Atkins nor does any other contemporary source. Noakes may have shortened the name in the diary, from Atkinson to Atkins. Jerry Atkinson and wife Oma had a large family at the Motts. They came from North Carolina. Ref. 1860 Census.

It was the worst murder committed here. He and three gamblers were playing cards in a room at the back of a drinking house and I suppose they got into a quarrel. Cox was shot with four bullets. It will pass off without notice, as usual. This Cox had a horse and mule which ranged near my place. This morning I found the horse dead, having froze to death in the night.

December 31 (Monday)

Home making pickling spice for my meat.

The comet is very bright tonight, the star being in the northwest and the tail reaching to the meridian. The entire country is in a deplorable state. Nothing is heard but war. Trade is stopped and there is no money. Expecting every day to be called up on military duty.

—July 2, 1861

THE WAR YEARS
1861

January 1 (Tuesday)
New Year's Day. I went for a ride with the Misses Ludewig and spent the evening there.

January 2 (Wednesday)
I went up to John Hinnant's and had some fun. The Hinnants gave a quilting frolic for all the girls around and a dance followed at night. There were too many men for the number of girls and it was in a very little room. I got tired about 10 p.m. and slipped off home. When I reached the place, I found Mrs. Ludewig and her two daughters serenading me for fun, thinking I was inside the house. We had some good fun then I walked them home.

January 3 (Thursday)
Horse hunting all day.

January 4 (Friday)
Went horse hunting with Mary Ludewig. I took my camping things along and the weather was very cold. We made a fire and cooked dinner in the brakes on the farther

prairie. We had a cold wet ride home. I stayed at Ludewig's all night.

January 5 (Saturday)

Miss Mary Ludewig and I rode down by the river and fetched a beef which they wanted me to kill for them. We found and roped him and rode off cattle hunting and fetched home their cow and calf. I rode out to find my horse and failed. Stayed all night at Ludewig's so I could kill the beef first thing in the morning.

January 6 (Sunday)

Killed the beef and rode home. Spent the evening at the Ludewig's and stayed all night.

January 7 (Monday)

Went fishing on the river with Miss Mary Ludewig.

January 8, 9 (Tuesday and Wednesday)

Sometimes at home and sometimes at Ludewig's.

January 10, 11 (Thursday and Friday)

Worked in my shed making a wash-box and wash-board. Planted some peach stones.

January 12 (Saturday)

Cold and windy weather.

January 13 (Sunday)

I spent the day at Ludewig's. Marriage declaration on 13th January 1861. At last I have made up my mind to be married and to wait no longer for better luck and better times. I have proposed to Miss Mary Ludewig and been accepted, and the old folks also being agreeable to the match. We will be married as soon as I can bring it about. As I can plainly see, I cannot do a thing without a wife and if we can manage to get along as times are now then I know we can do so at any time.

January 14 (Monday)

Warm. Spent the morning at Ludewig's and after dinner Mary [Marie] and I came down home for a walk and to get my saddle. Mr. Ludewig and I intend to go to Corpus tomorrow.

January 15 (Tuesday)

I slept at Ludewig's and went to catch Mr. Ludewig's horses. Could not find them so could not go to town.

January 16 (Wednesday)

Went to Corpus with Ludewig but could do no business. I could not get a cent of money either for my cart or anything else. I found the people had left my house two weeks before, and without paying the rent. I came home quite discouraged. Remained at Mr. Ludewig's all night.

January 17 (Thursday)

Weather fine. Stayed at Ludewig's.

January 18, 19 (Friday and Saturday)

At Ludewig's getting out lumber to fix some cart wheels for him and did some work at home.

January 20 (Sunday)

Came from Ludewig's this morning. Caught my black horse last night.

January 21 (Monday)

Home jobbing around.

January 22 (Tuesday)

Rode out and brought my mares in and penned them at Orchard's. Branded my colts and one of Orchard's. Saddled up, rode to Ludewig's, and stayed all night.

January 23 (Wednesday)

Jobbing at home.

January 24 (Thursday)

Busy gardening, planting figs and grape vines and a bed of shallots which Mr. Ludewig gave me to set out.

January 25 (Friday)

Snowed and covered the ground about two inches deep. At Ludewig's all day.

January 26 (Saturday)

Miss Mary Ludewig and I rode out to look after their horses. I then rode to Corpus to fetch a barrel of flour and to try to settle with Cannon about my cart, but without doing so. I returned to Ludewig's and remained all night.

January 27 (Sunday)

Cool and pleasant.

January 28 (Monday)

Working in the garden planting vegetable seeds.

January 29 (Tuesday)

Working in the garden and jobbing about.

January 30 (Wednesday)

I cleaned out my shed, put up a bed, and, assisted by Miss Ludewig, cleaned up my old clock.

January 31 (Thursday)

I varnished the bedstead and did other work at home.

February 1 (Friday)

I was digging in the garden and doing other things at the house.

February 2 (Saturday)

I worked at home in the morning and in the evening went to Mr. Ludewig's to try to catch his horses.

February 3 (Sunday)

I was at Mr. Ludewig's most all day.

February 4 — 8 (Monday — Friday)

Worked at home most of the time.

February 9 (Saturday)

A strong wind from the south. The previous part of the week has been fair with frosty nights.

February 10 (Sunday)

Stayed home all day.

February 11 (Monday)

I have been helping plow fields for Mr. Ludewig. We finished this morning and this evening I brought the plow home to be ready to plow my field soon as I can. I rode to Corpus with Mr. Ludewig, bought some seed and a barrel of flour, and commenced a suit on Cannon's notes, putting the matter into the hands of Chief Justice Russell.

I procured a marriage license at the County Clerk's office and left a notice of my marriage at the office of the Corpus papers to be advertised.[80] I returned home to Mr. Ludewig's.

After supper I took the horses, riding one and leading the other, and went home and dressed myself. Then, it being quite dark, I took the horses to Mr. [Henry] Taylor's in the Motts, he being justice of the peace, and fetched him to Mr. Ludewig's. There Mary and I were married, unknown to everybody but the old folks and Mr. Taylor.

We did not wish to have any fuss. For my part, I could not have had a party if I had wished to, as 30 cents was the most cash I possessed. I had not even the money to pay for the license, but Mary being willing to take me as I am, I thought it a waste of time to wait for better times. After Mr. Taylor was gone, or at least after I had taken him home, Mary and I, with Mr. and Mrs. Ludewig and sister Ellen, started for my place, each carrying some part of the bedding. I had not had time to get it all down before. The others then went home and left Mary and me alone in our glory.

February 12 (Tuesday)

Mary and I spent the day at home fixing up the shed, which we turned into a sleeping place.

February 13 (Wednesday)

Plowing in the field with Mr. Ludewig.

February 14 (Thursday)

Same. Plowing my field with Mr. Ludewig.

---

[80] The notice was printed in the Feb. 16, 1861 edition of the Ranchero: "Married — At the residence of the bride's father, near Nuecestown, February 11, 1861, Mr. Thomas J. Noakes to Miss Marie Elizabeth Ludewig." Noakes was then 29 and Marie was 19. Ref. 1860 Census.

February 15 (Friday)

Plowing all day. In the evening I shot some kirlews [curlews].[81] We had company from Corpus while I was gone.

February 16 (Saturday)

Plowing all day. Mr. [Henry] Taylor came to see us in the evening.

February 17 (Sunday)

We spent the day at Mr. Ludewig's after I had written a letter to my brother-in-law, Adolph Ludewig.[82]

February 18 (Monday)

Plowing all day, driving the steers myself.

February 19 (Tuesday)

Plowing all day.

February 20 (Wednesday)

Indication of rain. Finished plowing.

February 21 (Thursday)

Weather fair, but trying in vain to rain. I was too unwell to work, being completely broke down from previous work.

February 22 (Friday)

Plowing corn all day. Mary helped by driving the steers to plow out the furrows.

February 23 (Saturday)

It blew up a norther, but a mild one. I was plowing corn, sowing turnip and kale seeds in the garden, mending Mary's guitar, and fixing my saddle until evening, when

---

[81] Noakes may have been referring to the Eskimo curlew which was once common along the Texas coast. "There were tremendous numbers of these small curlews until about 1875. The gunner's name for them was doughbird." Ref. Helen Cruickshank, "A Paradise of Birds."

[82] Adolph Ludewig, his brother-in-law, was living in Austin but he had been at Corpus Christi. The 1850 census lists an Adolph Ludewig, saddle maker, as a resident.

Mary and I walked out to the Motts and called on Mr. [Henry] Taylor and Judge Doakes.[83]

February 24 (Sunday)

I suffered all day from a toothache. I could do nothing. I made an iron rod red hot and tried to burn out the nerve in the hollow of the tooth but I suppose I did not reach it as I suffered perfect agonies afterwards. After supper Mary and I walked up to the old folks' place. My tooth continued to get worse. We stayed all night.

February 25 (Monday)

I was in bed most of the day, worn out with my tooth. I tried all in my power to get a horse to go to Corpus to have it drawn, but could not. By night my face was swollen up so much that I could not have had it drawn if I had found a horse. Just at dark I walked to the store and got a bottle of whisky. On going to bed I took a big drink and got to sleep.

February 26 (Tuesday)

I feel better, but did little the first part of the day. Planted some grape cuttings in the north end of the field. Mr. and Mrs. Ludewig dined with us and then we walked up to the old folks' place and caught their horses.

February 27 (Wednesday)

Mary and I rode to Tule Lake to see about a horse that strayed from Mr. Ludewig's but we could find nothing about it. We did find a cow which Mr. Ludewig lost a year ago and the cow's large unmarked bull yearling, which we drove down to their place, and came home to dinner. Then went up there again and killed a yearling. Returned home to bed.

---

[83] Noakes made no mention of the big issue to be decided by the voters that day on whether Texas should secede from the Union. The results of the election in Nueces County, published in the March 2 Ranchero, were 164 votes in favor of secession and 42 against. For some reason, polls were not opened and no votes cast in several precincts, including Precinct 2, Nuecestown. Ref. Ranchero and Eugenia Briscoe, "City by the Sea."

February 28 (Thursday)

I was plowing corn till near nightfall when Mary and I went up to the bluff for a ride.

March 1 (Friday)

I plowed corn till dinner then Mary and I rode out and fetched home my mares and caught my black horse.

March 2 (Saturday)

A strong wind from the south. I rode down to Corpus to attend court as I was compelled to sue Cannon for the amount due me on the cart. I obtained a judgement but cannot collect the money for nine months, as a state law has just been passed to that effect, so as to give rascals every encouragement. I also found that the note I hold on the dredge boat company is of no earthly value, so all hope of obtaining any money is knocked on the head.

I received a letter from Emily. I went down to have my tooth drawn. I am badly in need of several of the necessaries of life, but cannot get any money to purchase them. I reached home at sundown and after supper Mary and I went fishing. We caught a bucket full of mullets, which we cleaned, salted and smoked.

March 3 (Sunday)

In the morning I rode and caught Mary's horse and after dinner rode out and drove home a cow and calf.

March 4 (Monday)

Planting corn all day. Finished the field tonight.

March 5 (Tuesday)

Samuel Couling, George Reynolds, Mr. Ludewig and myself altered Mr. Ludewig's colt in my pen.[84] I went with Reynolds and his wagon and fetched home a load of posts I cut last winter.

---

[84] "Alter" meant "castrate."

March 6 (Wednesday)

Reynolds and I hauled another load of posts. After which I planted beans, cabbage, cucumbers, kershaws [cushaw, squash] and various other seeds in the field.

March 7 (Thursday)

Weather warm and fair.

March 8 (Friday)

Some work at home.

March 9 (Saturday)

I felt unwell. Mary baited a line and put it in the river last night and this morning there was a large catfish on it. We cleaned it and took some to Reynolds. I finished his fence about noon, took dinner there, and came home but, feeling unwell, I did nothing more.

March 10 (Sunday)

I rode out and brought home my dun horse which strayed from the other horses. Spent the evening at Mr. Ludewig's.

March 11 (Monday)

I got up three cows with young calves, two of which were heifers with their first calf, and the other was a fighting cow. It took me most of the afternoon to fight her and pen the calf.

March 12 (Tuesday)

I rode out and found another cow and calf but lost them in the thicket on the way home. I brought home Mary's horse. After dinner I planted watermelons and kershaw [cushaw] seed in the field.

March 13 (Wednesday)

Mary and I started in the morning for a day's cattle hunt, camping for dinner on the Oso Creek. From there we rode across Blucher's Prairie and then home, getting there about dark.

March 14 (Thursday)

This morning I planted a small patch of cotton, fixed my saddle, and worked on the field fence.

March 15 (Friday)

I assisted Orchard with a wild mule. Brought home my roan horse which Mr. Orchard fetched home from where he had strayed. Passed the rest of the day talking with Adams, who stayed to dinner. He brought news to the effect that Indians had killed one of Bryden's shepherds and some other men and that a great deal of mischief had been done by them. I do not think it was Indians but have no doubt that it is the commencement of rough times.

March 16 (Saturday)

Everything is wanting rain. I did not feel like work so I rode out and brought home a cow and calf. After dinner I rode out again but found nothing. This evening, Mr. [Henry] Taylor and his mother and Mrs. Wade called to see us. The winter birds are leaving and the snow birds are arriving.[85] The trees are in leaf and everything looks like spring.

March 17 (Sunday)

I rode out in the morning. In the evening Mary walked to the old folks' place.

March 18 (Monday)

Last night we had a frost, which did considerable damage to the vegetables. I was fixing the upper end of the field fence. Mary and I went for a walk with the gun in the evening. We have been catching some large catfish in the river lately, one being on the line every morning. Some we cure and some we give away.

March 19 (Tuesday)

I finished the fence. Mary caught another large fish; we cleaned it and took a piece up to Mrs. Reynolds and a piece to Mrs. Taylor.

---

[85] It's not clear what Noakes meant. A "snowbird" was a pejorative term for a soldier who enlisted in the fall, to secure a warm berth for the winter, then deserted in the spring. It seems unlikely Noakes was referring to that particular bird.

March 20 (Wednesday)

I rode into the Motts and met the ass'or to get my ass'ment made out.[86] Got some things at the store and hunted among cattle at the river. In the evening Mary and I walked out to shoot something and to call on the old folks. I killed some golden plovers, which we found there in large flocks at this time of the year. The country is greatly excited at the present time, occasioned by the murderous depredations of what is reported to be Indians. The country according to reports is full of them and several persons have been killed.

James Bryden had one shepherd killed and everything at his ranch thrown into the greatest confusion. In consequence, his Mexican shepherds will not leave the house and the flocks are all mixed up. The accounts we hear are so conflicting and erroneous that little can be depended on.

I doubt whether they were Indians, but one thing is certain: There are some very mean people about of some sort or other and if the state does not at once devise some means of preventing such outrages, we shall see some bloody and dreadful times.[87]

March 21 (Thursday)

I was shifting a door in the old hut and fixing up a milk room.

March 22 (Friday)

Reynolds and I rode out and collected our horses and penned McKenzie's for him. After which I was fixing up

---

[86] Noakes went to see the assessor to get his assessment made. He was showing a rare flash of humor.

[87] The Ranchero reported on March 23, 1861 that "a company of minute men was organized in this city for the purpose of operating against the Indians who lately visited this section." Another report in the Ranchero in April, citing dangerous conditions on the frontier, said, "During the month of March last, Nueces County was invaded by hostile Indians who murdered 32 persons and drove off large and valuable quantities of livestock."

the milk room and took a walk with Mary and killed some more plovers and a rabbit and caught a fish before bedtime.

March 23 (Saturday)

We had a light rain which we needed. I understand the corn up the country is all destroyed by the late frost. The first thing done this morning was to go to the river to look at the fish line which we always bait the night before. Mary and I went down again after the cows were milked, where we found two large fish on the line, there being two hooks, and a short time afterwards Mary landed a large turtle which was full of eggs. Salted the fish and turtle intending to smoke them.

March 24 (Sunday)

We caught another large fish.

March 25 (Monday)

Weather fine. Received a letter from Edmond. After dinner I started on a cattle hunt to Gregory's Ranch. I rode to Mr. Holmes' well on the Oso Creek, the appointed place of rendezvous, where I met 27 more hands, some from Nuecestown, some from the river, and some from Corpus. We camped for the night.

March 26 (Tuesday)

Rode to Gregory's, took our dinners, then divided into three parties. We arranged our camping places for the night in such a manner that each party was nearly on the outside of the range in an opposite direction of the others. Our party, the Motts' boys, camped at a water hole on the bank of Agua Dulce Creek. About sundown two Mexicans came into our camp and gave us a long yarn about the Indians. They said they lived in the bushes so the Indians could not find them.

March 27 (Wednesday)

Morning foggy. On the move by daylight and had the cattle rounded up by one o'clock. We finished cutting out our cattle in three hours, dismounted for a little while, took some muddy water and bread, then sent some hands on to Gregory's with the herd, a distance of nine miles. The rest were left to round up another lot of cattle. We reached Gregory's a little after dark and penned our cattle. There we met Rufus Byler from Banquete.[88] He brought word that a party of Indians, some 300 in number, were within a few miles of Nuecestown and San Patricio and that some men had a fight with them at the latter place.

That was startling news for men who had left their homes unprotected. Some were for immediately starting for home. By turning the thing over in my mind, I came to the conclusion it was a tale made up by an opposite hunting party attempting to break ours up. There were some inconsistencies in the tale. I told the others my suspicions and they didn't agree with me.

We felt satisfied that if anything serious was likely to turn up, we should hear directly from the Motts, as we had a man leave us for his home that day and he would know where to send word to find us. We determined to keep on with the hunt until we heard something more definite. We killed a yearling in the dark and got our supper.

March 28 (Thursday)

We rounded up at Gregory's house but had very few cattle. We started the herd for the Encinal, hunting the country as we went, making the last roundup at Eagle Ranch. The rest of the party took the herd over the Oso Creek to pin them at the Encinal while the Motts' boys camped at the Eagle Ranch for the night.[89]

---

[88] Rufus Byler, Frank Byler's brother, was murdered in South Texas traveling from Austin to Banquete at the end of the Civil War. Ref. Eli Merriman, "Old Banquete" newspaper article and J. Frank Dobie, "The Longhorns." Dobie's mother, Ella Jane Byler, was from the large Byler family that ranched in the area from Banquete to Bluntzer. The 1860 census shows the Bylers as stockmen originally from Alabama.

[89] Map (No. IX from 1849-1861, U. S. Coast Survey, Washington, D.C., 1861) showed the location of the Eagle Ranch, which was beyond Fullerton's Encinal Ranch and south of Oso Creek, but did not indicate the owner's name.

March 29 (Friday)

Morning misty. We rounded up at Flour Bluff and crossed the creek to the Encinal where we penned. We killed another yearling and camped for the night.

March 30 (Saturday)

We rounded up the cattle at the Encinal and cleaned up [sorted out] our herd, getting ready for an early started in the morning. By that time, it was night. The Corpus people left with their cattle for home. We found out that the report of an Indian scare was a lie.

March 31 (Sunday)

We started with the herd soon after daylight and reached the Haris well about noon where we stayed a short while to rest the calves and get something to eat, Madame Haris kindly giving us some bread.[90] We reached the Motts at sundown, watered the cattle and penned them in Reynolds' pen. I made for home, feeling anxious to know how things had gone during my first absence. I was disappointed to find no one there and the place as dark and lonesome as it used to be in my single days. I got some bread and butter for supper then Mary returned, having been to her home. The casualties of the trip were two men slightly hurt from falls and one horse gored.

April 1 (Monday)

We cut out our cattle and helped Couling kill a cow, each getting some beef. This evening I took a bath in the river. We badly need rain, the river being quite salty. I received a letter from William today.

---

[90] Noakes had a fine hand but his writing is not always easy to decipher. In the original, it looks to be Haris but may have been Jaris or something else. The 1860 Census shows a Gregory, Antonia and Jenia Jaris, listed as herdsmen originally from Mexico, living in that general area. Spanish surnames were mangled in that census. Hinojosa was spelled as Ynojosa, Cantu as Cantoo, Soliz as Solice, Valdez as Valdias, and Juarez as Quaris. Who knows what the original name was for Haris/Jaris.

April 2 (Tuesday)

Last night, or rather early this morning, we had a nice little rain. It came up from the west accompanied by thunder and a wind that blew tremendously for a short time. Today we have a very strong south wind. I rode to Corpus, returning late in the evening, put in my cows, watered the horses, and cooked some supper. Mary was at the old folks. I fell asleep and didn't wake until morning.

April 3 (Wednesday)

Mary came home just as I was about to start for the Ludewig's. As I had my black horse to get up, we rode back together. We took breakfast at the old folks and then drove up my mares and caught the horse to ride on a cattle hunt, which will start tomorrow. But Mary was unwell so I resolved not to go.

April 4 (Thursday)

I rode down to the Oso Ranch and brought home a runaway horse for Reynolds.[91] He agreed to bring back my cattle on the hunt.

April 5 (Friday)

I was at home putting in watermelon seed and thinning out the corn.

April 6 (Saturday)

I caught up my dun paint colt and rode him a little.

April 7 (Sunday)

Spent the day at the old folks' place.

April 8 (Monday)

Mary and I drove up all the cattle we could find of Mr. Ludewig's and I altered the earmark.

April 9 (Tuesday)

Everything dying for want of rain. I did little jobs at home, amongst which I branded a yearling we found

---

[91] This was the ranch of the late Alden McLaughlin which once belonged to Henry Kinney. McLaughlin died in Havana in January 1860. Ref. Ranchero, Feb. 4, 1860.

yesterday. The cattle-hunting crowd returned and I helped with the herd.

April 10 (Wednesday)

I drove up my horses.

April 11 (Thursday)

The Banquete crowd came so we rounded up the cattle at the Motts, both above and below, then made one more round-up in Sampson's Bend.[92]

April 12 (Friday)

We rounded up Sanford's cattle.[93] Some of us went after we had finished and camped at the Round Lake [near San Patricio].

April 13 (Saturday)

We made three round-ups and returned as far as Sanford's. We took our dinner by the river, after which we came home with few cattle to drive. I had none.

April 14 (Sunday)

I rode out and drove up my horses to change for tomorrow, did various little jobs and penned a cow and large unmarked calf of Ned Rains.

April 15 (Monday)

After cooking my rations, I started for a five-day hunt down the Oso. We met and camped at the Haris [Joris] well. The night was cold, the wind northwest.

April 16 (Tuesday)

Our party divided into two companies to hunt on opposite sides of the creek. The one I was on hunted to [Capt.] Fullerton's. The other went on to Flour Bluff and

---

[92] George Sampson's Rancho Bueno Vista was four miles upstream from the Motts, adjoining the Barranco Blanco Ranch.

[93] Albert Sanford, from Massachusetts, owned one of Henry Kinney's old ranches, the Barranco Blanco, 18 miles above Corpus Christi on the Nueces River. Kinney had also owned Rancho del Oso, south of town, the Rancho del Alazan, 30 miles from Corpus Christi on Baffin Bay, and a ranch on Mustang Island. Kinney lost his ranch holdings to creditors after the failure of his Lone Star Fair in 1852.

we met at Fullerton's Encinal Ranch where we penned. Killed a yearling and camped.

April 17 (Wednesday)

We rounded up at Fullerton's, which took us till evening, then drove our herd to water and re-penned them and camped for the night.

April 18 (Thursday)

We were in the saddle early and drove our herd to the Rincon below Corpus.[94] We hunted the country as we went. We cooked our dinner then saddled up and hunted around the town, returning to camp at sundown. We camped on the shell at the entrance of the Rincon close to the bay so as to prevent our cattle from getting out. We had nothing to shade us from the hot sun or to break the cold night wind from the bay, however we made as merry as we could with the help of a little whisky.[95]

April 19 (Friday)

We drove as far as Turkey Creek.[96] We penned the cattle at Juan Saenz Ranch.[97] Killed a yearling and took our dinner, after which we drove home.

April 20 (Saturday)

We get no rain. The river is as salty as the bay and there is not a blade of grass to be seen.

---

[94] Earlier name for North Beach.

[95] Noakes didn't mention it but the making merry with a little whisky was surely connected to the news of the fall of Fort Sumter, which reached Corpus Christi that day. The Ranchero on the following Saturday said, "The event was celebrated Thursday night in this city amidst much rejoicing and firing of cannon. Ten guns were fired, seven for the Confederate States, one for Jeff Davis, one for Gen. Beauregard, and one for Gov. Clark." The pro-South Ranchero was ecstatic: "Irrepressible conflict has commenced! War has commenced!"

[96] Turkey Creek, La Calera Guajalote, emptied into the Nueces River not far below Nuecestown.

[97] Juan Saenz Ranch was seven miles west of Corpus Christi where today's UpRiver Road crosses Clarkwood Road. The community of Juan Saenz took its name from the original ranch owned by Juan Saenz Garcia.

April 21 (Sunday)

I rode up the river among the cattle in the morning, was at home till supper, after which Mary and I went up to the old folks for a walk.

April 22 (Monday)

I was at home all day. Mr. [Joseph] Almond called in the morning. I commenced to water the vegetables in the garden and field.

April 23 (Tuesday)

I got a cow in with a calf and drove up my horses and mares. I tried to rope my wild horse but he broke the fence again and ran off. I caught my colt and soon after that Mr. Garner called to get his mare, which was with mine.[98] We penned them again.

April 24 (Wednesday)

I fixed the cow pen in the morning. After dinner I commenced making a bucket for the well. Toward night Mary and I walked to the old place where we stayed till late.

April 25 (Thursday)

We had a good rain, helping our prospect of making some corn, just at the very moment we were ready to give up everything as gone. I finished the bucket and when the rain stopped at about 11 o'clock, I planted some cabbage and lettuce Mr. Ludewig brought us. In the evening Mary and I caught the horses and took them up to the old place, leaving the mare for Miss [Ellen] Ludewig and bringing the horse "Joe" home.

April 26 (Friday)

Mary, her sister and myself rode up the river to Ward's place and spent the day getting green grapes, mulberries, and dewberries. We returned before sundown, tied out the

---

[98] Noakes didn't use a first name but it was probably James M. Garner who lived in the area, not to be confused with Jim Garner who was later hanged in Corpus Christi.

horses, saw to the cows, and walked to the old folks' for supper.

April 27 (Saturday)

I have been working all day in the field thinning the corn and hoeing weeds.

April 28 (Sunday)

I rode around on the colt till noon. Mary and I walked to the old place to dinner, returning home for supper.

April 29 (Monday)

I was working all day in the field, pulling suckers from the corn and hoeing weeds. I also had the pleasure to find that the river, which lately has been as salty as the bay, was running rapidly from a freshet occasioned by the rain, so altogether things have put on a bright look.

April 30 (Tuesday)

Early this morning thunder warned us that more rain was about and soon after daylight it commenced, with a good deal of thunder, and lasted for two hours. It rained steadily. We have not had such a rain here in a long time.

May 1 (Wednesday)

Rode out to see my mares.

May 2 (Thursday)

At home. Heavy rain all day.

May 3 (Friday)

Raining still. Busy at home — set fish lines, killed some rabbits. Hope for corn and vegetables. The reports on the war front are not very encouraging. We are to be blockaded and the deuce knows what by the North. Cortina and his band are going to wipe us out, the Mexicans are going to take Texas from us, and what is left will be made into sausage meat by the Indians. Between one and the other, according to rumor, we stand a poor chance.

May 4 (Saturday)

Soon after daylight we had a good rain. I remained at home. Caught a large fish in the morning. Today we had squash for dinner. Mosquitoes are bad.

May 5 (Sunday)

Mary and I spent the day at the old folks' place.

May 6 (Monday)

Attended a meeting of the citizens of the Motts in the evening. The meeting was called by Mr. [Henry] Taylor to devise measures for the protection of our ranches in this country in case of Indians and Mexicans coming upon us. Mr. Taylor was called on to do so by a committee in Corpus, it being the intention of Corpus Christi to raise three companies, one of which is to consist of 100 mounted riflemen. They are to elect their own officers and will not be sent out of the county. Eleven of us volunteered for this company. As soon as this business was ended, we made up to start on a cattle hunt next Wednesday.

May 7 (Tuesday)

Out all day hunting my horses.

May 8 (Wednesday)

Went on a cattle hunt. Rode to our camping place about 10 miles from the Motts, a short distance beyond the West Oso at a mott of trees where some fresh people have just settled. Twenty of us met there.

May 9 (Thursday)

Made several roundups and penned at Bee's pen. Hunted around [Charles] Worthington's.[99] We made a round-up and took our cattle to Bee's pen, let out those we had there, and penned them at Terrell's.[100] We camped at Haris's well and killed a yearling.

---

[99] Charles Worthington, who married Forbes Britton's daughter Rebecca, owned a ranch between Britton's and Hamilton P. Bee's, eight miles south of Corpus Christi.

[100] William Blackburn Terrell, from Virginia, moved to Nueces County in 1857 and established a cattle ranch on the Oso.

May 10 (Friday)

Made a big roundup at Chocolate Motts.[101] After separating the up-country cattle, we drove and penned at Sam Glenn's.[102] We took our dinners at Glenn's then drove home.

May 11 (Saturday)

At home. Killed many rattlesnakes lately.

May 12 (Sunday)

Jobbing around home.

May 13 (Monday)

I started for the Almon Ranch where we had agreed to meet and camp. Took dinner at a waterhole on the prairie and reached camp at sundown. A rainstorm caused us to saddle up after we had some coffee, ride to a ranch, and take up quarters in a new unoccupied house. Heavy rain continued.

May 14 (Tuesday)

Remained in quarters, still raining. It cleared up by noon and we started to round up the cattle but the prairie was too wet. Another storm coming. We struck for home and arrived at sundown.

May 15 (Wednesday)

Hunting mine and Ludewig's cattle all day. Ate supper at Ludewig's and Mary and I came home.

May 16 (Thursday)

Rained all day. I was at home.

May 17 (Friday)

Cutting firewood, still raining.

---

[101] Chocolate Motts was on the Oso Creek, known as the place where Conrad Meuly killed an Indian. Ref. "Perilous Trails of Texas," John "Red" Dunn.
[102] Sam Glenn had a place on the Oso, Grulla Motts, which once belonged to Mustang Gray. Glenn was later the caporal for Martha Rabb's ranch. Ref. "Perilous Trails of Texas," John "Red" Dunn.

117

May 18 (Saturday)

Mr. Ludewig and I fetched a load of firewood. A storm came up and prevented us from doing work so we turned out the steers. I came home after dinner, took a short ride on "Joe," then put a handle on a pocketknife.

May 19 (Sunday)

Home all day till after supper, when Mary and I walked up to the old folks to visit.

May 20 (Monday)

Weather hot. Worked all day with Mr. Ludewig.

May 21 (Tuesday)

Weather still hot. Worked in the garden for part of the day. River flooding the country.

May 22 (Wednesday)

George Reynolds and I started down the Oso by Britton's Motts and to Corpus cow-hunting. We camped on the flats below the town.

May 23 (Thursday)

We hunted home, with Reynolds getting his work steers and I nothing. When I got home, I found the whole of the lower field covered with water, and it is still rising.

May 24 (Friday)

Worked on some wheels which I wanted to repair for my cart.

May 25 (Saturday)

The flats are still covered with water. Worked all day on the wheels.

May 26 (Sunday)

At home till evening, when I took a ride.

May 27 — May 30 (Monday — Thursday)

At home working.

May 31 (Friday)

This Friday brought gloomy news to our community. The rumors are not by any means encouraging. We are to be blockaded, bombarded, and the deuce knows what the

North. Cortina and his band from Brownsville are going to wipe us out and Mexico is going to take Texas back again. After that the Indians will finish the rest of our wives and children with the tomahawk. If only one of these rumors is correct, we have a poor chance to go on building homes and civilization in this country, with only a minimum of food, no farm implements but homemade ones. We are not prepared.

June 1 (Saturday)
Working at home.
June 2 (Sunday)
The weather this past week has been fine. The river is still on the flats. Have been at home all week, employed on the wheel and hoeing in the evenings when it was cool enough. The cattle hunters this week have been on the Palo Alto.[103] They went as far as Banquete and brought home two head, one a yearling. I wanted to get it, it only being marked and not branded. I branded it at Reynolds' pen.

Times are much better than they have been. There is plenty of grass and water and no mosquitoes. There is plenty of corn, and no money to worry our heads about.
June 6 (Thursday)
I have been working each day this week on the wheel. Yesterday Marie and her sister rode to Corpus to buy a few things from the store. I rode out and brought home my mare and changed my horse. Then Mary and I walked to the old folks, where I met and was introduced to Mr. Jones.[104]

---

[103] Palo Alto Ranch, 22 miles west of Corpus Christi, was originally the Mathias Garcia grant. The 83,000-acre ranch was later purchased by Martha Rabb. In 1884, D. C. Rachal bought Martha Rabb's old ranch then sold it to Robert Driscoll, which became part of the Driscoll Ranch and foundation of the Driscoll family fortune.

[104] Noakes alternated between calling his wife Mary and Marie. Census records identify her as Marie, although later historical accounts continued the confusion between "Mary" and "Marie."

June 7 (Friday)

I went to help Mr. Ludewig get a tree home, which he cut for me to make an axle for his cart, and Mary went to do some sewing. As soon as we reached the Ludewigs we found things changed. Mr. Jones had proposed and been accepted by Ellen, my sister-in-law. It was of course a matter for congratulations, so we let the work slide and gave the day to merriment.

June 8 (Saturday)

Busy at home getting in shallots and corn. After dinner Mary and I went up to the old folks' for a spell.

June 9 (Sunday)

Mary and I spent the day at the old folks visiting with Mr. Jones. We rode out, Mary on "Joe" and I on the colt.

June 10 (Monday)

After breakfast Mary and I walked up to the old folks. Mr. Ludewig and I went to Blucher Ranch and brought home a tree with the steers to make an axle for the cart. I came home and after dinner worked on the axle. Times are bad and likely to get worse. First cool weather today.

June 11 (Tuesday)

Mr. Ludewig came down and we heated the tires and put them on the wheel. I worked on the axle.

June 12 (Wednesday)

Worked on the axle. Mrs. Ludewig and Miss Ludewig were down all day washing.

June 13 (Thursday)

Spent the day with Marie at Mr. Ludewig's. It was my birthday today.[105]

June 14 (Friday)

Busied myself about the place. Cleaned some Doura corn.[106] I ground it and made bread with it the same way as

---

[105] Noakes was 32.

[106] This was a sorghum grain that was also known as "Indian corn" or "Guinea corn." The Nueces Valley on Oct. 10, 1857 described it as Doure Corn and said

to make cornbread, as an experiment. Mary and I tried it for supper and found it equal if not superior to cornbread. Not feeling well.

June 15 (Saturday)

I painted some flowers till dinner time. Shot a hare and jobbed at home. We hear nothing but talk of fighting and hard times.

June 16 (Sunday)

I finished my painting of flowers and walked up to the old folks' to visit.

June 17 (Monday)

Very hot. The gate to the pen was down and my cows were gone. Rode out and got them all back. Fixed the pen gate. Rode out and brought my horses home.

June 18 (Tuesday)

Rode down the Oso to Worthington's to find a strayed cow. I camped to watch the water hole.

June 19 (Wednesday)

Did not find my lost cow but brought home another cow and calf.

June 20 (Thursday)

Rode to two cattle round-ups but got nothing.

June 21 (Friday)

At home branding calves and making paint, after which Mary and I went for a ride.

June 22 (Saturday)

Busy all day with cart, axle, and painting.

June 23 (Sunday)

Rode around and walked up to Ludewig's.

---

the seeds were brought from Austin by Henry W. Berry. The Doure corn, said the Valley, "is very prolific, producing even in very dry weather, from 60 to 100 bushels per acre, with the same cultivation as Indian corn."

June 24 (Monday)

Reynolds and Ludewig came and helped me to burn the lampers [lampas] out of my black horse.[107] Worked on the cart.

June 25 (Tuesday)

Started to Corpus on a cattle hunt, catching up with the crowd at John Dunn's. We camped at Dunlap's.

June 26 (Wednesday)

We hunted around Corpus then drove to the Encinal Ranch and penned. We camped near the house after rounding up the cattle from the lower part of the range.

June 27 (Thursday)

We made a good round-up, worked the cattle and drove to the Oso Ranch and penned, gathering all the cattle there, cut out our strays then took dinner. We crossed the creek and rode down towards the Laguna [Madre] about seven miles, rounded up the cattle, and returned to camp. Being short of provisions, we killed a calf, ate supper, and turned in for the night.

June 28 (Friday)

We rounded up at Worthington's.[108] We then went to Terrell's Ranch where we penned. We had to camp till the next day.

June 29 (Saturday)

Reached home with the herd at 11 a.m. After supper Mary and I walked up to visit with the old folks.

June 30 (Sunday)

We spent the day at the old folks' house. I saw a comet tonight with a long tail.[109]

---

[107] Defined as a harmless condition that caused swelling of the roof of the mouth. Severe treatment in Noakes' time was to lance the palate, to make the swelling go down, or to burn the roof of the mouth.

[108] Charles Worthington's Ranch on the Oso Creek was between Britton's and Bee's ranches, eight miles south of Corpus Christi.

[109] The Ranchero also took notice: "The comet — the fiery-headed, long-tailed comet — has received a great deal of attention from star-gazers this week."

July 1 (Monday)

Put the cart together and thrashed some Doura corn.

July 2 (Tuesday)

Rain. Marie and I rode to Corpus to purchase some necessaries at the stores. We stayed at Mrs. Swift's and returned to Mr. Ludewig's a little after dark.[110] Samuel Couling brought up our things on his wagon. The comet is very bright tonight, the star being in the northwest and the tail reaching to the meridian.

The entire country is in a deplorable state. Nothing is heard but war. Trade is stopped and there is no money. Expecting every day to be called up on military duty.

July 3 (Wednesday)

Home all day.

July 4 (Thursday)

Brought in my horses. Took Mr. and Mrs. Ludewig to Blucher's Ranch and brought home a load of moss for a mattress.[111]

July 5 (Friday)

Painted the cart and jobbed around.

---

[110] Mrs. Susan Swift, a doctor's widow, ran a boarding house on Water Street, next door to Elizabeth Hart's store. The 1860 census lists her as a hotel-keeper and said she came from Kentucky and had four children, Leona, Grace, Marcella and William. The Swift home on Water Street was demolished in 1899 to make way for Eli Merriman home that was built on the site.

[111] Noakes doesn't say whether the Fourth was celebrated at Nuecestown. It was observed in Corpus Christi, though stripped of the usual patriotic sentiment, though the Ranchero noted that the signers of the Declaration of Independence in 1776 were also "rebels." Young scholars demonstrated their talents in an annual Fourth of July event held at the courthouse. Rev. J. P. Perham gave the opening address, preaching on the "sacred institution of slavery." The Knights of the Golden Circle marched through town to a banquet held at Ziegler's Hall, and the La Retama Saloon set out "a most sumptuous free lunch, the best public dinner we ever partook of in Corpus," said the Ranchero.

July 6 (Saturday)

Made a sieve to clean the Doura corn. We have tried the Doura corn and find it makes very good bread, and it is a good substitute for coffee.

July 7 (Sunday)

Took it easy all day.

July 8 (Monday)

Finished the axle and cleaned some corn.

July 9 (Tuesday)

Jobbing at home.

July 10 (Wednesday)

Attended a meeting in the Motts called by Mr. [Henry] Taylor, Justice of the Peace. The brigadier general of the district [Hamilton P. Bee] has ordered the muster of all men between 18 and 40 to serve as minute men in case of need. They were to elect their own officers, from the rank of captain down.[112]

July 11 (Thursday)

There was a picnic at the Motts, but Mary and I did not go until evening, when we met the party coming home.

July 12 (Friday)

Spent a lazy day.

July 13 (Saturday)

Rode 16 miles up the Nueces River to see a Mexican who had goats to trade. He could not understand a word of English so I could do no trading. Wanted to trade beeves for goats.

July 14 (Sunday)

Rode around and walked to Reynolds' place.

---

[112] This was the Reserve Company militia, Precinct Two. Elected officers included Frank Byler, captain, Thomas Noakes, first lieutenant, John Emory Frost, second lieutenant. Ref. "Muster Rolls of Military Companies Organized in Nueces County During the Civil War" compiled by D. E. Kilgore. See Appendix 4 for the complete listing.

July 15 (Monday)

Lazy weather, very hot.

July 16 (Tuesday)

Jobbed around and worked on corn.

July 17 (Wednesday)

Same as before.

July 18 (Thursday)

Same as before.

July 19 (Friday)

Working on corn.

July 20 (Saturday)

Hot and dry. Gathered and got in my corn today. Cattle hunters brought me a cow and calf.

July 21 (Sunday)

Took a cow and calf to Ludewig's. Stayed at home otherwise.

July 22 (Monday)

Rode to Corpus with Mr. Ludewig. I stayed to take down my house in town. I pulled down a good part of the kitchen by night.

July 23 (Tuesday)

Thunder and rain. Worked all day at the house. Took my meals at Adams' house.[113] I gave him some posts and fencing to offset.

July 24 (Wednesday)

Worked at the house.

July 25 (Thursday)

I finished taking down the house and fence. I put up a piece of fence for Adams in the place my house had occupied. Tried to do some business in Corpus.[114]

---

[113] William and Robert Adams recalled that their father, Robert Adams Sr., built their home just west of the 1854 courthouse. William Adams in 1938 said, "We lived near the courthouse. The present courthouse grounds probably include the lot where we lived." Noakes' home in town was next to the Adams' place.

July 26 (Friday)

Reynolds and Ludewig came with a wagon and cart and loaded up the lumber from my house and started for home. Reached it at 4 p.m., got dinner, and unloaded.

July 27 (Saturday)

I strained my back helping Reynolds with the steers and can scarcely move.

July 28 (Sunday)

Back painful. Preparing to return to Corpus for another load.

July 29 (Monday)

Reynolds, Ludewig and I went back to Corpus for another load.

July 30 (Tuesday)

Reynolds and Ludewig took the rest of the house home. I rode out and brought my cow and calf home.

July 31 (Wednesday)

Home unloading all day.

August 1 (Thursday)

Rode around and worked at home.

August 2 (Friday)

Felt bad all day but attended a political meeting at the Motts.

August 3 (Saturday)

Still unwell. Mary got me some medicine.

August 4 (Sunday)

Rode a little, but still unwell.

August 5 (Monday)

During the day I acted as clerk at the election in the Motts.

---

[114] In previous entries, when Noakes wrote that he "tried to do some business" he meant that he tried to collect a debt owed him, either by the dredge company or by John Cannon for the sale of a horse cart.

August 6 (Tuesday)

Mr. Ludewig and I took the cart to get some salt from the lower part of Oso Creek. By dark we had the greater part of our load collected, the salt fine and good.[115]

August 7 (Wednesday)

Early morning, we loaded up the cart and started home with 25 bushels of salt. We reached home about noon and unloaded the salt.

August 8 (Thursday)

Jobbing around.

August 9 (Friday)

Went back to the Oso to get salt. Found little fine salt so we worked at the coarse salt till dark. We were tired. We had to collect it with our hands and bring it out of the creek through a foot and a half of sand and up the bank into the cart.

We had little bedding and only bread and butter to eat. Besides our own, there were five wagons belonging to people from the Motts getting salt.

August 10 (Saturday)

We began at daylight and finished our load. All the other wagons followed and we made quite a wagon train. We got home at sundown with 35 bushels of salt in the cart.

August 11 (Sunday)

Took it easy all day.

---

[115] With the coast blockaded by Union warships, outside sources of salt were shut off and the salt deposits around the Laguna Madre and Baffin Bay became a valuable commodity. Because of the scarcity inland the price of salt soared to $10 dollars or more a bushel. The salt could be traded away from the coast for bacon, cornmeal, sweet potatoes or sold for Yankee dollars.

The Ranchero said, "Quite a brisk business is being done here in the salt line. Vessels and wagons are bringing up large quantities from the Laguna Madre. From here the salt is being taken to Indianola, San Antonio, Austin and other places in the state. Salt abounds in the vicinity of Corpus Christi in sufficient quantities to supply the whole country." Ref. Ranchero, July 13, 1861. See Appendix 5.

August 12 (Monday)

I started for the Palo Alto, William Rogers' ranch.[116] We heard that Mr. Ludewig's colt had strayed there. I reached the ranch at noon but after hunting for some horses in vain, I struck west for the San Fernando Creek, a distance of 15 miles, expecting to find water for myself and mare, of which we were badly in need.

I followed no road, steering by the sun. I ran down a fawn as I went along for something to eat, as I had come with provisions for only one day. When I reached the San Fernando, I found not a drop of water. I had no matches to make a fire. It was about ten miles to the next creek, the Santa Gertrudis, and the sun was about down. I had to keep going; the mare and I were much distressed for water.

I found a little water thick as gravy and although I could not touch it the mare had to make do. I rode two or three miles farther on and unsaddled, leaving the mare to find what she could. I put the saddle in a tree and took the fawn on my back and began to walk until I reached Bryden's Ranch on the Santa Gertrudis. Mr. and Mrs. Bryden received me very kindly, giving me supper and everything I needed. I remained all night with them.

August 13 (Tuesday)

After a good breakfast and leaving a description of the colt with Mr. Bryden, I started for Capt. King's ranch to make inquiry.[117] I then started for home and reached there about 11 o'clock that night.

I think Texas is the most inhospitable country under the sun. You may ride for a whole day in the burning sun and if necessity compels you to call at a ranch (unless it is some

---

[116] William Long (Billy) Rogers' ranch, Palo Alto, was located 22 miles west of Corpus Christi. This was later the Driscoll Ranch. Rogers survived a massacre on the Rio Grande in 1846. He later was elected sheriff of Nueces County and became a prominent businessman and rancher.

[117] Noakes must have recovered his saddle and mare at some point, but he didn't enlighten us.

friend) for information about strayed cattle or horses or anything else, it is seldom you get a satisfactory or even civil answer to your question. They tell you anything to get rid of you. As for inviting you to come in under the shade and rest awhile, it is a thing they do not think of. Nor do they offer to give you a drink of water.[118]

August 14 (Wednesday)

After dinner Mr. Ludewig and I, with the colt and the steers, drove to the salt diggings. Made it there at midnight. We took our supper and laid down.

August 15 (Thursday)

We had our load of salt collected in the cart by nine a.m. We made a start for home, but after going a mile or so we had to take the steers out of harness and get in the shade. The heat was so bad it took us till 10 p.m. to reach home. We had 35 bushels of salt.

August 16 (Friday)

Fishing in the river and taking it easy.

August 17 (Saturday)

I unloaded the salt and rode the colt after dinner. I did little besides shooting some rabbits.

August 18 (Sunday)

I took a ride on the colt.

August 19 (Monday)

I rode among the cattle and in the evening went fishing.

August 20 (Tuesday)

Busy at home and in the evening rode the colt.

August 21 (Wednesday)

I rode to the mouth of the river in search of one of Mr. Ludewig's steers. We wanted to go for a load of salt.

---

[118] Noakes didn't produce any evidence for that statement. His bitter reaction seems odd considering the hospitality he received from James and Janet Bryden, whom admittedly he knew. His diary is filled with instances in which travelers are taken in and given accommodations. It was considered standard practice at far-apart ranches to offer travelers a meal, a place to rest, and sometimes a fresh horse if needed.

Returned home for dinner and hunted again in the evening without success.

August 22 (Thursday)

Hunted for the steer all day but could not find him.

August 23 (Friday)

I was hunting for the steers all day in the rain but came home without having seen them.

August 24 (Saturday)

Mr. Ludewig found the steers this morning but it is too late to get any more salt. The rain washed it away. It was our only chance to make anything and luck would not allow us to make that. Some of the people around here who are smart have got several hundred bushels for which they are getting a ready sale right here at home. Mary and I walked to the Motts and called on Mr. [Henry] Taylor.

November 17 (Sunday)

We elected a brigadier general for this district. In April the first shot of the Civil War was fired at Fort Sumter but Texas has been slow or indifferent to its pledge to the Southern cause, although it was one of the first to vote "secession." This will be more disastrous to the progress and culture of Texas than the Indian depredations.

December 21 (Saturday)

Yesterday I received an order from our major to put the company on a war footing, which I acknowledged by letter to him today.

* * *

A missing portion of Noakes' journal includes the period from Aug. 21, 1861 to the end of the year, except for one lone entry on Dec. 21. This was a time when the effects of the Union blockade of the Texas coast began to cause some hardship with the

shortage of food and manufactured goods
and it was a time when there were increased
fears that Corpus Christi and the Aransas
Pass channel leading into the bay would
become targets for enemy action. —M. G.

* * *

We have the most startling prospects of famine. Flour is $24 per barrel and cornmeal is $2.50 a bushel. Both are very scarce at that. We have seven or eight cows in the pen and can only get enough milk for coffee, as there is no grass and nobody is able to plant anything.

—March 15, 1862

THE WAR YEARS
1862

January 20 (Monday)

Capt. [Frank] Byler called soon after breakfast to request me to write some notices to be stuck up in three different places within the precinct to call our company together on Monday, the 27th. I did so.

January 27 (Monday)

I rode "Joe" into the Motts to attend to the matter of our company. After drilling a short time, we made plans for a cow hunt and dispersed. I came home.

February 8 (Saturday)

This was muster day. About 11 o'clock I rode "Joe" up to the Motts, where I found seven of the men. The captain and the rest of the company deemed it too cold to turn out. I had the muster roll called and dismissed the company and returned home.[119] After dinner the captain called to say that in consequence of the Northerners being on Mustang

---

[119] Reserve Company in Precinct 2, Nuecestown, was formed on July 15, 1861.

Island, we were to hold ourselves in readiness to turn out at a moment's notice.[120]

February 22 (Saturday)

Today is muster day for our company. I shall be glad when the war is over. They are putting a war tax on us and increasing all the other taxes. I do not know how to buy the necessaries of life now. There is nothing but paper money in circulation. If you sell anything, you cannot pass it only at a great disadvantage.

February 27 (Thursday)

I took some meat to Judge Doakes and heard the news of another victory gained over the Northerners at Bowling Green.[121]

March 1 (Saturday)

I was at home getting ready for an early start tomorrow morning. The officers and non-commissioned officers have been ordered to attend a camp of instruction at Beeville, 45 miles from here.

March 2 (Sunday)

At daylight I was up and soon ready to start for the place of encampment. After waiting a long time in the Motts for the others who were going, I started alone, being tired of waiting in the cold wind. The rest overtook me in a short time. We took dinner on this side of the river at San Patricio. We crossed and rode some time into the night and

---

[120] Capt. Byler was probably referring to raiding forays of Lt. John W. Kittredge, commander of the Union blockading squadron off Aransas Pass channel. In early February, Kittredge sent a shore party to attack and run off Capt. Benjamin F. Neal's artillery battery on Mustang Island. It was no doubt this event Byler was referring to. Mustang Island wasn't occupied by federal forces until November 1863 during Gen. Nathaniel Banks' invasion of the Texas coast.

[121] Some victory. On Feb. 13-14, 1862, Confederate forces evacuated Bowling Green, the Confederate capitol of Kentucky, after reports that Forts Henry and Donelson had fallen to the Union. Confederate troops headed south for Nashville.

camped on the open prairie without water and very little wood.

March 3 (Monday)

The night was very cold and this morning there was ice on the only canteen we had. We ate breakfast without coffee and rode on. We got to Green Gay's on the Aransas about noon.[122] There was a great many horsemen and buggies departing for the encampment. We fell into the stream and after a ride of three or four miles we arrived at our destination.

We found the spot chosen for the camp a most beautiful one in every respect, in the bend of the river, covered with live-oak trees and on rather high ground. It was well-suited for a military encampment, with good water, good grass, and plenty of shade. We were only four in number. The rest of the officers of our company were detained at home on different excuses, the want of inclination being the true one I suspect in most cases.

We made our camp under a large live-oak tree. After eating our dinners, we repaired to headquarters, which was known by a flag stuck in a tree, with a few chairs scattered underneath. There must have been four or five hundred men on the ground, all commissioned officers of the brigade. We formed in a line when the roll was read. After answering to our names, we agreed to form ourselves into companies and to choose our officers in order that we might better instruct ourselves in the duties and drills of soldiers. We drilled awhile then returned to our camp.

March 4 (Tuesday)

At daylight we mustered for roll call then took breakfast and attended to our horses. About eight o'clock we mustered for infantry drill and drilled till nearly noon. After

---

[122] Green Gay's cotton farm and ranch was where the Aransas River crossed the road between San Patricio and Goliad. Ref. Thomas A. Dwyer, "From Mustangs to Mules," article in "Mustangs and Cow Horses," edited by J. Frank Dobie and Mody Boatwright.

dinner, all hands mustered on horseback. There were five companies with each bearing its colors. We drilled for three or four hours then tied our horses.

About four o'clock we formed into companies and marched to headquarters on dress parade, our brigadier general being in full uniform, that being a blue shirt tucked into his pants, a citizen's hat, and a sash and sword. After going through several kinds of drills, and presenting arms, and all the other forms required on such occasions, we were dismissed. At eight o'clock we mustered again for roll call and a guard for the night was detailed. Those not on guard could go to roost.

March 7 (Thursday)

We drilled in the morning. At three o'clock we mustered for dress parade. After going through the regular forms, a proclamation was read from the governor of the state calling for 15,000 more men and warned that if the required number was not forthcoming by volunteering within the next 30 days then the state must have recourse to the draft.

We heard that the South had suffered a severe defeat, having had 12 regiments taken prisoner besides a great number killed and wounded. We were dismissed about half past four and started for home, reaching there at noon the next day.

March 15 (Saturday)

We have the most startling prospects of famine. Flour is $24 per barrel and cornmeal is $2.50 a bushel. Both are very scarce at that.[123] We have seven or eight cows in the

---

[123] Joseph Almond, one of Noakes' neighbors, noted in his diary later that year, in October 1862, that the price of cornmeal had climbed to $8 a bushel in Corpus Christi. He bought a load but when he reached home, he found that he had been short-weighted by 16 pounds. On Jan. 15, 1863, the Ranchero reported that rumors that corn was selling for $16 a bushel in Corpus Christi were untrue. "The fact of the matter is, corn has sold here for $26 a bushel and were there today corn for sale in this town, it could be sold for $100 a bushel. Hunger will force the payment of any price, so long as a dollar is to be had."

pen and can only get enough milk for coffee, as there is no grass and nobody is able to plant anything.

March 28 (Friday)

Today was our election for brigadier-general, major, and company officers. [Frank] Byler and myself were elected to our old offices.[124] The other offices were also filled.

April 5 (Saturday)

Today was muster day and I drilled the men for the greater part of the time.

April 30 (Wednesday)

The Confederate States Congress has passed a conscription law which compels every man, from the age of 18 to 35, to go into active service.

May 3 (Saturday)

A company of infantry camped here today. They are from San Antonio and are a fine lot of men. They are going to Corpus Christi.

May 6 (Tuesday)

I ascertained that the wives of the men who go to the war are to receive $10 a month. Marie is satisfied for me to go. Consequently, the first thing this morning I went to the Motts and joined that company.[125] They have allowed me till Thursday to get ready to march.

May 9 (Friday)

After we drilled, we were marched into Corpus Christi and the company was taken to a place above the town where a couple of deserters were hanging in a tree.[126] We

---

[124] Byler was re-elected captain of the company and Noakes first lieutenant.

[125] This was John Ireland's Independent Company, Texas Infantry, later designated as Company K. Besides Noakes, the muster roll shows that Adolph Ludewig, Noakes' brother in law, was in the company.

[126] The two men were probably Confederate deserters though no court-martial records have been found. Ref. "The Maltby Brothers' Civil War" by Norman Delaney. In a deposition after the war, Joseph FitzSimmons, city secretary, said

were allowed half an hour to buy mess utensils then marched back to camp.

May 18 (Sunday)

I went to church, looking into the Roman Catholic church as I went by. I went to the Episcopal Church and returned to camp for dinner. Our provisions are anything but satisfactory, being deficient in quantity and quality.

***

One of Noakes' missing journals covered the period from May 19, 1862 through November 13, 1863. At least one major event occurred during that time: the bombardment of Corpus Christi by Union warships on Aug. 18, 1862. Noakes was there as a member of Capt. John Ireland's company. He later painted a likeness of what he remembered of the battle. The painting by Noakes depicted the high point of the fight when Union ships fired at a Confederate battery of three guns located on the shore. Union forces landed and were repulsed by Confederate cavalry.

A few details of Noakes' activities during this period can be found by correlating the entries in Joseph Almond's diary for the same period. There were several cattle-hunting trips by the men of the Motts in July and September. Noakes may not have been along if he was still with his company; it's not clear when he received a medical

---

the two men hanged were from New York and their only crime was being too free with their opinions. He said placards were attached to the hanged men that read "Traitors Take Warning" and "Union Men Beware" and that some of the town's pro-Union supporters were marched at gunpoint to see the bodies.

furlough. But he was at home in April 1863. Almond said several of the neighbors joined in a grape-gathering expedition to Ashton Bottoms on the river, a mile above Nuecestown. Thomas and Mary Noakes were among the participants. On Aug. 27, 1863, Almond said that Johnny, the 11-year-old son of James and Janet Bryden, died of what was described as a congestive chill. Noakes helped make the coffin. On Sept. 22, 1863, Almond noted in his diary that he saw Noakes and John Hogarth. "They had been tailing and altering Hogarth's lambs. Hogarth intended to go to the Aransas Creek next day and Noakes to the Lagarto."

We return to Noakes' diary on Nov. 14, 1863 when he and a group of men went to pick up a consignment of goods at Miller's Ferry at Santa Margarita. They found that the freighter had left the goods with Miller but had overcharged on the bill, which Miller had paid. They went on a chase in search of the freighter to recover the excess money. —M. G.

***

The last day of a miserable year. Bitterly cold.
The whole atmosphere is thick with sand
and dust. We sat by the fire making shoe pegs
and mending Marie's shoes. The company of
men that passed me the other evening went to
Corpus where they took a man named Dix
prisoner. It was said that he was a traitor who
been communicating with the Yankees.
So ends a miserable year.

—*Dec. 31, 1863*

THE WAR YEARS
1863

November 14 (Saturday)

Weather cool. Wind from the north. I was up at daylight
and rode to the Motts. From there we went to Sanford's
Ranch [Barranco Blanco] where we made up our
complement of men. We rode to San Patricio and called at
Miller's at the ferry.[127] The goods were left with him but
the freighter had charged 30 dollars more than had been
agreed upon. We concluded to follow him and make him
give it up, as Miller had paid for the things.

We rode all day, crossed the Aransas River, and could
still hear of him ahead. We expected to overtake him at

---

[127] The ferry at the Santa Margarita crossing below San Patricio was operated
by Samuel Reed Miller. After the war, S. G. Miller ran a ferry at Lagarto.
Samuel Reed Miller's ferry was later known as Quinn's Ferry, run by Alonzo
Quinn.

Beeville. We arrived there after dark. We had not stopped to eat since we left home. We made coffee and ate some bread and meat and pushed on again to the next creek.

We were told by some cattlemen that the train of wagons we were after was still ahead. Our horses were tired out, so we unsaddled and laid down till nearly morning.

November 15 (Sunday)

Weather fine, but cool. During the night it was cold. We were in the saddle and on the road before daylight. About sunrise we came upon the train we were after, which consisted of four wagons loaded and one empty.

There were four white men and two [N------s] along.[128] The man himself was a stout determined old fellow and we had some high talking until we showed him that we were determined to have what we came for. He couldn't bluff us off.

He handed over the money, but at the same time requested the names of all of us in the party. All gave him their name but I was overlooked.

We rode back to Beeville then to the Aransas, where we were given a good dinner at a house on the bank of the river. We reached home about 10 p.m. Since we had started, we rode about 150 miles. I cooked myself some supper and went to bed.

November 16 (Monday)

Weather clear and warm. The country is awfully dry and the cattle are suffering. I repaired my harness and did different jobs. I felt very stiff and tired this evening.

November 17 (Tuesday)

Weather still warm and dry. I grained the deer hide and then tried my new horse with the cart, with which I was

---

[128] After some mental debate, I decided not to repeat Noakes' use of the N-word. While my intent is to remain true to his written record, that can be done without being legalistic or obsessive. Noakes was a product of his time, but we are products of our time and we should avoid using racial slurs that inflict hurt. As for Noakes, we should not judge him based on the morality of today.

well-satisfied. I also wrote a letter to Adolph Ludewig, but could not send it. In the first of the morning we heard heavy guns from the direction of Mustang Island.[129]

November 18 (Wednesday)

Weather warm and windy from the south. I took my horse cart and went down the Oso to try and kill a deer but had no luck.

We have fresh news every day of the approach of the Yankees. There are 1,200 reported at the mouth of the Rio Grande and another seven or eight thousand prepared to take Corpus Christi.

The greatest alarm prevails all over the country with people scattering in all directions, some going east and some in the east going west.

Corpus Christi people are moving out into the country to get away from the Yankee.[130] The country people are moving to Corpus for fear of the Mexicans. Every man able to carry a gun is being called out. There is every prospect of our soon seeing all the horrors of war.

November 19 (Thursday)

Weather hot and windy from the south. It changed around and blew cold and the air and sky were filled with dust. Gen. [Hamilton P.] Bee passed by here last night with or five or six hundred men bound for Corpus.

This morning I felt too unsettled to do much. I watered the cows and calves at the well and made some hoops for a water keg.

At the present moment there is little that is cheerful to be seen or heard. The country is dried up. The cattle and

---

[129] After capturing Brownsville, Union forces under Gen. Nathaniel Banks landed at Corpus Christi Pass at sundown Nov. 16, 1863. Soon after daybreak on the 17th they attacked Fort Semmes on Mustang Island and after fire from Union gunboats in the Aransas Pass channel, Confederates in the fort raised a white flag.

[130] Noakes often used "the Yankee" in singular form for federal troops.

horses are starving for want of water. The river is too salty for them to drink.

The Yankees, Mexicans and Indians are advancing from every side and to all appearances this part of the country will be given up.

We are to take our choices, to abandon our homes and property and go east to starve, or stay here and let them murder us.

November 20 (Friday)

Weather cold. I walked over to James Bryden's to hear the news.[131] In the evening I dressed and worked a buckskin.

November 21 (Saturday)

Weather warmer. I took the horse and cart down the Oso and hunted deer all day, without success. After I came home, I heard that four Yankee vessels were in sight of Corpus Christi.

November 22 (Sunday)

Weather warm, wind from the southeast. I lent my horse and cart to Mr. Terrell, who broke a part of the harness. A clerk in Hobby's regiment, an Englishman, called and dined with us.[132] After he left, I walked to Mr. [Henry] Taylor's and had a talk. Yesterday's report that the Yankees were at Corpus is unfounded.

November 24 (Tuesday)

A norther came blustering up last night, accompanied by a few sprinkles of rain, and although the first part of the night was very warm, this morning it is very cold. I took a walk up to Judge Doakes' to hear the news.

In the middle of the day I was making an ax handle and a spade handle.

---

[131] James Bryden moved his family from their remote ranch on the Santa Gertrudis to Nuecestown for greater safety. He later moved to the Diezmero Ranch 24 on the Nueces River 24 miles from Corpus Christi.

[132] Maj. A. M. Hobby commanded the Eighth Texas Infantry.

November 25 (Wednesday)

Weather cold, wind from the north. I found out yesterday that the troops at Corpus have had to move up the river, there being no water for them below.[133]

I took the cart and fetched home a sheep from Mr. Ned Taylor's flock, making the second I have had from the six owed me on the trade with my horse. Soon as I reached home, I killed the sheep. When I finished watering the cows and calves at the well, I grained the sheepskin then worked on the spade handle till dark.

The excitement about the Yankee is considerably abated; some of them reportedly have left Brownsville and they have made no farther advances on Corpus as yet.

November 26 (Thursday)

I watered the cows and calves, finished the spade handle, and commenced work on a saddle tree. Toward sundown I rode out toward Blucher's Ranch to find a piece of wood for a saddle tree.

When I returned home I found Mr. [Samuel] Edgerly there.[134] Mr. Edgerly, a quartermaster sergeant, was accompanied by a Mr. Hire, with three wagons and 15 [N------s] on their way east of here, as the federals are landing at Black Point [on Copano Bay] in force. They are expected at Corpus in a day or two. The [N------s] camped

---

[133] Gen. Hamilton P. "Hamp" Bee withdrew his forces from Corpus Christi, a strategic retreat that was bitterly resented by the people of Corpus Christi who suggested the general was too timid to fight. Bee reported to his superiors from Corpus Christi that, "About 3,000 of the enemy are at the Aransas Pass. I shall virtually abandon this place tomorrow. There is nothing for the cavalry horses to eat and, from the latest developments of the enemy, he will either march up St. Joseph's Island and attack Saluria or he will land at Lamar and cross over to Indianola, thus cutting off Fort Esperanza. I need not say that I find my position annoying. There are three points of attack for the enemy — Corpus, Lamar, and Saluria — the first is the least important to us."

[134] Noakes knew Edgerly well. Samuel Edgerly and his younger brother Oscar, from New York, came to Texas to take care of a herd of sheep, on shares, for William Headen, a Corpus Christi wool merchant. When the war broke out, the brothers joined the Confederate army. The Edgerly brothers also kept a diary.

145

at my well and killed a heifer.[135] Mr. Hire and Edgerly passed the evening with me.

November 27 (Friday)

Weather very warm with a strong wind from the south. Mr. Hire and Edgerly took breakfast with me at daylight. I took my horse and cart and went with them as far as Sampson's Ranch. Mr. Hire gave me a sack of flour in payment for the heifer they killed the night before.[136] We are now left without protection from the federals, there being no forces here now to oppose them. They will do with us as they please.[137]

I drove down to the river bottom and cut a piece of wood for a saddle tree, then returned home and brought the sack of flour for Mr. [Ned] Taylor in the cart. When I reached home, I put the hide in lime and did various jobs till dark.

November 28 (Saturday)

Early this morning a cold norther blew in and this morning it is too cold to work outdoors. I sat by the fire and worked a sheepskin which I am dressing. I repaired the well and walked to the Motts to find if there is any fresh news about the Yankee, but could hear nothing worthwhile.

November 29 (Sunday)

Weather cold, the coldest day we have had yet. This morning there was ice on the tub standing by the house and in the kettle. I broke and mended the wood axe and my

---

[135] It is not clear what this movement was about but Gen. Bee had ordered the evacuation of all slaves from the region. Bee's order said, "Under no circumstances were Negro men to be left behind." As a last resort, Bee ordered, they were to be shot, "for they will become willing or unwilling soldiers against us." Ref. War of the Rebellion, Series 1, Vol. 53.

[136] In his own diary, Samuel Edgerly, in Bee's command, noted on Nov. 26, 1863: "Left Corpus for Victoria. Going with the quartermaster's department." Ref. Diary of Sam and Oscar Edgerly.

[137] Henry Maltby, editor of the Ranchero, shared this opinion. He moved his office, bag and baggage, press and type trays, to Santa Margarita on the Nueces River above the Motts and noted that an invasion of Union forces was imminent. "We are in the hands of God." Ref. Ranchero, Dec. 17, 1863.

hammer handle and watered all the cows that came to the well, but the wind was too cold to do much outside.

November 30 (Monday)

Weather cold. I commenced to work on another saddle tree, roughing out the piece for the fore tree. I also put some meat up in the chimney of the old house to smoke. Yesterday two small kids [goats] came to the house and have taken up quarters here.

December 1 (Tuesday)

Weather cool but not so cold. I walked to the Wrights to see them about some wethers.[138] Soon as I returned, I went to work on the saddle tree.

December 2 (Wednesday)

Weather warm and everything exceedingly dry. I got in two cows and two calves, Marie helping me to drive them in on foot. We have only one of our own in the pen (to milk) so we do what everybody else here does, get in anybody's we can find. With the exception of watering the cows, I was at work on the saddle tree the rest of the day. The excitement about the Yankee seems considerably diminished. They have not yet arrived at Corpus although it is open to them whenever they want to take possession of the place.

December 3 (Thursday)

Weather warm, misty in the morning. I killed a yearling for meat and put the hide in lime to work for a cover to a saddle I am making. I scraped off the hair from the hide I had in lime, after which I worked on the saddle tree.

December 4 (Friday)

Weather inclined to be showery, but we had no rain here. Worked all day on the saddle tree.

---

[138] Defined as dry ewes without lambs.

December 5 (Saturday)

Weather showery, but we had hardly enough to settle the dust. It was foggy early in the morning. I worked at the saddle tree and scraped the hair off the hide and staked it out today.

December 6 (Sunday)

Weather warm early in the morning. We had a thick fog from the east which soon cleared and by evening we had a small shower. I finished the saddle tree and prepared the hide to cover it. I was compelled to do so or it would have spoiled.[139] This evening I walked over to Judge Doakes to hear the news and get a book to read. He has some that belongs to a person who has gone east. I hear that the Yankee has taken Saluria and captured several guns and all the ammunition there.[140]

December 7 (Monday)

Weather fine and warm, wind from the south. I spent most of the day covering a saddle tree.

December 8 (Tuesday)

Last night we had a few spatters of rain and this morning the wind is from the east and cool. I trimmed off the saddle tree and worked a sheepskin which I had grained. I watered over 70 head of cattle at the well, a daily occasion.

December 9 (Wednesday)

Weather fine and cool. I was hunting deer all day, without success.

December 10 (Thursday)

Weather fine, wind east. I was busy over several jobs till about 11 a.m. when a deer and fawn came within sight of our house. I took my gun for a shot at them and followed them to Blucher's Prairie but could not get a shot.

---

[139] With the use of the word "compelled," I think Noakes was making an excuse for working on Sunday.

[140] By Saluria, the town on Matagorda Island, Noakes apparently was referring to the nearby Fort Esperanza which guarded Pass Cavallo. Union troops under Gen. Nathaniel Banks captured the fort and its guns on Nov. 29, 1863.

Returning through the thicket, I came across a wild sow and five small pigs. I gave chase and caught one, which I took home. We (or rather Marie) have undertaken to suckle it. We also have two goats, which found their way here two weeks ago, and what with them, the pig, and three cats, we have plenty to feed. When I reached home, George Reynolds was there putting a colt in the pen. In the evening I was making a rawhide to go over the saddle horn.

December 11 (Friday)

Weather cool, morning foggy. I worked on my saddle rigging, making it out of the leather which I have tanned. After dinner, Marie and I and the little one went out in the cart and I shot a buck.[141] We were in hopes of finding another pig but did not. I also brought home a little firewood in the cart.

December 12 (Saturday)

Weather warm and dry. Until dinner time I was skinning and salting the deer, salting the hams and graining and tanning the hide. Mr. Reese came along and took dinner. In the evening I was working on a strip for the saddle.

December 13 (Sunday)

Clear sky but quite cold. Marie has made a nice pair of gloves out of the sheepskin I dressed. We do not get any war news; the mails have ceased to run from or to here and the Corpus newspaper has been stopped. A great many people have gone from here and more are leaving for fear of the Mexicans. As yet I have heard nothing to be immediately scared about, although the situation in which things stand in general are most threatening.

December 14 (Monday)

Worked on the saddle rigging.

---

[141] The "little one" referred to Noakes' son Thomas John Jr., who was born on Dec. 17, 1862 while his father was away in the Confederate Army, a soldier in John Ireland's company, Texas Infantry, later designated as Company K.

December 15 (Tuesday)

Making the leather-work out of the leather I tanned. Mr. Wright [Joseph Jr., "Joe"] called me to bid goodbye. He has to join his company in Louisiana.

December 16 (Wednesday)

The atmosphere has been filled with dust, making the already desolate country look even worse. Finished the saddle about noon. It is a homespun affair throughout. I made everything about it, even the buckskin. This evening I split out some shoe pegs. To judge by the number of cattle I have left, out of 50 cows that I ought to have by my book, we have only one cow of our own in the pen. We have been following the custom of the country and getting in any cows that come around with young calves. We have eight cows now, which Marie and I have got in afoot. When we see a cow with a young calf near the place, we each take a rope and whichever one gets the first chance, ropes the calf (which Marie can do as well as I can, if not better) and we get it into the pen, by driving or dragging. The boy is growing and is full of mischief. He can run about by himself and sometimes wanders off alone a long way from the house. He will be a year old tomorrow.

December 17 (Thursday)

Toward evening Marie and I penned an unmarked yearling to kill for meat.

December 18 (Friday)

Cold and icy. Killed the yearling and limed its hide to prepare for a saddle. After dinner I took half the meat from the yearling up to the old folks in my cart. I brought back two bags of flour which had been given to me by the military authorities at Corpus when the post was broken up there. The same was given to every soldier's family.

December 19 (Saturday)

I worked a deerskin and watered cattle till noon when I became ill with fever.

December 20 (Sunday)

Cold. Hunting my horse. Took a ride to Mr. Littig's.[142]

December 21 (Monday)

Killed two bucks. Brought the skin home and hung the meat in a tree.

December 22 (Tuesday)

I went early with the cart to get the meat I hung in a tree. When I got there nearly all had been destroyed by the buzzards. I brought home a load of firewood. Adams came to visit and stayed all night. A man named Gibbs came here.[143] He was here to get the flour from me, given to me at Corpus. He claims it as his and said that his son, who is in our company, bought it and sold it to him. But as his son is away and his tale is ridiculously contradictory, I told him that I meant to keep the flour till he could prove that it was his. The fact is that it was a conspiracy among them to swindle me out of the flour. It was only by sheer good luck that I obtained it.

December 23 (Wednesday)

I walked to Mr. [Henry] Taylor's and had a talk with him about the flour. Helped Taylor with a sick horse and called at Mr. Bryden's.

December 24 (Thursday)

Tried to find my horse, but failed.

December 25 (Friday)

Christmas Day. Tried again to find my horses. At dark we walked up to the old folks' where we spent the evening and had an eggnog. We made ourselves as merry as we

---

[142] J. W. Littig came to Corpus Christi in 1839 as a clerk for Henry Kinney. He married Mary Ann Beynon in 1856 and settled in Nuecestown. Littig and his wife Mary were friends of Felix and Maria Blucher of Corpus Christi. Maria Blucher in one letter said, "Mrs. Littig provides me with excellent butter." Ref. "Maria von Blucher's Corpus Christi."

[143] James Gibbs. 1860 Census lists him as a farmer, from England, with a wife, Charlotte, and two sons, James Jr., and Benjamin.

could under the circumstances, but present prospects are by no means favorable for merry-making.

We heard that Capt. King's ranch has been visited by a band of Yankees who took everything they wanted but King himself. King was away on a scout with several men of this place, George Reynolds being one of them. The raiders are reported to have fired into the house and shot a servant and they wanted to burn the premises, but their leader would not let them. What goods they did not take away, they made Mr. King responsible for, under threat that if anything was missing when they returned, which they intended to do the next night, they would burn everything. We believe Capt. King and his party have been taken, as they started in pursuit of some thieves nearly two weeks ago and have not been heard from. After the news reached here, Holt and Stevens started out with a horse wagon and have not returned. They went to warn Capt. King away. We are liable for a visit at any moment, for we are left at the mercy of any force that likes to come in on us.[144]

December 26 (Saturday)

I went early to the Motts to get the news. Found [George] Robertson of Corpus who had been run off by the Union party there.[145] He spent the afternoon here.

December 27 (Sunday)

Dr. Robertson was here in the afternoon.

---

[144] A few days before Christmas 1863, while Richard King was away, a Union raiding party attacked King Ranch. Henrietta King and four children were at the ranch. Shots were fired at the house and a servant was killed. The raiders rounded up cattle to drive to Brownsville. Ref. "King Ranch" by Tom Lea and the Ranchero, Dec. 24, 1863.

[145] On Christmas Day 1863, Maj. William Thompson, commander of the 20th Iowa garrisoned on Mustang Island, led a raiding foray into Corpus Christi. They chased Dr. George Robertson, John Riggs and another man to Mrs. Swift's boarding house. Dr. Robertson hid in a closet while Riggs and the other man crawled under a bed. But Riggs' long legs stuck out and he and the other man were captured. Dr. Robertson was not found and left later that day for Nuecestown. Ref. Eli Merriman memoirs and Maj. Thompson's letters,

December 28 (Monday)

After breakfast I went to the Motts to hear the news. Nothing fresh. I worked on the cart wheels and prepared the strands of a cowhide for plaiting a whip.

December 29 (Tuesday)

Close to sundown I went out to shoot a deer. I came across an old buck asleep under a tree. I shot him in the head so as not to damage the hide. When I went up to him, he appeared decisively dead, with a big hole in his head, so I did not take the caution of cutting his throat. I took hold of his horns and dragged him to an open space where all of a sudden, he sprang to his feet and was quickly out of shot. He left a blood trail, but I did not get him. An astonishing thing stopped me. I was following his trail from the timber to the open prairie, when I discovered 80 to 100 men close upon me, so close that concealment was out of the question. I was in a bad fix. I knew of no troops of our side in this part of the country. From the accounts we have received, we knew we could expect armed parties of Mexicans and Yankees from the Rio Grande at any time. I thought it was a troop of that sort.

I halted, resigned to take things as they were. Three of them started toward me and it was several minutes before I knew whether they were friend or foe, as they put me through a severe course of questioning. The captain came up and I could see by his uniform they were Confederates. I was glad. Being satisfied with my replies, they left me. Reynolds returned home today. He has been in Mexico after some cattle thieves with Capt. King. The party returned safe after traveling through dangerous country. Capt. King came home to find his beautiful house a wreck and his wife and children gone.[146]

---

[146] After the raid, Henrietta King took the children to San Antonio for safety, stopping on the way at San Patricio, where she had her fifth baby, a boy, whom she named after a family friend, Robert E. Lee.

December 30 (Wednesday)

I bought a bushel of corn from Mr. [Ned] Taylor.

December 31 (Thursday)

The last day of a miserable year. Bitterly cold. We sat by the fire mending Marie's shoes. The company of men that passed me the other evening went to Corpus where they took a man named Dix prisoner. It was said he was a traitor and had been communicating with the Yankees.[147] So ends a miserable year.

---

[147] John Dix, a retired ship captain, was an ardent Unionist. Confederates believed he was communicating with Union warships by flashing a lantern light to send pre-arranged signals. He was arrested and threatened with hanging.

No rain worth mentioning since last July, over
six months. Dead animals meet your gaze in
every direction, look where you will. The
atmosphere is quite oppressive on account of
decomposition. War and famine are all that
we see, hear, and talk about.

—Jan. 24, 1864

THE WAR YEARS
1864

January 1 (Friday)

Water and milk froze. Stayed in and boiled soap, the first
I have had to make, and I succeeded very well. I drove the
cart to [Ned] Taylor's and borrowed a bushel of corn.
Reynolds was here this evening and we talked of things
generally.

January 2 (Saturday)

I am not well. My lungs have bled.

January 3 (Sunday)

My lungs are very much out of order. I went to the Motts
and had a look at the Galveston papers at Mr. [Herman]
Vetters.

January 4 (Monday)

I put in a plow handle for Mr. Ludewig.

January 5 (Tuesday)

Exceedingly cold, with ice all day. Water froze close to
the fire. I put my horse in the old house to keep him from
perishing. I walked to the Motts and changed some books
at Judge Doakes.

January 6 (Wednesday)

Still cold, ice everywhere.

January 7 (Thursday)

I helped Mr. Wright pull out a cow of his that was bogged in the river. For two or three hundred yards down the river I counted 42 animals, cows, horses, sheep, all bogged down in the mud. And this is only the beginning. There are thousands of cattle on the other side of the river dying for something to eat.

January 8 (Friday)

Ice everywhere. Even the river froze over, bank to bank, in some places. Got three wethers from Mr. Wright, gave one to Mr. Vetters and brought the other two home to kill.

January 9 (Saturday)

I killed the two wethers and stretched the hides. Took off as much of the hide as I could get at from the dead cows bogged in the river. I also skinned a two-year-old steer which Marie and I pulled out of the river.

January 10 (Sunday)

At present there is a lull in the excitement of the war in these parts. We have heard no news of the Yankees, Mexicans and Indians. It may be because of the excessive cold. From the long drought and the cold, the cattle are suffering tremendously. They are dying very fast on the opposite side of the river. Even deer have become quite common in the settlement in search of food and water.

January 11 (Monday)

I repaired a chair for Mr. Taylor and took it to him in the evening.

January 12 (Tuesday)

Hauled firewood.

January 13 (Wednesday)
Worked a sheepskin out for a rug and burned dry cow dung for ashes to make soap. Shot a large buck on the flats but he got away and floated down the river.

January 14 (Thursday)
Rode around by Turkey Creek.

January 15 (Friday)
Warmer. After dinner I went with my horse cart to Blucher's Ranch and cut out some forks for saddle trees.[148] Mr. Ludewig went with me.

January 16 (Saturday)
I went in my cart to get some wood. When I returned, I found two men with a wagon camped at the house. They had a load of corn for sale, which they offered at two dollars a bushel, cheap for the times. I went up to Mr. Ludewig's to talk to him about buying some. He agreed to come down in the morning.

January 17 (Sunday)
Mr. Ludewig came down and we bought them out of their corn, about 10 bushels. We also bought lard and bacon for 25 cents a pound. I borrowed sacks from Mr. Ned Taylor to put the corn in. I made a box in the kitchen to store the sacks of corn. Went up to Mrs. Reynolds and helped her to measure some salt, which she had sold. Came home and helped Mr. Ludewig load his part of the corn in the cart and then helped Mr. Taylor hitch a horse of his to my cart. I have lent him my cart to go east to get some corn; he agreed to bring me five bushels for the loan of the cart.

---

[148] The typical saddle tree of that time was fashioned from the fork of a tree as the base, or frame, of the saddle, which was covered with rawhide. Noakes looked for tree forks among timber on Blucher's Prairie. He doesn't say what type of tree he preferred, but saddles were usually made from soft wood such as pine or cottonwood; hard wood tended to split. Good saddle-makers were real craftsmen and artists, as Noakes seemed to be.

157

January 18 (Monday)

Worked on a saddle tree, getting it ready to cover.

January 19 (Tuesday)

Worked all day covering the saddle tree.

January 20 (Wednesday)

Finished the saddle tree and scraped the hair off a hide and pegged it out to dry then took up another hide which had dried. James Bryden took supper with us. There is no mail now and we get no news of the war. The country is in a deplorable state for want of rain, with cattle and sheep starving and dying all over the country. The long cold spell killed great numbers of sheep. Mr. Perham lost all he had, three or four thousand head.[149]

January 21 (Thursday)

Attended to the same old jobs. Talked with the Wrights at the Motts.

January 22 (Friday)

Rode all day in search of a beef fit to kill, unsuccessful.

January 23 (Saturday)

Today I commenced work on a boat I want to build in order to cross the river when I want to.

January 24 (Sunday)

Nothing but the usual work. No rain worth mentioning since last July, over six months. Dead animals meet your gaze in every direction, look where you will. The atmosphere is quite oppressive on account of decomposition. War and famine are all we see, hear, or talk about. Everything in the country seems to be common property. The Mexicans, Yankees, and even our own soldiers are stealing everything, both animals fit to eat or ride. It has become the general rule for people to kill anything they please. The boldest thief is the best off.

---

[149] Rev. J. P. Perham, a Methodist minister, owned a sheep ranch near Banquete, on Los Pintos Creek.

January 25 (Monday)

Worked on the boat. Went up to Reynolds and ground two axes for Ludewig. About sundown a Negro with a wagon and team of mules camped at my well.

January 26 (Tuesday)

The man who camped at the well last night was sick with fever. He could not see to his mules and requested me to get somebody to drive his team to Corpus. I knew of no one to drive the team so I concluded, rather than see the man out of medicine and needing proper attention, to drive the team down myself. I harnessed the mules, tied my horse behind and drove to Corpus.

The wagon contained the baggage of Capt. Gilpin. He is quartermaster of some district or other and with whom I have been acquainted since I first came to this country.[150] Capt. Gilpin was very much pleased to get the wagon and treated me kindly. I took dinner with him and Mr. and Mrs. Ohler.[151] I was provided with plenty of corn for my horse. Gilpin also presented me with the sum of two dollars, not as pay but as a present, as I would only agree to take it on that understanding. I told him I considered it a case of compassion, to get the man to town, and that alone induced me to drive the team down.

January 27 (Wednesday)

Warm and pleasant. Marie and I penned a beef soon after daylight but he jumped out of the pen so I loaded my rifle and shot him, as we needed meat and grease, as did the Ludewigs. Marie went up to let them know and they came down in the cart. Meantime, Ned Taylor lent me a hand to skin the beef, after I watered the cows. By dinner time we

---

[150] Henry Gilpin was an early merchant engaged in the Mexican trade. He bought the Penitas Ranch, north of San Patricio, and was serving as chief justice of Nueces County at the time of Noakes' visit.
[151] Edward Ohler was a wealthy merchant who owned a store on Water Street. His wife was Matilda Ohler. They had two sons, Charles and William.

had the beef cut up and after dinner Mr. Ludewig took away half the meat and tallow.

I worked the hair off the hide that I had soaking in the river and tanned it out. I branded a calf in the pen and did my daily work, watering and getting salt grass for the calves. Ned Taylor returned from the east yesterday but he brought me only three instead of five bushels of corn.

January 28 (Thursday)

Weather very warm. I cut up and salted the meat, branded a calf, took back the corn that I owed to Mr. [Henry] Taylor. I rode to Blucher's Ranch and cut some timber to make a knee for the boat and a fork for a saddle tree. I cut some shrubs that resemble holly, with yellow wood, to make a yellow dye.

January 29 (Friday)

Weather still warm. I rode up to the Motts then skinned a small calf that had starved to death and repaired the watering place at the well.

January 30 (Saturday)

Weather warm and windy from the south. After dinner I did my usual watering at the well. I made a vat to make lye for soapmaking. Not having a barrel to hold water, I put four posts in the ground four feet apart, with forks at the top, five feet from the ground. I laid a cross piece from one fork to another, tied with rawhide strips, then hung up a deer hide to form a waterproof sack.

January 31 (Sunday)

Weather exceedingly warm. The wind was from the south till nearly night when it changed around and by sundown was from the north. After supper I did my usual work then rode up the river to see how things looked. I never felt more distressed with the conditions in the country than I did today. The general appearance is most desolate. The high wind blows the dust and sand, which covers everything, the clouds of dust filling the atmosphere and confining the range of vision to a small space.

There is the miserable and starved look of the cattle and the thousands (I can safely say) of the dead and dying that line the shore around the river. And there is the dismal look to the country, for there is not a green thing to be seen. One watering hole on this side was entirely blocked up with bogged cattle; there were 27 in one bunch. First there was a row of cattle bogged next to the shore then another row which had climbed over them to get at the water. And that way they were bogged three or four rows deep. You could stand at one place and count 120, some dead and some barely alive. The dust getting into my lungs caused them to commence bleeding. I returned home as quickly as I could, feeling depressed from the scene. If privation of every description, and a dreary life devoid of pleasure, would help a man get to heaven, I think that we who live in this part of Texas stand a good chance of getting there. I sometimes think that a man who has spent a lifetime of toil and disappointment seems to be doomed at the end of it to perpetual torment in a world that is in opposition to the merciful laws laid down for our guidance by a wise Creator. By far it would have been better for us never to have been born.

February 1 (Monday)
Weather cool. I was burning dry cow dung with which I mixed oyster shells that had been burned into lime. I watered the cattle and skinned a cow which died in the pen and put the skin to soak in the river to get the hair off.

February 2 (Tuesday)
Weather warm and changeable. As soon as I was up, I skinned a yearling that died a short distance on the salt flat in front of the house. I watered the cattle and hung up the salt beef I cured in a smoke in the old house. I worked the hair off a hide and in the evening, I filled up my vat with ashes and did various jobs till dark. I wrote a letter to Adolph, my brother-in-law.

February 3 (Wednesday)

During the night another light norther came up. This morning it is quite cool. I skinned another calf on the salt flats and hung the hide to loosen the hair. I rode up to Mr. Littig's to see Tom Banyon who was taken prisoner by the Yankees and is now home on a furlough.[152] After I returned home I commenced to make a trough with which to water my cattle.

February 4 (Thursday)

Weather warm. I worked all day at the trough, fixing it to four posts at the well.

February 5 (Friday)

Weather still warm. I worked at my lye-making operations, putting water on the ashes and commenced to boil it down as it dripped through.

February 6 (Saturday)

This morning at sunrise a norther came up. I killed our pig. He was getting too big for the amount of milk we had to give him. After scalding and cleaning him, I felt too unwell to do anything else, having a fever. I milked what cows I could then laid on the bed. In the evening James Bryden and Capt. Ware called to look at my saddle horse.[153]

February 7 (Sunday)

Weather cold when out of the sun. I watered a few cows and did little jobs but soon had to stop and go to bed. The fever became strong on me about the middle of the day. I felt a little better by night.

---

[152] Thomas Banyon brought home his friend, Peter Mullen, who was in his same company and was in bad health. Mullen, the son of Mr. and Mrs. Michael Mullen, died soon afterwards. Ref., "Pathfinders" by Mrs. Frank DeGarmo.

[153] Capt. James A. Ware, a former Corpus Christi attorney, commanded a militia unit called Ware's Partisan Rangers which, later in the war, was designated as Company F of the 1st Texas Cavalry. Toward the end of the war Ware was in command of the Confederate camp on San Fernando Creek near Banquete.

February 8 (Monday)

Cool, that is the air is cool, but the sun is hot. This morning I broke out with an eruption of spots all over, but thicker on my head and face. I do not know what it is, unless it is the measles. I have no medicine in the house. I was too unwell to do any work this morning.

February 9 (Tuesday)

Weather bad. I felt better today, but did little but read. Old Adams was here. The fever pimples are going away. I finished boiling and pouring the water from my lye vat. But I never could find any signs of lye about it and when all the water evaporated away, there was nothing left but salt. The cow-dung operation is a failure. I will next try river wood.

February 10 (Wednesday)

Weather cool last night and there was lightning. I felt well enough to water the cattle and walked to Judge Doakes and borrowed an encyclopedia to read. This morning Ned Taylor started for the east with horse and cart to buy corn, under the agreement that he is to bring me two bushels and keep ten for himself. The cattle are dying fast, everywhere.

February 11 (Thursday)

Two hours before sundown we had a thunderstorm, which came up from the northwest. It rained steadily for three hours, sufficient to settle the dust for about three days. In the morning I rode Ned Taylor's horse to try to find my horses, but could not after hunting for the greater part of the day. Toward night I was preparing for the expected rain, taking in a hide left out to dry and packing away the meat I had been smoking.

February 12 (Friday)

Weather fine and warm. I had a regular rawhide day. I skinned a calf that died on the flats and scraped the hair off three hides I had soaked in the river.

February 13 (Saturday)

Weather fine, but showing greatly for rain. I was watering the cattle and cleaning three more hides till dinner after which I walked out to the woods to try to kill a deer but didn't succeed. I nearly stepped on a rattlesnake, which I killed with a stick. His body was as thick as my arm, but about nine inches longer than my arm. I skinned it and brought home the skin. His head was about two inches between the eyes.

February 14 (Sunday)

Weather warm and windy from the south. The dust is blowing in clouds again. I took a ride out to try and find my horses but with no better success. This makes the seventh time I have hunted for them, without finding them, since I last saw them. At one watering place up on at the bluff I counted 163 head of cattle and three horses, bogged and dead. I only counted them on this side and for just a short distance. They are thick on both sides from the mouth of the river up as far as there is water sufficient to bog them. I crept in on a large alligator asleep and got within two yards of him before he smelled me. He was about 12 feet long.

A week ago, when I was up the river, I saw many other dead animals. There were two steers yoked together, one dead and the other standing next to it. I saw them again today, the dead one in a fair stage of decomposition and the other one still standing by it with its head fastened down to it yet still alive. Such scenes as this now seem a common thing, almost an everyday occurrence. The whole country stinks from the numbers of dead animals about.

The trees, shrubs and grass are commencing to come out and, in a few days, the brown earth will have a pleasant shade of green. We get no mail now, no news of the war. We are abandoned without the knowledge of even a mail carrier.

February 15 (Monday)

Last night we had thunder and lightning, which came up from the north, but no rain today. It is cool. I was working three hides till dinner time, after which I rode up to the bluff and down to Blucher's Prairie to try and find my horses but could see nothing of them.

February 16 (Tuesday)

Weather dry, wind east but toward night shifted to the north and became quite cold. I worked on the hides, watered the cattle, then worked on the boat till dark.

February 17 (Wednesday)

Weather cold, wind north which changed to the east toward night. I worked all day on the boat, sawing out the knees from lumber. It is reported that several hundred Yankees are encamped 50 miles from here, but I do not believe it.

February 18 (Thursday)

Last night we had a high cold wind from the east, which changed this morning to the north and was extremely cold. It was accompanied by a blowing mist. It was too cold in the morning to work on the boat so I killed a little starved calf near the old house. I grained its hide and tanned it. After dinner I worked at the boat, sawing out the knees.

February 19 (Friday)

Weather fine but cold. There was ice on the water barrels and the trough. I took in and hung up all my hides and did my usual work. Later I went to work on the boat till dark.

February 20 (Saturday)

Weather fine, wind south, strong and cold. Last night Ned Taylor returned after dark so this morning I went to John Williams where he stopped, measured out my corn and brought it home in the cart. The trip was successful for us both. He bought me 10 bushels of corn and the same for himself, without injury to horse or cart. Miss Wright took supper with us last night. I busied myself all day at the boat and washed out a sheepskin to tan, and did other jobs.

February 21 (Sunday)

Weather fine, wind south. Ned Taylor loaned me a horse and I rode out once more to try and find my horses. I succeeded in finding some of them, and these I must water. I drove them home and watered them at the well. The rest of the day I spent reading and watering the cattle. We hear nothing of the Yankee.

February 22 (Monday)

Weather fine and warm. I was repairing my cart harness and working on the boat.

February 23 (Tuesday)

Weather fine. I made a square water bucket for Mr. Byler and fixed up the cart for a journey. After supper Marie and I measured and sacked up 10 bushels of corn.

February 24 (Wednesday)

Weather fine. I was told that the Mexicans on the Pintos Creek were out of corn and would pay four dollars a bushel for it, so I concluded to start up there with my cart and take 10 bushels along, and on the trip pick up some tanbark.[154] I started this morning soon as I could get away. I took dinner near the Chocolate Motts then traveled down to the Palo Alto Creek.[155] It was raining and at dark I camped near the crossing.

February 25 (Thursday)

Weather fine, morning foggy. I drove up to Perkins' Ranch.[156] It was deserted except by Mexicans, but they wanted no corn. I continued on to a place where McClane

---

[154] The bark of some trees considered suitable for tanning hides.

[155] This may have been what is known today as Lost Creek, which is just west of Driscoll.

[156] James Perkins, from Louisiana, had a ranch near Banquete. He was a volunteer in Mat Nolan's Mounted Rangers. Ref., 1860 Census and Muster Roll, Appendix 4.

was staying.[157] I took dinner with him and talked for a couple of hours. He made me an offer to tend his sheep on shares but I wouldn't give him an answer till I thought it over. I learned that a wagon and two carts loaded with corn came by ahead of me the day before so I concluded it was my usual luck to be a little too late. I reached a Mexican ranch on the creek about sundown where I found a man named Parker who was returning with his corn. He was in a great scare about the Yankees, which he said were a short distance away. I was vexed to think that I should have come so far then have to return home with my corn. I determined to continue on, taking my chances with the Yankees. That night I lit no fire and camped away from the creek.

February 26 (Friday)

Weather fine, every morning is very foggy. I started soon after daylight and reached the Precenos Ranch.[158] I didn't see anything to run from. I sold my corn at Precenos but at a low price, to get rid of it. The Mexicans there were already supplied. I started home by another route and camped by the river.

February 27 (Saturday)

Weather fine. I was on the move early, crossing the Agua Dulce and continuing down the Banquete Creek. At Banquete, out of 12 or 14 houses, I saw only one or two that were occupied, the rest were abandoned, the people having fled east. A more desolate country can't be imagined. Go which way you will, you see dead horses,

---

[157] John McClane came to Corpus Christi in 1856 with a shipment of merino bucks for Richard King from his father's farm in Pennsylvania. McClane stayed in Texas and soon had his own flocks of sheep. After the war, he was appointed sheriff of Nueces County by the occupation authorities.

[158] Rancho los Precenos was 40 miles southwest of Corpus Christi and a mile east from today's Alice. The ranch was owned by Rafael Lopez, and later by King Ranch. Ref. Ranchero, March 23, 1861, "King Ranch" by Tom Lea.

cattle and sheep. All the creeks stink with them and you generally see several dead around every deserted place.

I went down the creek some distance where I camped and collected my tanbark. About 2 p.m. I drove to a mott where I camped. I dug out some wild onions to eat with my supper. These onions grow in clusters like shallots. It is astonishing how long they can live and the length of time they will lie in the parched ground if there is no rain for them to grow.

February 28 (Sunday)

Weather changeable. I reached home at noon. About sundown a dry cold norther came up, with black clouds. Toward night I rode to the Motts to hear the news. I found that the Yankees have been to Corpus within the week and have taken every Confederate man they could get hold of and it is reported that 500 Yankees and Mexicans are at San Diego on their way here.

February 29 (Monday)

Weather cold and misty at times. I skinned a yearling which died near the place and then went up to see Reynolds. I traded him a box of gun caps for a pound and half of gunpowder.

March 1 (Tuesday)

I was making a harness for the horse for my cart and in the evening, I rode up to the Motts.

March 2 (Wednesday)

Weather warmer. I was cutting out and plaiting a hide rope with which to make braces for the cart harness. After dinner Marie and I went up to the old folks and killed a beef, being out of meat.

March 3 (Thursday)

Weather warm. Besides my daily work of watering cattle, I finished plaiting the rope, after which I cut it into the desired lengths and made them into braces. I took my

168

cart and horse and drove to Woessner ranch to try to sell some corn but not succeeding. I returned by the old folks and brought Marie and a beef hide home. Marie had gone up to help cut up the meat. I put the hide in the river to soak till the hair slips.

March 4 (Friday)

Weather warm. I fixed the iron work in the harness, put calf hide in the river, and commenced making a well bucket. In the morning Gibbs called to try to get the flour, but bringing no more proof of it belonging to him. I would not let him have it. We had a row and he called me mean. When I told him that if he was not an old man, I would give him a good whipping, he said that if he were as young as I he would whip me quickly. Our respective ages prevented a collision.

March 5 (Saturday)

Miss Marsh called in the evening. Weather cool and in the night the wind shifted to the north. I worked on the well bucket and finished it about 2 p.m. then cut out the strands of a calf-skin rope for reins for the lead horse for the cart.

March 6 (Sunday)

Weather warm and windy from the south. Adams was here in the morning, so I could do nothing but talk to him. After dinner I skinned a cow that died by the field fence. I then rode up in front of Littig's place where I saw some of my mares, one of them was a mare with a new colt. The Yankees make great times in Corpus, coming in every few days and taking prisoner all the Confederates they can get hold of. They commit a great many depredations.

The cattle are dying faster than ever. The trees and grass have made attempts to come out in leaf but have been killed by the late frosts. They are now making another attempt and the yuccas are in blossom.

March 7 (Monday)

Weather fine. I was plaiting a small hide rope for reins for my cart. After dinner I went to the Motts to act as clerk

169

for an election for chief justice but nobody was there so I returned home.

I learned from a small slip of paper that has been sent anonymously to a person at the Motts that the Yankee intended to pay the Motts a visit either last night or the next day, and as there were 150 of them in Corpus, I thought they might well intend something of that sort. They have taken all the Confederate men they could get in Corpus. I went home and prepared for them. I put everything of value under the ground, with nearly all our provisions, and at night I slept 300 yards from the house, with my horse and saddle ready.

March 8 (Tuesday)

Weather hot and cloudy. I rode around to hear the news. I heard that the Yankee left Corpus so I returned home and went to work. I skinned a cow that died and worked on some hides till night. After supper I plaited a whip lash and took some of the buried things out of the ground.

March 9 (Wednesday)

Last night we had a little rain and a good deal of thunder. It rained again soon after daylight. A thundershower passed over with a fall of hail, the largest I have ever seen, some of the stones being an inch in diameter. Luckily it was soon over. They hit the house so hard it made you think the shingles would split. I worked on the harness for the cart as Ned Taylor is about to start east for corn. I want to go with him with my cart.

After it cleared up, I rode out and brought home the horse Joe, with his mare, which I penned. Marie and I harnessed him to the cart to break him in. He cut up a little but soon gave in. I went to fixing up to start in the morning. Ned Taylor came along and we got both horses harnessed to the cart and they seemed to work very well.

March 10 (Thursday)

Weather fine but cold and windy from the north. I started with my cart in the company of Ned Taylor who was driving his wagon. We camped on the Nueces River timber on the west side of the river. Joe the horse behaved very well. The stink arising from the dead cattle in the river was very offensive.

March 11 (Friday)

Weather fine. We crossed the river and camped at night a short way beyond Papalote.

March 12 (Saturday)

Weather cool and fine. As soon as I started this morning, Joe commenced cutting up, giving me a good deal of trouble. In crossing the Aransas River, after driving through the stream, we had a steep bank to drive up. It was not till after a bout of bucking and pitching that we got him up and after he was up it was as much as I could do to manage him.

We were among post oaks growing in some places so close together, on each side of the road, that it would be difficult to drive a cart through them. Joe commenced to pitch and plunge more than ever, and in doing so struck the grey horse I had in the lead. This caused him to jump and snap the lines out of my hands and Joe's reins got tangled and jerked me out of the cart. I fell over and off went the horses and cart at top speed through the timber.

I put it down as a certainty that the cart would be smashed up in a few minutes. The horses ran to each side of a tree and snapped the strong rawhide traces like they were thread. Now being separated they took different directions.

After following the tracks of the cart for a half mile through the oaks I came on the cart lying on one wheel with the other up in the air. Joe was still fastened to the shaft, the harness hanging in pieces, and the contents of the cart scattered on the ground.

I examined the horse and found him uninjured. After hitching up the cart, I was astonished to find nothing broken besides the harness. Ned came up with his wagon, having followed the cart trail. We fastened the cart behind his wagon and agreed to drive a few miles down the road and camp while I mounted Joe and rode in search of the grey.

After following the trail for five miles, I found him in the Aransas River standing by the water. We galloped back till I came to Ned's camp. I cooked something to eat, tied up the harness with rawhide, and in one hour we were on the road again. I tied Joe behind Ned's wagon.

March 13 (Sunday)

We drove all day and crossed several creeks without incident. I put Joe in the lead of Ned's wagon to compel him to behave.

March 14 (Monday)

Camped last night on the bare prairie. It was cold, drizzling rain, and there was no firewood. We crossed the San Antonio River and drove through Goliad. The town is prettily situated and though small there is a substantial look about it. Unlike most Texas towns, a good many of its houses are built of stone and in very good taste. Wind bitterly cold.

March 15 (Tuesday)

We drove five miles and camped in the shelter of some trees. I took Joe and rode around to inquire for corn. Found some for sale and drove our teams to the house and made a bargain with the man, a German. I went with the cart and fetched a corn sheller from a neighboring ranch and we shelled about half of the load that evening.

March 16 (Wednesday)

We slept in the house, the people being very kind, and passed the evening talking over the fire with two Americans who were driving teams, although one was a medical man by profession. The first thing this morning I traded Joe to the doctor for a work horse, as I could not get my load home if I depended on Joe. The doctor gave me five dollars to boot. We loaded our teams with corn and sweet potatoes and after dinner started for home, driving eight miles. My new horse worked fine.

March 17 (Thursday)

We drove through Goliad then took another road for home. After driving about 20 miles, we camped for the night.

March 18 (Friday)

We passed through Refugio, a poor-looking place, crossed a river by the same name, and kept on till night. After camping, I caught a rabbit in the hollow of a tree, which I cooked for our supper. We had not had fresh meat on the trip.

March 19 (Saturday)

Drove all day through a dry and desolate-looking country for want of rain. Every river or creek we passed was full of dead cattle and they dotted the prairie all over. Thousands and thousands of cattle are dead and everywhere in the neighborhood of water or trees the air is so offensive that we cannot camp there. Sometimes more than a dozen carcasses lie in one heap.

March 20 (Sunday)

We crossed the Nueces about 12 and reached home after dark. I found no one at home to welcome me. All was dark, cold and miserable. I had to get into the house by prying open one of the windows. I tended to the horses, feeling very tired, then laid down and took a little sleep before making a fire and cooking supper.

March 21 (Monday)

Marie came down after a few hours. I made a bin for the corn and repaired the harness till night. Mr. McMaster spent the evening with us.[159]

---

[159] The 1860 Census shows that John McMaster and his younger brother Simon came from South Carolina. John was often called "Pink" McMaster. He later moved to the Lagarto area. A place name near Nuecestown was McMaster's Hollow.

March 22 (Tuesday)

I was busy all day fixing my harness and getting ready to start on another trip. I sold my best saddle today to Couling for 14 dollars and another saddle tree, which I can fresh cover and sell. Since I have been away there has been a fight in Corpus or rather a skirmish between our men and the Yankees.[160] There was another fight between our men and a party of Mexicans. The Mexicans were defeated and our men took a good deal of property from them.[161]

March 23 (Wednesday)

Killed my pig, dressed it and did various jobs. Rode up to Couling's and brought home a piece of beef, which he had killed. I now have everything ready to start on another trip tomorrow.

March 24 (Thursday)

Wind blew hard all day and in spite of rain the dust moved in clouds. Ned Taylor and I started on another trip and crossed the Nueces at Miller's [Ferry] where we camped and fed our horses from moss from the trees. We cut down the trees by the river to obtain the moss. As soon as we began cutting down the trees, cattle came running up and it was only with great difficulty that we could get any

---

[160] On March 17, 1864 Maj. Matthew Nolan with 70 men encountered a Union force near Corpus Christi picking up confiscated Confederate cotton. Nolan reported that his force encountered Union pickets and drove them into the city with one killed, one wounded, and an Enfield rifle captured. The only Confederate casualty, said Nolan, was Lawrence Dunn, who was wounded. Union Maj. William Thompson had a different story. He reported that his pickets held off charging Confederates and that one Confederate was killed and three were wounded, but not one of his men got a scratch. Ref. Briscoe, "City by the Sea."

[161] A Confederate force of 62 men under Maj. Nolan attacked the camp of Cecilio Balerio, who commanded an irregular Union cavalry squad of 80 men that had recently attacked King Ranch and driven off cattle. Balerio's camp was at Los Patricios 50 miles below Banquete. In the engagement, two of Nolan's men were killed and five of Balerio's. Balerio and his two sons escaped and fled to Mexico. This fight took place on March 13, 1864, four days before the fight in Corpus Christi. Ref. Nolan's report to Col. John S. Ford at San Antonio.

174

of the moss for our horses. The starving cattle fairly took it by storm. We could not drive them away. Very sad. They first ate the moss and the leaves and then the branches up to an inch and a half thick.

March 25 (Friday)

We drove beyond Papalote Creek and camped.

March 26 (Saturday)

Crossed the Aransas River and Medio Creek.

March 27 (Sunday)

We crossed the Blanco, the Mogner, Goat, and several other creeks and camped within three miles of Goliad.[162]

March 28 (Monday)

We crossed the San Antonio River, passed through Goliad, and reached our destination two hours before sundown.

March 29 (Tuesday)

I loaded eight bushels of corn on my cart, Ned Taylor taking 20 bushels, then we drove about two miles to a steam mill to get it ground. We camped for the night near the mill.

March 30 (Wednesday)

After getting our corn ground into meal we returned to the place where we bought it and bought sweet potatoes and shallots and camped there for the night.

March 31 (Thursday)

Drove to within a mile or two of Goliad where we camped near two Irishmen who were going along our road. Not long after we camped, Stevens from the Motts came along with his wagon on the same errand we were on. He camped with us.[163]

---

[162] There was no "Mogner" Creek in Goliad County; this may have been Noakes' variation of Manahuilla Creek.

[163] James E. Stevens lived next door to the school house at the Motts. The 1860 Census lists him as a farmer, from Pennsylvania; he and his wife Mary had four children, Louisa, 8, Alice, 6, James, 4, Henry, 2.

April 1 (Friday)

Weather fair. As we went through Goliad, I bought 30 pounds of coarse sugar for 120 dollars in paper money, that being at the rate of nearly 20 paper dollars to one of specie. I obtained that money over a year ago in payment for a horse and a yoke of work steers.

April 5 (Tuesday)

We reached home in safety about noon, having had fine weather, but windy. I found Marie at home and everything nice and satisfactory. In the evening I unloaded the corn and skinned a dead calf.

April 6 (Wednesday)

Weather showing for rain, wind southeast. I was fixing hides and doing various jobs. I brought the flour that we had buried back into the house and Marie sifted it. In the evening Adams came along and I wasted my time talking with him. Today I had a small wild pig given to me as a pet. The javelina is a native wild hog which differs in several respects from the domestic hog.

April 7 (Thursday)

Weather warm. I was arranging my corn and meal. I returned the sacks I borrowed from Mr. Ned Taylor, prepared a saddle-tree covering and skinned another calf which had died.

April 8 (Friday)

Last night a furious norther came roaring up and this morning it is cold, windy and dusty. I covered the saddle tree I got from Couling and skinned a calf.

April 9 (Saturday)

Weather dry, cold and windy from the west. I worked on another saddle-tree till near noon when I helped Adams pull a cow out of the bog. We got dinner, after which I cleaned a calf hide. As I can get no sacking, to make a sack which I badly need I made one out of a yearling hide which I had prepared for that purpose. I intend to make more if I find I can make them answer. I skinned a calf and part of two cows in the river.

April 10 (Sunday)

Weather dry and windy from the south. I passed a tolerably lazy day doing nothing but what was necessary. I took my gun out of the hole. I have now taken nearly everything out, but I expect every day that we will hear of something that will cause us to bury everything again. And so we keep on. But I am so accustomed to alarms that they bring no sense of fear. We are all now so nearly ruined that to be quite ruined has lost its lesson and we get accustomed to the idea.

The state of the country is even worse than it has been. Our prospects blacken. We are now nearly into summer and winter has not yet left us. There is nothing growing and the country presents a sandy waste. We will get no spring, as the hot months are too near.

The cattle must now be about two-thirds dead and the balance going fast. There is nothing here that is fit for food, either beef, mutton or anything else. Away to the east, where we might get supplies, things are getting just as scarce, with no prospect of making any crop.

We hear daily the warnings of Yankee forces and Mexican guerrillas advancing on us, but they are not here yet. About half the people in Corpus have deserted to the Yankee and when you are talking to your most intimate acquaintance, you cannot be sure that you are addressing friend or foe politically. Instead of people working together for their mutual good, such times as these seem to cause a greater feeling of selfishness and a general mistrust of each other as well as a greater license of all the evil propensities.

Everybody appears afraid that someone else will not be ruined as soon as they are, and it seems they will do all they can to make sure everybody else is ruined first. While they secure their last remaining morsel to themselves, with a greedy clutch with one hand, they employ the other hand to snatch the last crust of bread from the mouth of their neighbor, and if they accomplish this they exult over the deed. No one but those who have experienced such times can form any idea of the wickedness of human nature when it is stripped of all restraints and its usual covering of formalities.

April 11 (Monday)

Skinning cows and calves before noon then walked to the Motts to hear the news.

April 12 (Tuesday)

Skinning calves and working hides through the morning. In the evening worked on a saddle tree.

April 13 (Wednesday)

A fine rain, running like a river in the hollows. Worked on hides and finished the fore tree of a saddle. This morning we heard the sound of heavy guns from the east.

April 14 (Thursday)

Wind, thunder and rain. Worked on the rawhide till noon then finished the saddle tree, now ready to cover. We are swarming with fleas. Air was so cold I worked with my greatcoat on.

April 15 (Friday)

Worked all day on rawhides.

April 16 (Saturday)

Worked all day covering the saddle.

April 17 (Sunday)

I sold the saddle tree which I got from Couling as part payment for the one I sold him. I repaired and freshened it and sold it for $8 cash to a Mexican neighbor. My ink is gone and I have to write with what I make myself from black paint. I also make my own shot to kill small game by beating lead into thin sheets then cutting it into small squares. It answers very well.

We have every reason to hope that the Yankee is withdrawing from this part of Texas. Anyway, we hear nothing of them and most of the excitement of a short time back has subsided. The rain has changed everything. A slight covering of green has spread over the entire country.

April 18 (Monday)

I worked two hides I had in the river and finished some calf hides for sacks.

April 19 (Tuesday)

I was trading with several Mexicans, sold them 22 dollars' worth of corn, cornmeal and flour. I fetched a hide from Mr. Ludewig's and the rest of the day I made rawhide sacks.

April 20 (Wednesday)

Today I turned blacksmith and made some iron staples out of stout wire with which to fix the wooden bows to my cart.[164] Repaired the cart then Mr. [Henry] Taylor and Miss Marsh came and spent the evening.[165]

April 21 (Thursday)

More rain. Our prospects seem brighter, as to the war and the country. I have completed six rawhide sacks, enough to try as an experiment. I occupied the day working with staples and bows on my cart.

April 22 (Friday)

Weather cloudy, wind from the south. I skinned a cow that died nearby and the rest of the day worked on the bows for the cart, lashing them together at the top with rawhide.

April 23 (Saturday)

Soon after daylight this morning the wind, which had been blowing from the southeast, shifted to the north. It blew and rained and thundered for an hour. We had a good

---

[164] Noakes attached wooden hoops ("bows") to his cart to hold a covering, similar to the covered wagons called prairie schooners.

[165] Both were schoolteachers. It's not clear whether Jane L. Marsh, a young woman from Connecticut, taught school at Nuecestown, but she taught in the Dix home in Corpus Christi at the end of the war and was appointed postmaster of Corpus Christi in December 1865. She died in the yellow fever epidemic in 1867.

rain but it soon ceased and we had a cold, dry, strong north wind, which lasted till night. Marie and I planted some seeds for watermelon and mushmelon (cantaloupe) and I finished the bows for the cart.

April 24 (Sunday)

Weather cool and beautiful. Everything is green. The birds are singing and nature seems to have returned to new life. The geese are leaving and the beautiful spring birds, which remain with us for so short a time, have arrived. The starving cattle appear to have taken a new lease on life. I should think that there is no country in the world that can revive so quickly after a rain as this one.

In the morning I cleaned a calfskin to keep it from spoiling. We cooked some weeds I found in the field as greens for dinner and in the evening, I took a ride. There is no news of the war.

April 25 (Monday)

Weather fine. Marie rode Tony to Corpus. I worked on hides, sewing them together to cover my cart and I turned a fly whorl [pulley] for Mrs. Hammond's spinning wheel with an apparatus that I made for the purpose.

April 26 (Tuesday)

Weather fine and warm. I finished the cover for my cart and put it on. I was cutting a weed, a wild species of tobacco, which grows in the field to dry for smoking.

April 27 (Wednesday)

Weather fine, but windy from the south and looking like rain. In the morning I fixed sideboards to the cart and went up to George Reynolds and helped Ned Taylor throw a horse to doctor him. The treatment was to puncture the affected shoulder with an awl, pour turpentine into the hole and heat it with a hot iron. After dinner I worked on repairing the cart harness.

April 28 (Thursday)

Weather the same as yesterday. I rode over to the old folks' then to the Motts to mail some letters and from there down the Oso where I saw my mares. I rode on to Mrs. Hammond's to take her the whorl. Soon as I reached home, I pegged out a hide and worked on the cart harness.

There are various reports afloat about a great victory having been gained somewhere on the Red River, but one day we hear that it was by the Yankee and the next by the Confederate so we do not yet know who gained the victory. Very likely there has not been a fight at all.

April 29 (Friday)

Weather fine. I worked on the cart. I sold more corn to a Mexican.

April 30 (Saturday)

Near sundown a norther came up accompanied by rain and thunder, but we did not get much rain. I finished the cart, made a whip handle, mended my shoes, fixed some hides, and had everything ready to start on another trip.

May 1 (Sunday)

Weather cold and cloudy. Last night I was alone: Marie was at the old folks' and the rain kept her from coming home. I was up early and rode to Mr. Littig's to get an order from Mr. Lovenskiold for some salt to take east and trade for corn. I had heard that Mr. Lovenskiold was there.[166] I was provided with the required order with the understanding that I would work out the value of the salt by hauling for commission. The rest of the day I took it easy.

May 2 (Monday)

Weather hot with very little wind, which blew from the east. I went up to Reynolds' and repaired a cradle for Mrs. Reynolds. I came home and made some hoops for a cap and

---

[166] Col. Charles Lovenskiold was the provost marshal at Corpus Christi.

put them on then went to pounding oak bark to tan with, till night.

May 3 (Tuesday)

Weather fine. I sold all my corn, cornmeal and sugar to some Mexican and Reynolds brought me a piece of beef, which had been killed for the soldiers' families. I boiled some tanbark and made a strong orange dye. I put a buckskin, calfskin, and jacket of mine to dye. I worked one buckskin.

May 4 (Wednesday)

Weather clear, windy from the south. Marie and I and the baby took a ride to Corpus in the cart. I went to get some corn which I had lent Mr. Mussett and Marie went to buy some things for the house. We have been without a mattress for the bed or a mirror to comb our hair by, both of which we needed. We found Corpus in a state of desolation, everything gone to ruin and hardly a living soul to be seen. We took dinner and spent an hour with Mrs. Swift then returned to Mr. Russell's and Marie bought her things. We got home a little after dark.

May 5 (Thursday)

Weather fine with a strong south wind and little rain. I spent all day dressing and working buckskins, boiling tanbark, and fixing hides to tan.

May 6 (Friday)

Weather inclined to rain. I repaired the ox cart for the old man then we were going out to get a load of firewood but the sky looked too much like rain and we gave it up. I trifled away the rest of the day with my tanning.

May 7 (Saturday)

Weather showing for rain, but none came. I rode among the cattle and worked with the hides.

May 8 (Sunday)

Weather the same as the last four days, so cloudy that it looks as though it must rain any minute, with a strong wind from the south. I rode up to see Stevens. Finding that he intended starting east with his wagon tomorrow to get corn, I returned home, penned and killed a yearling, then fixed up to start with Stevens. I distributed the meat among my neighbors. Marie made me a nice waistcoat out of some of my own buckskin and I have been dying it. The report now is that the Yankee is landing a cavalry force on Padre Island, but I do not believe it.

May 9 (Monday)

Weather misty in the morning but it soon cleared off. Stevens and I started east for corn. We camped for the night near Scott's Ranch.[167]

May 10 (Tuesday)

At sunrise the wind changed around and came greatly up from the north, increasing in violence toward night. In crossing the Nueces River, which had just fallen from a rise, Stevens' wagon got stuck in the mud and we spent half the day working to get it out, digging away the mud with our hands. When we reached San Patricio, we took in our salt, which we had an order for from Mr. Lovenskiold, and I procured a pass from the provost marshal to travel by.[168] After driving five miles we made camp. During the night my cough was very troublesome.

May 11 (Wednesday)

Last night the wind blew strongly from the north and this morning it is cold. We camped at night about three miles from the Aransas River on the plain.

May 12 (Thursday)

Weather fine, wind south and very hot. We crossed the Aransas River and the Medio Creek and camped three miles beyond.

---

[167] This was John Wesley Scott's place, Rancho Seco, near Santa Margarita (today's Bluntzer).

[168] The Confederate seat of government for Nueces County and the Corpus Christi newspaper Ranchero were moved to the Santa Margarita/San Patricio area after Corpus Christi was bombarded by Union warships in August 1862.

May 13 (Friday)

Weather fine. We crossed the Blanco, Goat, and Sarco creeks and camped on the prairie three miles from Goliad.

May 14 (Saturday)

Weather pleasant. We made a short but rough ride, first having about a mile of deep sand to get through then the river and a bad creek to cross. We stopped at a [N------] blacksmith's and had some repairs done. We drove about five miles and camped.

May 15 (Sunday)

Weather hot. We drove to the Coleto Creek where I purchased corn for my horses. At night we camped three miles from Clinton. This day's driving was through a very beautiful country, with oak groves and green glades, but thickly settled.

May 16 (Monday)

Weather fine. We drove through Clinton, a small place with a few stores and two or three good buildings, on the Guadalupe River, which we forded. On the opposite side we met two teams from San Patricio. The man admired my new cart cover of rawhide sacks very much, as did many others we met along the road.[169]

We heard of a planter seven miles away who wanted salt, so we drove to the place and traded our salt to the overseer at the rate of two bushels of corn for one of salt. We drove two miles on to the [N------] quarters where the corn was and camped in the yard by the corn crib.

May 17 (Tuesday)

Four [N------] women shelled the corn for us and we passed the day fixing our harness, greasing our wheels, and attending to the horses.

---

[169] Noakes with his orange-dyed buckskin shirt and cart covered with rawhide must have presented quite a sight.

May 18 (Wednesday)

Weather showed indications of rain. First thing in the morning we weighed our corn, loaded up our teams, and after buying eggs from the [N------s] we started home. We found the [N------s] perfectly content with their lot and their master and having no desire to change either. To judge from what they told us, and from what we saw, they are well-treated and there are thousands of white men that might envy them.

We drove on to the ferry at Clinton and camped. After dark a young man in a buggy came along. He was some kind of government expert. He camped with us and I gave him some eggs and bacon for his supper and we talked into the night.

May 19 (Thursday)

Weather fine. We crossed the ferry in safety and by night reached a mill on Coleto Creek where we stopped to get our corn ground. We camped near the mill.

May 20 (Friday)

Passed the day very pleasantly, reading, eating, sleeping.

May 21 (Saturday)

We were through grinding our corn by 10 o'clock. I took only one bushel of meal and Mr. Stevens took 10. I then drove to the place where I had purchased my corn on the last trip and bought some bacon. We drove on to within five miles of Goliad, where we camped.

May 22 (Sunday)

Passed through Goliad and forded the San Antonio River. After getting through that horrid sand we stopped awhile to cool the horses. We found that Goliad people are scared from expecting the Yankee is about to make a raid on them from the coast. We left the road we came on and took the road by Beeville and the rest of the day we passed through post-oak country.

May 23 (Monday)

We drove all day and camped at night on the Tabbycat Creek.[170]

May 24 (Tuesday)

We passed through Beeville, a poor, deserted-looking place. Nearly every house stands on the bare prairie without a fence and giving the general appearance of so many wooden boxes standing about at intervals. Beeville is on flat land near Poesta Creek. We rested our horses at noon at the Aransas River where two Irishmen from San Patricio fell in with us. We camped at night by a small creek about six miles from the Aransas River. As we came by the soldiers' camp, they gave us some beef, which they had been killing. I met a Scotchman named Boyd who came to this country on the same ship that I did.

May 25 (Wednesday)

Reached San Patricio where we camped.

May 26 (Thursday)

Arrived home about two hours before sundown. I found no one at home and had to break down the door to get into the house. I unloaded the cart and attended to the horses. After dark Marie came home and then Mr. [Henry] Taylor and Miss Marsh called and it was nearly midnight before I could get any supper. I bought a new milk bucket at Miller's Ferry and brought it along.

May 27 (Friday)

Everything is as dry as ever and the Nueces River is salty from the Gulf. Weighed my corn and put it in the bin. Worked about the place. In the evening I killed a yearling for some meat and as usual I sent one-fourth of it to the old folks. I buried the hide to slip the hair.

---

[170] Noakes was no doubt referring to Taipacate Creek in eastern Bee County. He didn't take particular pains with the correct spelling of Spanish place names.

May 28 (Saturday)

Worked at tanning, watering cattle at the well, and brought in the cows and calves.

May 29 (Sunday)

We hear rumors of great Confederate victories but experience has taught us that it is best not to believe them. I was compelled to clean the calf hide I had buried to keep it from spoiling.[171] I read and wrote letters.

May 30 (Monday)

Weather fine. I hunted among the cattle and made a rawhide sack.

May 31 (Tuesday)

Weather fine. I hunted among the cattle and branded one of the mares and my bay cart horse. We sold some buckskin to Mr. Clark and some corn and cornmeal to a Mexican. I made two more sacks out of the hide of the yearling I killed the other day. Marie and I are richer than we have been since we have been together. We have one hundred dollars on hand and plenty to eat in the house.

June 1 (Wednesday)

No rain, but much is needed. Two of the Mussetts stayed with us last night.[172] I fetched home some beef; the county commissioners are distributing beef to all the families in the precinct, once a week, by order of the commanding general. After dinner I drove a cow and calf home from the old folks and made a pad for my cart saddle.

June 2 (Thursday)

About ten in the morning a thunderstorm came up and we had a heavy rain. The salt flats in front of the house were covered with water. Such a heavy rain has not fallen

---

[171] Noakes again seems to be trying to explain why he was working on Sunday.

[172] Elias Tyre Mussett settled at Corpus Christi after the Mexican War and raised a large family. The Mussett ranch was one mile from Corpus Christi in the vicinity of where Miller High School is now located. Noakes' visitors may have been any of the oldest of Mussett's seven sons.

in a long time. The river was running fresh this morning, even before the rain, so it must have rained somewhere above.

June 3 (Friday)

Another small shower passed over. I cut and plaited two rawhide ropes.

June 4 (Saturday)

A shower passed over us again and there was a great deal of lightning after dark. I plaited bridle reins and busied myself about home.

June 5 (Sunday)

Weather as it has been for some days, excessively hot in the morning and towards night thunderstorms hanging around. The river is running at the top of its banks and everything is green again. The Yankee is reported in Corpus again. I rode up to see Stevens about starting down to the Salt Lake for salt.[173] We agreed to start tomorrow if nothing turns up to prevent us. After dinner I walked up to have a talk with Bryden. I sold some more corn to a Mexican today.

Since the trip I made up the country, my health has greatly improved and I feel better than I have since I left my own country. While I was away Marie weighed the boy and he now eats as much as I do and is growing fast. Mischief has been his sole occupation between eating, drinking and sleeping.

June 6 (Monday)

Weather fine. Stevens and I started down to the Salt Lake to get salt to take up the country and trade for corn. The lake is 50 miles from here on the coast. Salt had been gathered and laid up in piles at the commencement of the war, but in consequence of the danger from renegade Mexicans and Yankees, it has been abandoned. Now, with

---

[173] Baffin Bay was called the Salt Lake or Salt Lagoon in Noakes' time. Maps of the coast during the Civil War show it as the Salt Lagoon.

things seeming a little more secure, we determined to run the risks and get a load if we could. We camped at night on the Palo Alto Prairie. There was lightning in the northwest, but none came near.

June 7 (Tuesday)

Weather threatening rain. A little after sundown a black norther passed over us, behind which was a thunderstorm but we had only a few spatters of rain. The prairies are green and the grass good. We camped at night within three miles of the Salt Lake. The prairies down there are swarming with tarantulas. I counted over 70 in the distance of a mile.

June 8 (Wednesday)

Weather very hot. Rain passed around us. We drove by a Mexican hut where we sold a little corn. We went on to the lagoon where we loaded our salt. I put mine into my hide sacks. The salt lay in large long lumps which crusted over to the thickness of six or eight inches. The crust was hard as rock. We had to chop it with our axes. We drove back 12 miles and camped on the prairie.

June 9 (Thursday)

We had a heavy shower pass over as we drove along in the morning. We crossed the Palo Alto Creek by noon. After getting dinner and resting the horses, we drove on 12 miles and camped on the prairie.

June 10 (Friday)

Last night we had a heavy thunderstorm from the northwest, with considerable rain. My rawhide cart cover kept me perfectly dry. We were on the move early but the roads were awfully heavy and we did not cross the Oso Creek till noon. On the prairie we saw an animal that appeared to be a cross between a dog and a wolf. It was a yellow color and very large, strongly built, its ears were round and it was much shorter than a wolf. It appeared to be very bold.

We reached home two hours before sundown. I found the mosquitoes troublesome. The salt marsh in front of the house and all the country was under water from an overflow of the river, which was still rising.

June 11 (Saturday)

Weather very hot. I rode into the Motts, calling at Mr. Blackwell's, Stevens', and Littig's. I rode around to hunt a cow and called at the old folks. In the evening I weighed and emptied my salt and mended a sack.

June 12 (Sunday)

Weather fine and hot. The river is all over the flats and still on the rise. I was at home all day.

June 13 (Monday)

Weather hot and fine. I worked all day on a saddle tree I am repairing for a man named Dunn and I worked on two rawhides.

June 14 (Tuesday)

Weather the same as yesterday. I worked at the saddle and then took a ride to the Motts and this evening cut out two beeves for distribution, greased my cart, and fixed up for another salt trip. The river is too high to allow us to cross it to go east, so Stevens and I have concluded to start for the Salt Lake tomorrow. The river has fallen a little but the flats are still under water.

Our wild pig is growing fast. It lays quite close under the house during the heat of the day. It eats very little, about two quarts of milk a day is all that it can eat. Its color has changed since it was small, being now more of a blue with lighter colored marks down each shoulder. It is affectionate to those who treat it kindly, but to those whom it dislikes it is very savage, sniffing at them like a dog. It is master of all the dogs.

June 15 (Wednesday)

I started in my cart with Stevens and his wagon and Herman Doakes with a cart for the Salt Lake [Baffin Bay] for salt. We camped at night on the prairies.

June 16 (Thursday)

Weather fine and very hot. We crossed the Palo Alto Creek after laying in a supply of water for ourselves and horses. We will get no water at the Salt Lake, which is a distance of 24 miles from the crossing on the creek. We reached the salt about two hours after sundown.

June 17 (Friday)

Weather fine. We loaded up our teams and drove back about 15 miles and camped on the prairie.

June 18 (Saturday)

Weather very hot. We crossed the creek, which was up, without accident and camped for the night a few miles on this side.

June 19 (Sunday)

Weather very hot. We drove on to Murdock's place.[174] There were two or three women living there with their families, their husbands having deserted to the Yankee. One of the women had a child die the previous evening and there was not a man or boy big enough to make the coffin and dig the grave. We offered our services, which were thankfully accepted. We turned out our horses and I made the coffin (there were tools and lumber there) while Stevens dug the grave. We buried the child and reached home about sundown. I found no one at home so walked over to Bryden's and had a talk.

---

[174] William Murdock's family lived on the West Oso 10 miles west of town on Rancho de Lanoria. Murdock was later murdered on Aug. 19, 1872. He was tied up, a heavy plow placed on him, and his house set afire. Ref. Nueces Valley, Aug. 24, 1872.

June 20 (Monday)

Weather fine and very hot. The river is still over its banks but falling. I rode around in the morning and unloaded my salt in the evening.

June 21 (Tuesday)

Weather very hot and thunderstorms passing around. I worked all day on a saddle which I am repairing and fresh-covering for a man named Dunn.

June 22 (Wednesday)

Weather hot and showery but no rain fell. I rode to the Motts and got our weekly rations of beef and took the old folks' piece to them. I finished the saddle tree and rigged a tree for myself.

June 23 (Thursday)

Weather hot. I rode among the cattle and penned a cow and calf for the old folks and one for myself. I branded the calves in the pen. The river is still running high but has fallen considerably.

June 24 (Friday)

Weather showery. Marie and I took a ride to Blucher's Prairie and found two of our cows with calves. We started to drive them home but one got into the thicket and we had to leave her.

June 25 (Saturday)

Showers all day. I took our last sack of flour out of our secret hole. In the evening Mr. Stevens called. I sold a dollar's worth of corn to a Mexican.

June 26 (Sunday)

Weather showery. The salt flats are under water and the river is rising again. From information I received, I was induced to bury nearly all my corn in the hole today. The rest of our provisions may soon have to follow. I hear now that the Yankee has left the island down on the coast.[175] If

---

[175] Union troops garrisoned on Matagorda and Mustang islands were withdrawn to New Orleans by the middle of June 1864.

so, it will be bad for the families here that have been supplied with provisions from them. We get no news or communication from the east in consequence of the overflow of the river.[176]

June 27 (Monday)

Heavy rain here. I was paid five dollars for the saddle tree that I covered the other day. I went to Corpus to get some sacks. I got some sacks, a little bread and black pepper, which we have not had for a long time. Corpus looks more desolate that ever. The Yankees have been preying on Confederate property and the Confederates have been making a pounce on the Yankee property there. Furniture can be bought for a mere song and pretty well all the lumber houses have migrated, some to the Yankees and some into the country.[177]

June 28 (Tuesday)

Made the boy a cart in the morning and after dinner assisted in killing the Confederate beef. I took one hide.

June 29 (Wednesday)

Heavy rain here. Sold some more corn to a Mexican and worked on my boat. I rode down to the Motts and penned McKenzie's horses for him.

June 30 (Thursday)

Weather fine. Worked all day on the boat.

July 1 (Friday)

Cleaned the hides I had in soak and after dinner Marie and I rode out and brought home a cow and calf.

---

[176] When the Nueces flooded, as Noakes noted, communication across the river ceased, travelers would unyoke their teams and camp by the river and wait until the high water receded.

[177] Maria Blucher in a letter to her parents in Germany wrote, "The Yankees have demolished and destroyed every house that has been abandoned. There were more houses than families, and consequently they were not all occupied. Ref. "Maria von Blucher's Corpus Christi."

July 2 (Saturday)

I received a parcel from mother containing a letter from her, one from Uncle Richard, and one from Mr. Gill, our lawyer, together with the form of a power of attorney, ready drawn up for me to sign, to enable mother to sell my land at Polegate, England.[178]

I also received notice from my brother-in-law Adolph that I must report to my company or be reported absent without leave. I walked to Mr. Bryden's to get Hogarth's address and borrowed some tar to tar the boat. Returned home and wrote a long letter to Capt. George to inquire into the matter of my order.[179]

July 3 (Sunday)

Wrote a letter to Mr. Hogarth and mailed Capt. George's letter. After calling on Mr. Holbein, the county clerk who is living at Hammond's place, I took a ride down to Blucher's Prairie.[180]

July 4 (Monday)

In trying to write a letter to mother, my eyes were very sore.

July 5 (Tuesday)

I had to write to mother, but my sore eyes prevented it.

July 6 (Wednesday)

I rode to Mr. Holbein's and got him to attest and Mr. Ludewig and Hobbs to sign the form [as witnesses] for power of attorney. I carried it up to San Patricio and mailed it to Judge [Benjamin] Neal for him to verify the genuineness of Holbein's signature. My eyes were sore and inflamed, so much so that I had to wear a shade. I met Joe Wright at San Patricio, who was on his way home from the war, having lost the middle finger of his left hand. He gave

---

[178] A town in East Sussex, England.

[179] Capt. William L. George, company roster.

[180] Reuben Holbein, a native of England, immigrated to Texas in 1846. He became a notary public and county clerk in 1852. He was later the business manager of King Ranch. His wife, Sarah Hobbs, was from Nuecestown.

194

me a very interesting account of some of the scenes he had been through. Some of them were laughable while others were heartrending.

July 7 (Thursday)

I fixed up and about noon started with Stevens to the Salt Lake for another load of salt.

July 8 (Friday)

We reached within three miles of the lake, having driven 30 miles since morning.

July 9 (Saturday)

We drove to where the salt lay and loaded up our teams (old Ned Taylor being along also) and started on our way back. Our horses suffered for water as there was none on the road after we left the creek at Wilson's. There and back made a distance of 18 miles without water, except for what we could carry for them.

July 11 (Monday)

Reached home about 11 a.m. and in the evening weighed my salt.

July 12 (Tuesday)

Wrote a letter to mother. Some soldiers called and directed me to report to the quartermaster at Banquete the amount of salt I hauled on the last trip. Towards sundown I went to Reynolds' pen and helped kill a beef.

July 13 (Wednesday)

I rode to the Banquete with Stevens and made it all right with the quartermaster about the salt. We took our dinner beneath some shade trees. The meal consisted of dry bread and stinking water.

July 14 (Thursday)

Dry, things burning up. I was preparing for another trip up country, making a new cart whip, and writing to Uncle Richard in England. Marie rode up to the old folks' and brought down a cow and some melons. The cow she found with a large calf.

July 15 (Friday)

I was still writing Uncle Richard. Mrs. Bryden spent the evening with us.

July 16 (Saturday)

Branded the calves, cut a whip lash and rode around in search of cows with young calves.

July 17 (Sunday)

Finished the letter to Uncle Richard and wrote one to Mr. Gill (for power of attorney). Rode up to see Mr. Littig on business.

July 18 (Monday)

Everything burned up. Prepared myself for another trip.

July 19 (Tuesday)

A little rain. Getting everything ready for the trip. Rode up to see Stevens then went up to the old folks to fetch some watermelons.

July 20 (Wednesday)

Stevens had agreed to start today but this morning he was sick and asked to wait until tomorrow. Worked over the cart cover with a mixture of lime, milk and glue to reflect the sun. Tried to catch a fish but failed and near sundown killed a hen.

July 21 (Thursday)

Started about 11 a.m. and drove to Round Lake and camped. Stevens and Ned Taylor being my companions.

July 22 (Friday)

Weather very hot and towards night thundershowers passed around. We ferried the Nueces, the river being on the rise.[181]

July 23 (Saturday)

Weather stormy last night. We were overtaken by another train of three wagons on the same errand as ourselves. We had a smart shower and before we reached

---

[181] Noakes no doubt meant they had to use the ferry and pay ferriage instead of fording the river and saving that expense.

camp there was a heavy thunderstorm. It was very severe and lasted until after dark. My cart cover kept my things perfectly dry. Stevens lost his bedding on the road, so his little son Jimmie slept with me in the cart.

July 24 (Sunday)

Thundered but no rain today. Roads were wet and heavy. We were in company with five other trains besides the first three we fell in with. We crossed the Aransas River and Poesta Creek and passed through Beeville and camped six miles farther on.

July 25 (Monday)

We drove through two bad creeks and camped after about 15 miles.

July 26 (Tuesday)

Weather fine. Our road today was over a rolling, varied country with limestone hills and bushes. We crossed Hondo Creek and one other and late in the evening another one, but we found the road led over a steep bank, about 25 feet deep, washed out by the water coming down as a torrent from the rain above. We saw that it was impossible to cross so we went a mile up and camped.

July 27 (Wednesday)

In consequence of not being able to cross the creek last night we had to drive to another crossing five miles up the creek with no road and through a rough and wet country and across any number of small branches. The crossing when we reached it looked as though it would ruin every train that tried to cross, but we all got safely over at last. We parted from the train and started for a ford which crossed the San Antonio River below Helena, about five miles.

This crossing was very dangerous, the bank going down to the river was almost perpendicular, but we made the crossing in safety. We camped a mile from the river. We are nearly out of provisions and can find no game on the road.

I was told by a soldier this evening that if I tried to pass through Helena without papers or furlough (which I have not) then I would be sent off to Houston. He advised me to go through early and quick so as not to be seen.

July 28 (Thursday)

We passed through Helena as early as we could and I got through without being molested. The place is a poor tumbled-down-looking affair. We crossed four or five creeks which were running and just barely fordable. We stopped to rest the horses. Stevens bought corn at San Patricio for 75 cents a bushel. We had to pay one dollar and a half at Helena. The country looks fair up here, and the grass is good.

July 29 (Friday)

We drove 15 miles through a low sandy country covered with live oak and post oak and the road nearly hid by tall sage weeds which grow as high as the wagon on each side. We passed poor-looking ranches but could get no corn for our horses. The men were at home and gave us as many watermelons as we could carry to our wagons. We crossed a big creek three times and a great many little bad creeks. Stevens got stuck in one and we had to pull him out.

July 30 (Saturday)

Road was so wet we could not travel more than six or seven miles. Most of the road was through a rolling mesquite country. The course of travel has been through a dreary and uninhabited country. What few ranches there were, were deserted and we could not purchase provisions of any kind, and our stores are nearly out. When we do meet anybody on the road, they always tell us there is plenty just a few miles ahead, but we never reach the place and it is always just a few miles ahead.

July 31 (Sunday)

We drove about 15 miles through a rough country of mesquite and post oaks and creeks every half mile. We were told so much about a particular ranch and assured that everything we might want to purchase could be had there in any quantity. When we reached this ranch, we found it consisted of six or eight deserted cabins tumbling down and was surrounded by tall weeds. A white woman and a Negro in a cow pen assured us that we had reached this ranch, but that what we saw was all that was left and that there was not a man on the place.

We drove mournfully on for some miles. By persuasion and a good deal of paying, we managed to get a little corn from an old man for our horses. We continued on this rough and uncertain road till it was time to camp.

When we left home, we were told that the distance to New Braunfels was not over 170 miles, but inquiring yesterday a man told us that we had 170 miles yet to go. The same man said that we are farther from Seguin than we were two days ago.

August 1 (Monday)

Where we camped last night, the wild grapes were most abundant. The oak trees were covered by the vines, which were full of fruit. We continued on until we came to the Guadalupe Bottoms where we drove through heavy pecan timber, also elm and hickory. This is the first day that we have seen hickory and walnut trees. We came to the [Guadalupe] river, which we crossed in safety. I was coughing up blood and did not pay sufficient attention to my horses and found myself in deep water, with a swift current. By whipping the horses, I managed to get through without harm, as my salt was in waterproof rawhide sacks. We camped five miles from the ford.

August 2 (Tuesday)

We reached Seguin about 3 p.m. after driving through a country of mesquite and post oak and steep rocky hills and creeks lined with black walnut, pecan and other trees. The farms today have a more substantial look with expensive improvements. My first impression of Seguin was

199

favorable. I think that, if it were not war-time, it would be a lovely and interesting neighborhood. There are some nice-looking houses and the schoolhouse is quite a tasteful building. Seguin is near the Guadalupe River with a flat prairie both north and west. I saw the first lieutenant, Ellis, who was home on furlough.[182] He received me very kindly. We camped two miles beyond Seguin on the New Braunfels Road. I have been coughing up blood again today.

August 3 (Wednesday)

Weather very hot. We reached the ford of the Guadalupe about three hours before sundown after a rough day's drive. We then drove into New Braunfels. I was surprised to find it so extensive a place. The principal street must be three quarters of a mile long, with some very fine buildings. The houses present a clean and attractive appearance, with nice shady gardens. The best streets have shade trees that are mostly china [chinaberry]. The courthouse is a substantial building of light-colored stone. From the general appearance of things, you can see at once that the town is either German or French.

I went with Stevens to the place where he was to deliver his load of furniture for a man named Phifer.[183] After we had got through, we drove to the outside of town to the Comal Creek, where we turned out and let the horses loose to graze. We found everything in New Braunfels enormously dear [expensive] except for salt and the market was glutted with that commodity. I found at once that I could do no good trading there. I felt very unwell, still spitting up blood.

---

[182] Thomas J. Ellis, company roster.
[183] He was probably referring to George Pfeuffer, married to Susan Gravis, who owned a sheep ranch and planned to construct a gunpower mill in Corpus Christi in 1862. He was from New Braunfels.

August 4 (Thursday)

Weather exceedingly hot, with no breeze. We were walking all day over the town, trying to trade salt for flour and to purchase such things as we needed, but everything was ridiculously high. We had to pay 15 cents for a small glass of beer and everything else was in the same proportion. I felt very unwell all day and towards night I became worse and by sundown I had a high fever on me.

August 5 (Friday)

Weather hot. I spent a restless night from the fever in my head and early this morning I coughed up a considerable quantity of blood. Our horses were missing this morning and it was three or four hours before Stevens and Ned Taylor could find them. We hitched up, although I felt as if I could hardly stand. But having no grass for the horses we were bound to get to some.

We drove to Tony's mill where I traded a sack of salt for the same quantity of seconds' flour. I had had nothing to eat on the road and we intended to go out on the Austin road and try to trade salt for flour from the wagons that were bringing it down the country. After waiting two or three hours in the town, while Stevens had his wagon fixed, we drove out and crossed the ford.

Getting a little weak, after crossing the river, it brought on a regular hemorrhage. I swallowed some salt and soon stopped it. We had to drive three or four miles before we could get to a camping place. Soon as we had crossed the ford, a strong wind blew up from the northeast, which added to my discomfort, as we had to meet it.

The previous part of the day had been hot, with no breeze. The wind came from a thunderstorm but the storm went around us. We were on one of the principal roads by which the cotton is transported to the Rio Grande. It was crowded with teams, most of which had five pairs of mules or seven or eight yoke of oxen.

August 6 (Saturday)

Weather fine but thunderstorms in sight. I felt unwell and had severe pains in my chest. However, I had to attend to my horses, but not being quick enough to suit old Ned Taylor, he started off without us. Stevens and I started and had not driven far when a man directed us to another road about a mile from the road we were on. This road led to San Marcos. We had to drive over rocky ground, which jolted me considerably, till we reached the other road. We tried to sell salt or buy some eggs at the houses on the road but could not.

At length we stopped to rest the horses. At noon a person came along on horseback who told us about a man who had flour to trade for salt and we decided to call on him. We drove on to the house and made a trade with him. He took my salt and gave me flour, pound for pound. I unloaded my salt and Stevens and I drove up a hollow in the hills and camped. Today's drive has been at the foot of rugged hills covered with trees, among which can be seen the cedar. We also saw some good peach orchards.

August 7 (Sunday)

Last night a severe thunderstorm passed over, but the rain did not amount to much. Just as we were hitching up, along came Old Ned. We cannot shake him off. He had returned and hunted us up after finding no sale for his salt at San Marcos. He was with Mr. Davis, the person to whom I had sold my salt, and I was lucky to have made the trade or he would have spoiled it, if he could. We found that he had already done as much for Stevens, who had nearly traded a mare he brought along for flour.

I felt much better this morning but as soon as I commenced lifting the bags of flour the bleeding began again and I had to give it up. Mr. Stevens did my work for me.

Last night Mr. Davis agreed to take Stevens' mare and pay him in flour. But Old Ned offered him his salt at such a low price that he tried to give up on Stevens' trade in order to make the trade with Taylor. I hinted that we expected him to stand up to his first bargain and he agreed to send for some more flour that he had two miles away to pay Stevens for the mare.

We agreed to stop at a certain place and he would send the flour and take the mare the next morning. After a poor dinner we drove to the designated place. Old Ned tried to get us to go farther on to camp which, I believe, was intended to break up Stevens' trade. We saw through his designs and Stevens told him so. He and I turned back to the proper place and Old Ned turned out where he was. The old beggar has been nothing but a curse ever since we left home.

August 8 (Monday)

Thundershowers passed around all day. Stevens and I shifted our camp a few hundred yards and then laid still, I for the quiet I needed and Stevens to wait for his flour, which came in the evening. I was getting dirty and had to wash out some clothes, which made me feel unwell for the rest of the day.

At night Old Ned came to try and persuade Stevens to make a start. I told them that if they wished to go to go on and start but that for me, if I did not wait and get the bleeding stopped, I would not be able to stop it at all. I said that I was determined to stay right there. Stevens said he would not leave me and would wait as long as I wanted to stay. Old Ned went off mad.

August 9 (Tuesday)

Weather very hot. I had a disturbed night, coughing very much, and this morning feeling quite worn out. I kept quiet as I could, but to be quiet is impossible on the road. Old Ned left this morning for home. He doesn't believe in coddling sick men. Stevens is very kind and I know he won't leave me but to be rid of Old Ned Taylor is a relief.

203

I find Mr. Davis a very intelligent and, I expect, educated man. He is the teacher at a school close to where we are camped. I had quite an interesting conversation with him yesterday while alone.

One of the schoolboys, a lad about 11 years old, came over to our camp to buy a chaw of tobacco from Mr. Stevens this morning. When I said that he had commenced chewing early, he said he had chewed tobacco for four years. At recess he came over for another chaw. Mr. Stevens handed him the plug and he bit off a large mouthful, enough to make me sick in five minutes.

I had no appetite for food and fancied fruit. I gave Stevens a dollar and he went search of some. He returned with a bucket full of peaches, having paid only half a dollar for them, the only cheap thing we found on the trip. From that time on I began to get better. The peaches seemed to cool my feverish blood.

August 10 (Wednesday)

Weather cooler. I felt better and we drove to within a few miles of Seguin. We traveled on the road which for some distance was lined with sunflowers growing higher than horseback and the ground was covered with rocks. A great part of the country between Seguin and San Marcos was covered with sunflowers, which grow five feet high with blossoms two inches in diameter, and very numerous.

August 11 (Thursday)

We had a little rain in Seguin. We bought corn for our horses and I went in the rain to get some liquor at any price, since I needed some to make a tonic. Stevens had his wagon fixed and I drove on to find grass and wait for him. We camped that night about 14 miles from Seguin, on the [Guadalupe] river.

August 12 (Friday)

Weather fine, with a nice breeze. I feel a great deal better this morning. We left the road by which we had come up and took one which crossed the river below Belmont [in

Gonzales County]. We traveled the rest of the day over a hilly, rocky, and sandy country. We passed two or three comfortable-looking homesteads, but Belmont looked as though somebody had taken a notion to live there but got out of the notion before they finished the place.

We forded the Guadalupe at Fowler's. The crossing was not bad but we had a steep slope to get out. We drove a long distance on a trail which we were directed to take till we came to the end of it in a thick wood. We saw that it was a logging road so we had to return and hunt another road. After driving all evening, we had to camp out three miles from the ford. The country on each side of the river had high, steep hills, rounded and covered with rocks and gravel.

August 13 (Saturday)

Weather fine. I feel better. We started on a rough road with dead trees lying across it every few hundred yards. After a few miles we came to a farm, where I traded some flour for bacon, pound for pound. The owner directed us to a water hole a little farther on, where we turned out and waited while Stevens rode around and traded among the people. The heat was very great and the flurry of exchanging my flour brought the fever on me again and I had to lie still till near night. We hitched up and drove to a house in the woods about a mile farther on, where Stevens had been making some trades.

August 14 (Sunday)

We wanted to get to Yorktown [in DeWitt County] and were driving over the country in search of a road. Everybody we saw directed us to a fresh road and at length we came to a house where we were given some nice watermelon and the man gave us directions on how to strike the Yorktown road.

The trail we were told to follow dried out and we had to do without one till we came to a fork of what we afterwards ascertained to be Sandies Creek. We were brought to a stand by not being able to cross. We unhitched and Stevens rode down the creeks and found a crossing three miles down. We went down and crossed and finding a house received directions which took us onto a road which, I expect, will take us somewhere. I took a bath in the creek, as I felt so dirty.

August 15 (Monday)

Weather fine. I do not feel so well today. We drove a mile when we came to a house where we expected to get directions about the road but the man was not home and the women knew nothing. We continued on till we were convinced we were wrong and after crossing a bad creek we stopped and turned out, thinking to see somebody ride by from whom we might inquire.

Not a soul could be seen. Towards night Stevens rode back to the house we had passed in the morning and saw the man who gave him the proper course. I washed my clothes and did various jobs. This morning we were told that we were eight miles from Yorktown but Stevens found from the man that we were 22 miles away and on the wrong road. We would have to re-cross the bad creek and cross it again about two miles farther down.

August 16 (Tuesday)

Weather hot. Last night we got no rest from mosquitoes which were worse than they had been anywhere else on the trip. I felt very unwell and this morning I can eat nothing. Up to noon we traveled through a hilly and woody and in some places rocky country, having to climb over piles of rocks, which I thought must break something.

We came to a house about noon and passing the pen saw that they had been killing a calf, so we went and got some meat, which I relished and it seemed to do me good. After getting our dinner we drove four or five miles over a low hilly country and after crossing a creek, the water of which was deep enough to get into my cart, we camped.

August 17 (Wednesday)

Weather showery. We drove over rough hills till at length we really did reach Yorktown, which is a poor, scattered-looking place. It looks as though all the ranchers for 50 miles around had congregated there. I bought saddle leather, shoes and some bread then we drove down to a mill and I bought one-half bushel of corn meal and we drove over a bad creek and camped.

After getting some cold coffee, I took care of my horses and rode back two or three miles and bought some shallots, soap, and beans.

August 18 (Thursday)

As we were hitching up we had a shower and after driving two hours we called at a house to try to buy some corn. The shower commenced again and it rained for two hours. We halted at the house. We then drove through a post-oak country till we came to Middletown.[184] It consisted of four or five poor-looking houses. We continued over hills bare of trees till we were within five miles of Goliad, where we camped. The roads were rough and heavy. I feel better today.

August 19 (Friday)

Weather showery. Roads heavy and wet. We crossed Mogner [Manahuilla] Creek and called at homes as we entered Goliad to buy corn for our horses. I was told while getting the corn that the military authorities were taking up every man who tried to pass through the town. If he could not show a proper furlough or permit, he was taken from his team and put into jail till they could send him to his company.

As I had no papers of any kind, I thought I was gone for certain. Then, with the advice of those present, we took a road that led around the town and as Stevens had to get

---

[184] Middletown was between Goliad and Clinton. The name was later changed to Weesatche. Ref. "Handbook of Texas."

something that he wanted, I kept on till I reached the river which I forded and waited on the other side for Stevens, without having been noticed. My health is improving every day and I now have a good appetite. We drove about 10 miles and camped after crossing the ferry on the San Antonio River.

August 20 (Saturday)

We drove to the Blanco River where I sold some flour and after dinner we drove on to the Tabbycat [Taipacate] Creek.

August 21 (Sunday)

We drove through Beeville and called at Mr. G. Wright's. We camped at night on a creek about 12 miles this side of Beeville. No rain from the time we crossed the Tabbycat Creek till we came to the Papalote, where there has been plenty.

August 22 (Monday)

We started from camp before day, as our horses had had no water, and drove a short distance to the bayou, where we crossed it. We camped at night near Skidmore.

August 23 (Tuesday)

I sold a little flour in San Patricio and we ferried the Nueces River and drove home. I reached home about 3 p.m. Marie was not at home but came along about dark.

August 24 (Wednesday)

I unloaded the cart and rested. I got a letter from Capt. George, ordering me to return as soon as I can and saying that he had done everything he could to get me discharged. Now they will discharge a man only after he's been dead 10 days, and even then, they do it reluctantly. The captain said I must come to Galveston and be examined and if found unfit to put in the ranks, they will put me in the quartermaster or ordnance departments. I have to fix up to go. After getting enough good provisions to last me and Marie all winter, I must go and live on the worst kind of cornbread and poor beef. I weighed out some flour, bacon and shallots for Mr. Ludewig, who came down.

August 25 (Thursday)

Took the things up to Ludewig's in my cart then came back and wrote a letter to Capt. George to say that I would be at Galveston as soon as I could. I took up a few shallots for James Bryden.

August 26 (Friday)

Transcribed my journal and read.

August 27 (Saturday)

Made preparations for leaving home. Mended up my marching tricks. In the evening I rode into the Motts on business.

August 28 (Sunday)

I rode up to meet Mr. Rogers to see about some mares, but he did not come. I hear that my company is ordered back to Corpus so I shall not start to Galveston till I am certain.

August 30 (Tuesday)

I put my tools and stuff to rights, preparing to leave home. Saw Mr. Rogers.[185] I got no satisfaction about the mares. I traded my favorite colt two years ago for two mares and seventy dollars. The mares had colts the following spring, soon after which I fetched them home, paying [Rev. J. P.] Perham $5 in specie for taking care of them. As soon as I had them home, they went off again, before I had the colts branded. Since that is nearly two years ago, I shall lose the colts, and as I can hear nothing of the mares, I expect I shall never see them again.

The paper money we kept till it was worth nothing, and that is a good example of Texas trading. Shot a hare and caught a few fish.

---

[185] William L. Rogers' Palo Alto Ranch, 22 miles southwest of Corpus Christi, was later the Driscoll Ranch.

August 31 (Wednesday)

I hunted my mares and branded two colts. Marie being the only help I could get, we altered [castrated] a two-year-old colt, the first one that I have tried my hand on. I branded the calves. I shall not brand half as many calves this year as I did the first year. I bought the cattle, about seven years ago, although I have sold none and bought some more.

September 1 (Thursday)

Making a trunk to take my clothes in. Took the cart to pieces and stored it in the shed.

September 2 (Friday)

Fetched all the salt from the old house and put it in the corn bin. Ran in a calf and branded it.

September 3 (Saturday)

Rode out to see my colts and brought a cow with a large calf.

September 4 (Sunday)

Branded the large calf and rode around among my cattle.

September 5 (Monday)

I rode out to the Pintos Creek to have one more search for the lost mares. Did not find them but rode on to Perham's place to see Mr. Richardson.[186] Mr. Richardson was away from home so at the invitation of Mrs. Richardson I remained all night.

September 6 (Tuesday)

Mr. Richardson returned about sundown. I gave the mares and colts into his care until after the war. I started home at daylight and came by Banquete and drew pay for a beef which the quartermaster had on his books that was killed for the troops. The beef was worth $15 but I was paid

---

[186] James Richardson was described as caporal of Perham's sheep ranch, not to be confused with another James Richardson who worked for Richard King and commanded a Confederate cavalry company that was active during the war.

$2, and that is the first pay I have had for several they have killed.

Before we were in any danger, we had to feed the soldiers with our beeves. As soon as danger threatened us, we were abandoned and now that we are once more out of danger, by the withdrawal of the [federal] army, the [Confederate] troops are being sent back to live again on our beeves.

The tax collector was the first to remind us that the danger was over by his demanding the war tax on property that, only a few months ago, we had been ordered to abandon to the enemy. I branded a large steer in the place of one that had been stolen from me. I feel so disgusted at the manner in which I have been treated and robbed that I am going to adopt the rules now in vogue and get back what property I can.

September 7 (Wednesday)

With Marie's help I branded two more unmarked animals, about two years old. Everybody is branding all they can get and I mean to do the same. Unmarked stock is public property. No fresh meat today.

September 8 (Thursday)

Rode down to Corpus to get some flannel for underclothes but could get none. Spent the evening with Mrs. Swift and reached home at midnight.

September 9 (Friday)

Penned and branded a yearling and ran in a cow and calf.

September 10 (Saturday)

Marie and I rode to Tule Lake on a cattle hunt. We drove home and branded four yearling bulls. Everybody tells me I have as much right to the yearlings as the others who are branding them. As long as I am at home, I shall do my best to get my share. My health is better.

September 11 (Sunday)

Had a row with George Reynolds. He falsely accused me and Marie of having given information about a steer that certain parties have charged him with stealing.

September 12 (Monday)

Branded a heifer yearling and two bulls in the evening.

September 13 (Tuesday)

Made Ludewig an axe handle. Branded a bull.

September 14 (Wednesday)

Went to Corpus and bought two woolen undershirts. Returned with James Gibbs, who is on furlough.

September 15 (Thursday)

I rode to Banquete to consult the military authorities about my returning to my company. I was advised to be examined by the surgeon at that post and let him forward his certificate to headquarters and await further orders. I saw Dr. Merriman.[187] I agreed to ride out again on Sunday for an examination.

September 16 (Friday)

Everybody is in great hopes of the war ending this fall. Present events give us reason to expect a change may come soon. It is reported that the Mexican General Cortina is threatening or actually invading us on the Rio Grande.

September 17 (Saturday)

Very important event happened. Mr. Ludewig came down and told me there was a vacancy at Banquete for clerk in the commissary department. I rode out and saw Capt. Alsbury, the quartermaster, to make application for it. I took my paintings along and they soon gained me an introduction when I was promised the place. I rode over to Dr. Merriman's but he had no time to examine me. I

---

[187] Dr. Eli T. Merriman owned a ranch and horse-stock operation at Banquete and practiced medicine in the region. During the war, Dr. Merriman served as a commissioned officer in the Confederate ranks. His son Eli became a newsman in the 1870s and was one of the founders of the Corpus Christi Caller.

returned to Mrs. Morgan's where I had been all day and got my supper.[188]

September 18 (Sunday)

Rode over to Dr. Merriman's and he examined me, sounding my lungs. He told me my right lung was entirely useless and advised me to take particular care of myself. He gave me, at the same time, a certificate of disability.

September 19 (Monday)

I wrote to Capt. George to request him to give me a detail as clerk to Capt. Alsbury, the quartermaster at Banquete. I heard the first geese and sandhill cranes crossing over.

September 20 (Tuesday)

Weather fine and dry. I was at home till dinner, after which Marie and I took a ride around Tule Lake, calling at Mr. Barnard's to get some liquor to make a tonic, which I was advised by Dr. Merriman to take.[189] But we could get none. We rode back up the river.

September 21 (Wednesday)

The last few days has been unhealthy weather, the sun very hot and every once in a while a cool wind from the northeast, our usual fall weather. I rode up the river to get some willow bark to make tea with. I also brought home a horehound plant to assist in making an experiment. In the evening I rode up to Ward's place to get a sheep from Wright's flock, the last due in payment for a horse trade.

Young Mrs. Wright rode up with me. Joe Wright was with the sheep and at sundown we penned them. Mrs. Wright killed one and skinned and cut it up while Joe and I

---

[188] This was the Byington boarding house and store operated by Samuel and Rachel Byington. After Samuel died in New Orleans in February 1860, she married a man named Morgan in 1862 and the Byington store and boarding house became known as Mrs. Morgan's. Her husband, James N. Morgan, was a Confederate captain who commanded a militia company at the start of the war. Ref. Old Bayview web site, 1860 Census.

[189] James R. Barnard owned a saloon, the La Retama, in Corpus Christi.

caught mine, which I killed. Joe could not do much, having lately come home from the war minus one finger and part of a hand. I tied my sheep on the horse while Mrs. Wright carried hers in a sack. As we were riding home in the dark, Mrs. Wright's horse pitched her off into the road, along with the meat. I attempted to carry her meat for her but my horse would not let me.

September 22 (Thursday)

Weather fine, wind south. I carried Mrs. Bryden and the old folks some of the sheep after I cut it up. I rode around a little among the cattle and the rest of the day I amused myself reading.

September 23 (Friday)

Weather fine. I rode among the cattle that came down to the river to water. As I watched, I saw that Reynolds and several others were swimming two yokes of steers across the river. After dinner Marie and I went for a ride among the cattle and drove home and branded more mavericks.

September 24 (Saturday)

We had a heavy rain, which lasted a short time in the morning, then light showers were in sight all day. I rode around till the rain came on, after which I remained indoors reading. I have been reading "Hudibras".[190]

September 25 (Sunday)

Showers passed around all day. We had a small shower in the morning; there must have been a heavy rain to the west. To pass the time I cut and plaited a lariat, or hide-rope. I saw a few geese today. We have no war news at present.

September 26 (Monday)

Weather fine. In the morning I shot a rabbit as I was hunting for my bay horse. In the evening Maria and I rode among the cattle, but brought nothing home.

---

[190] Samuel Butler's "Hudibras" was set during the English Civil War in the 17th Century.

September 27 (Tuesday)

Weather fine. I was cutting an eight-strand plaited rope and a calf rope.

September 28 (Wednesday)

Weather fine. Marie and I took another ride among the cattle to hunt for cows with young calves. We brought home a brindled fighting cow and a maverick. We had to get the cow out of the pen before we could rope the calf, and the only way we could do that was to tie a rope to the gate and when the cow ran out, pull it closed, and keep the calf inside. Marie did this while I drove her out. We branded the calf and the maverick together with two that we had in the pen.

Marie and I branded 20 mavericks. But from the number of calves I am missing, I do not consider that to be half what I am entitled to. By my book, I ought this year to get over 50 calves and at present I have only been able to get 16 cows with calves of my own. Not being able to get away to hunt them, other people get their calves and I am determined to get as many as I can of the public stock.

September 29 (Thursday)

Weather fine. I plaited the rope that I cut out on Tuesday.

September 30 (Friday)

Weather fine. I went to John Williams to try and buy some corn but could not. I sketched the javelina pig to keep a correct likeness of him, as I will have to kill him. He has gotten to be so savage to strangers that he flies at anybody who comes near him except me, Marie and the boy. I fixed the lid of a box for John Williams.

October 1 (Saturday)

About nine a.m. we had a strong wind blow up from the northeast, quite chilly with hard rain which lasted some time, but it was no more than the ground could soak up. I killed the javelina pig and dressed the meat and the hide.

October 2 (Sunday)

Weather fine and hot again. I was reading till after dinner when Marie and I walked up to the old folks and spent the evening.

October 3 (Monday)

Soon after breakfast we had another norther blow up with a little rain. I was making a shelf for the old folks and painting the pig. Towards night the wind increased in strength and coldness. We were glad to set over the fire.

October 4 (Tuesday)

Last night was very cold. We could hardly keep warm, even with two or three blankets over us. I was riding all day before I could find my cart horse, which had gone off hobbled.

October 5 (Wednesday)

Weather fine and warmer. I was painting a likeness of the boy and the javelina. I also penned a maverick and branded him.

October 6 (Thursday)

Weather fine and warm. I was painting up to noon when I fetched up the horses and Marie and I went for a ride and brought home a yearling to kill. After dark we walked up to the old folks and stayed awhile.

October 7 (Friday)

Weather warm and fine. I rode around a little then resumed my painting.

October 8 (Saturday)

Last night we had another norther blow up and this morning the wind is quite cold. I killed the yearling I had in the pen, cleaned the flesh from the hide, and buried it to slip the hair. I went to work on Mr. Ludewig's water barrel, making hoops out of fencing wire and putting them on. He and Heward took dinner with us. I carried the meat around to the neighbors and sold a beef to McKenzie for $10.

October 9 (Sunday)

Weather fine, wind cool, sun hot. I cut up the meat and salted some and jerked some.[191] I rode around awhile to see my cart horse but could not find him. Ellen took supper with us after which we all walked back home with her, where I met a captain somebody and Mr. [Richard] Schubert.[192] I commenced to copy one of my paintings today.

October 10 (Monday)

Weather fine but cool. I worked the hair off the calf hide I had buried and the rest of the day I was sketching the painting that I call the first gun.

October 11 (Tuesday)

Weather fine. I was painting till near dinner when I helped Mr. [James] Kiser pen and neck up the steer I sold him the other day. In the evening I went to see Bryden.

October 12 (Wednesday)

Last night or early this morning we had a small shower, hardly sufficient to settle the dust. Today I sent the letters I wrote nearly three months ago to mother, Uncle Richard and Mr. Gill by Bryden to Capt. Alsbury, the quartermaster at Banquete, who is going to Brownsville.[193]

October 13 (Thursday)

Weather fine. I was painting all day.

---

[191] Jerked meat, called jerky from the Spanish word charqui, consisted of lean meat rubbed with salt and black pepper. It was cut into thin strips and hung out to dry in the hot sun until it lost its redness and turned dark brown.

[192] Richard Schubert, a family friend of the Blucher's, had a gun shop in Corpus Christi. At the end of the war, he opened a large general store at the corner of Chaparral and Lawrence. He later moved his trading house to Duval County, at Concepcion and San Diego, and then returned to Germany.

[193] This was probably the first chance Noakes had to send the letters to England. With Brownsville back under Confederate control, the letters could be forwarded from there by foreign ships, which arrived to take on cargoes of cotton. In his diary, Joseph Almond noted in June 1863 that he managed to get a letter to his father in England by way of Matamoros. The Cotton Road served an ancillary purpose of carrying out the mail to foreign destinations.

October 14 (Friday)

Weather fine, everything drying up, the grass all gone. I was painting on the same piece.

October 15 (Saturday)

Weather fine till night when we had a small shower. The wind which had been shifting all day changed to the north and blew strong and cold.

October 16 (Sunday)

Weather cold last night. Rain was quite dried up this morning. The sky today has been overcast and towards night a steady rain commenced which has continued to the present time, 8 p.m. I spent the day painting to pass the time.

October 17 (Monday)

The rain that started last night has continued more or less up to this evening. We have had a steady rain that will do some good. I was at my painting all day.

October 18 (Tuesday)

Weather cold. I finished my piece that I have been painting and rode out to hunt my cart horse, without success.

October 19 (Wednesday)

Weather cold and wet till noon, when the rain ceased. I commenced painting another small piece, representing a boy and a girl in a boat on a lake. I attempted this piece to get practice in drawing the human face. This evening I rode out to hunt the calves.

October 20 (Thursday)

Weather cold. I rode out and brought home my cart horse then rode to the Motts on business. I took dinner at Bryden's. I had called there for some letters; one was from Adolph Ludewig and the other from the clerk of my company acknowledging my last letter to Capt. George and directing me how to act. The yellow fever is bad at Galveston. I returned home after dinner when I had one of my old fevers come on. I sweated till it broke but I felt unwell for some time.

October 21 (Friday)

Weather cold and misty in the morning. I was painting all day.

October 22 (Saturday)

Weather cold and sky overcast but no rain. I was painting all day except a short while in the morning when I tried to shoot a rabbit with a charge of shot. I missed and there was an end of our hope for fresh meat today. I finished the piece I have been painting since yesterday. I am in need of something to read of a night.

October 24 (Monday)

I rode to Banquete to see Dr. Merriman about my certificate. I stopped at Mrs. Morgan's, who keeps a boarding house where I took dinner. At Mrs. Morgan's I met Maj. Ingledow.[194] He gave me advice about the medical disability and, having arranged everything satisfactorily, I left for home. I got there after dark, calling at Bryden's as I came along.

October 25 (Tuesday)

Weather fine and warm. I did nothing worth mentioning, feeling unsettled as I may be called upon any day to Banquete and I do not like to begin a job for fear of not being able to finish it. In the evening Marie and I went up to the old folks where we took supper and I brought home a bushel of corn which Mr. Ludewig bought for me.

October 26 (Wednesday)

Weather changeable, light wind from the northwest. I commenced to make a saddle tree, till noon, after which I rode out and brought home my horses.

October 27 (Thursday)

Weather fine with a strong cold wind from the west and a hot sun. I worked at the saddle tree.

---

[194] Maj. Isaac Ingledow was the Confederate enrolling officer at Banquete.

October 28 (Friday)

Weather warm and cloudy. I took a ride up the river, giving myself a Texas holiday. This consists of riding a broken-down horse all day in search of game that you never find and having nothing to eat. I could find no turkeys or anything else but a pie melon or two growing on the salt marsh which I brought home.

October 29 (Saturday)

Weather changeable and warm. I was writing some lines for my brother-in-law, up to noon, then worked on the saddle tree.

October 30 (Sunday)

Weather cold and cloudy, but thunderstorm-like wind from the northeast. Very peculiar weather. I rode up to Stevens and brought a bushel of corn meal. I hunted in vain for one of my cart horses and after dinner I went and had a talk with Mrs. Bryden.

October 31 (Monday)

Last night and today it has been cool and wet from the northeast but no quantity of rain fell. Thunder passed around before daylight. I worked all day on the saddle tree.

November 1 (Tuesday)

Weather warm, wind from the south, and every now and then spatters of rain fell till noon. I rode out and brought home my bay horse but it cleared off. I was working on my saddle tree and killed two large rattlesnakes. I took their fat, but had nothing to put it in, so I skinned one of the snakes without ripping or puncturing the skin. I made a bag of that one and filled it with fat and tied a knot at each end.

November 2 (Wednesday)

The coldest day we have had this winter. Early this morning there was thunder and rain from the northeast and about daylight the wind blew up strong and cold from the north. The rain ceased but the wind continued to blow strong and very cold. I worked on a saddle tree. I am making two, as well as an axe handle.

Yesterday as I was working at the bench, Marie being there, she discovered a large tarantula crawling up my back and nearly to my neck. She knocked it off and we killed it. Shortly before I had been out with the gun to shoot a rabbit. The tarantula must have jumped on me as I was walking through high weeds.

I saw today by the paper that every male between the age of 18 and 45 will have to return to the army. All those having exemptions, whether for sickness or disability, will have to report again. It appears hard for men who have been in the service and have been found entirely unfit for duty — in consequence of some kind of disease, such as consumption, and having been sent home with certificates to that effect — to have to turn out in the face of winter to a camp of instruction and thereby sacrifice their otherwise short lives. By doing so they do not render a particle of good to the country or anybody else.

The war fiend haunts every nook and corner of the country. It cannot rest while even the sick and broken-down are away from the horrid strife, but must drag them from their already ruined homes to perish from exposure and neglect, away from those whose endearing attention might offer solace for their few remaining days on earth. But that grim message of Death should come to beckon them away. Their final suffering might be alleviated by the presence of those dear ones whose natural ties would cause them to feel a deeper sympathy and promote them to a greater devotion than could be realized by any other earthly being. But no, declares the war fiend, these comforts are too great for these times. He must be torn away and dragged off to some distant camp and there die and be buried like a dog.

November 3 (Thursday)

I worked on the saddle trees.

November 4 (Friday)

I killed a poor yearling calf as we could not nothing fat, and Marie has been crying for meat for some days. I had to kill it, although there will not be five pounds of meat from it. I cleaned the hide and buried it to slip the hair. I seem to have lost my appetite for meat. I care for nothing now but mush made of cornmeal and milk. The gruel is eaten with cold unboiled milk. I can eat this three times a day in preference to anything else we get now, for if we have meat there are no vegetables, and we never make any kind of pudding. If we do get anything that might be made good there is always something in the way and it has to be cooked up any way and eaten with bread instead of some nice light kind of pudding to make a change. If we intend to have anything now more than bread and meat, there is always something deficient. But mush does not require much trouble and no skill in seasoning it and when it is not burned and the meal and milk are fresh, there is nothing more required to compete the meal. I have settled down to mush for the rest of my life.

The better part of the day I worked on the saddle tree and talked to Mrs. Bryden. She called, but Marie was gone up to the old folks.

November 5 (Saturday)

I burned the lampers out of my bay horse, throwing him in the pen and burning them with a sharp, flat, hooked piece of iron which I made for the purpose.[195] The rest of the day I was busy at the saddle tree.

November 6 (Sunday)

I took a walk to Judge Doakes to hear the news. After dinner I went for a ride down the Oso.

November 7 (Monday)

Weather warm. I worked on the saddle tree.

---

[195] "Lampas" caused swelling of the roof of a horse's mouth. Typical treatment was to burn or lance the affected area.

November 8 (Tuesday)

Weather warm. I worked all day on the saddle tree.

November 9 (Wednesday)

Last night soon after I got to bed the wind shifted to the west and blew tremendously but soon shifted to the north and blew just as strong. I got up and braced up the house roof on the inside with ropes. I covered up the well and brought home a little horse (Tony) which I had staked out. The wind blew for two or three hours and stopped. This morning it was cold. I worked the hide I had buried till dinner time, when I was occupied writing Mr. Hagar about the Gibbs' place.

November 10 (Thursday)

Weather fine and cool. I worked on the saddle tree.

November 11 (Friday)

Weather fine, no wind, hot sun. I worked on the saddle tree and pegged out the hide.

November 12 (Saturday)

Weather fine and wind warm. I finished one saddle tree, now ready for covering.

November 13 (Sunday)

Weather fine and hot. Today should have been our day of rest, but my horses have all been gone for three days and I was out tramping on foot in search of them, from breakfast time till three in the afternoon, without finding them. When I returned home, they were there, having been to water during my absence.

November 14 (Monday)

Weather as yesterday. I worked all day covering one of the saddle trees.

November 15 (Tuesday)

Last night the wind changed to the northeast and today it is cool. I was finishing covering the saddle tree, till noon, when I started work on the other one. Marie and Ellen went to Bryden's to spend the day.

After supper Mr. and Mrs. Ludewig came down and passed the evening till Ellen came from Mrs. Bryden's and they went home together.

November 16 (Wednesday)

Raining, wind changeable till night, when it blew strongly from the south. I was working all day at the saddle tree, Marie caught some catfish in the river. As we wanted meat badly, they came very welcome.

November 17 (Thursday)

Weather fine and warm. I prepared a saddle tree for covering and worked the hide for that purpose. Marie caught more fish.

November 18 (Friday)

Last night a norther blew up and this morning it was too cold to work covering the saddle. Toward night we had a little rain.

November 19 (Saturday)

Weather very cold with more rain. I had to cover the saddle or spoil the hide so I worked till late at night and finished it.

November 20 (Sunday)

Very cold and a steady rain commenced in the middle of last night and continued more or less till sundown. It was the wettest day we've seen for a long time. I stayed in the house all day. This evening Mr. Stevens called and brought me a piece of beef he had just killed.

November 21 (Monday)

Weather cold, wind from the north. I was fixing a saddle tree, getting ready to cover it for Mr. Stevens, and getting firewood.

November 22 (Tuesday)

Cold this morning. There was ice on the water in the tubs beside the house. It was too cold to cover the saddle so I walked to the Motts, had a talk with James Bryden, and bought some soap at Vetters' store. After dinner I took

Judge Doakes two pounds of flour, which I lent him. I also bought a hat, pair of shoes and some coffee from Kingley, a peddler.

November 23 (Wednesday)

Weather warmer, wind from the south. I went to Kingley and bought some shoes for Marie. I worked on another saddle tree till night besides working the hide to cover the one for Stevens. Mr. and Mrs. Ludewig took supper with us.

The prospects of the termination of the war are gloomy. It is generally supposed that it will last another four years. If so, what will become of us?

November 24 (Thursday)

Weather as yesterday. I was preparing the hide to cover another saddle tree and fixing the tree.

November 26 (Saturday)

Weather still the same. I covered the other saddle tree.

November 27 (Sunday)

Weather still the same as the last three days. I amused myself with the saddle till evening when Marie and I went to the river and caught some fish for supper. Stevens came for his tree today and paid me $5 for it.

November 28 (Monday)

Weather warm. I was making and boiling wooden stirrups and working on the rigging of my saddle. I went up to the old folks and passed the evening. Mrs. Bryden was there.

November 29 (Tuesday)

Weather warm. I cut out and stamped the leather for my saddle which I partly rigged. The stirrup proved a failure. The wood was too knotty to turn. Ellen took supper with us and I walked home with her.

November 30 (Wednesday)

Weather fine and warm. The mornings for the last week have been damp and foggy. The grass is quite green. With the help of Marie, I finished my saddle tree about noon. I borrowed a horse from Mrs. Bryden and rode out to hunt my cart horses, but could not find them.

December 1 (Thursday)

Weather warm. I rode out and found my horses. We had some smart showers. After dinner it cleared off and I rode up to Hobbs' and bought some paint oil, after which I walked up to the old folks with Marie and the boy. On the way I shot and killed a goose which weighed ten and half pounds.

December 2 (Friday)

Weather fine and warm. I rode to Banquete and got my sick furlough extended.

* * *

A missing portion of the Noakes journals extended from Dec. 2, 1864 to July 9, 1865. This was a significant time that covered the last few months of the Civil War. At some point during that time Noakes moved his wife and son from the Motts to a rented home in Corpus Christi. They left the family home empty, like so many Noakes had seen on his corn-buying and salt-trading trips. The inhabitants had fled inland, "gone east" as Noakes put it. The same was true for Corpus Christi where two-thirds of the population left the city, reducing it from several thousand residents to about 400.

When Noakes and family arrived in early 1865, Corpus Christi was in a state of ruin, with abandoned houses pulled down for lumber and firewood by Union troops. Officials had decamped from the town after the Kittredge bombardment then Banks'

226

invasion in November 1863. Officially, they left for Santa Margarita, a crossing place on the Nueces County side of the river, but they were operating out of the village of San Patricio, out of reach of Union warships.

Food supplies were scarce in Corpus Christi. There was no regular mail service and no newspaper — editor Henry Maltby moved the Ranchero to Matamoros. Most of the stores were closed, there were no ships in the harbor and little commercial activity in the town. Private and public property had been neglected during the course of the war and the town's streets were littered with dead animals. One of the worst droughts in living memory left the land itself looking dead.

During this time in town, Noakes' second son, Nelson Edmondson, was born, on June 13, 1865 at Susan Swift's boarding house on Water Street.

A few weeks later, in July, two companies of Union occupation troops, black soldiers under the command of white officers, arrived. One resident, Mrs. Henry M. Hinnant, who was a young girl at the time, said, "The town was filled with Yankee troops, all Negroes. We were so scared." Rosalie Priour, a teacher, wrote in her memoirs that the occupation troops "were the most lawless set of people I have ever seen. No one was safe."

Other accounts said that except for a couple of incidents the black soldiers behaved very well. An occupation tax was imposed and some of the best homes were commandeered by Union officers and occupation authorities began to appoint pro-Union residents to official positions in local government. That was the state of Corpus Christi in July 1865 when we return to Noakes' diary as he and three men were planning a trip to Padre Island to salvage a boat that had washed up on shore. —M. G.

* * *

Marie (Mary) Ludwig Noakes, undated.

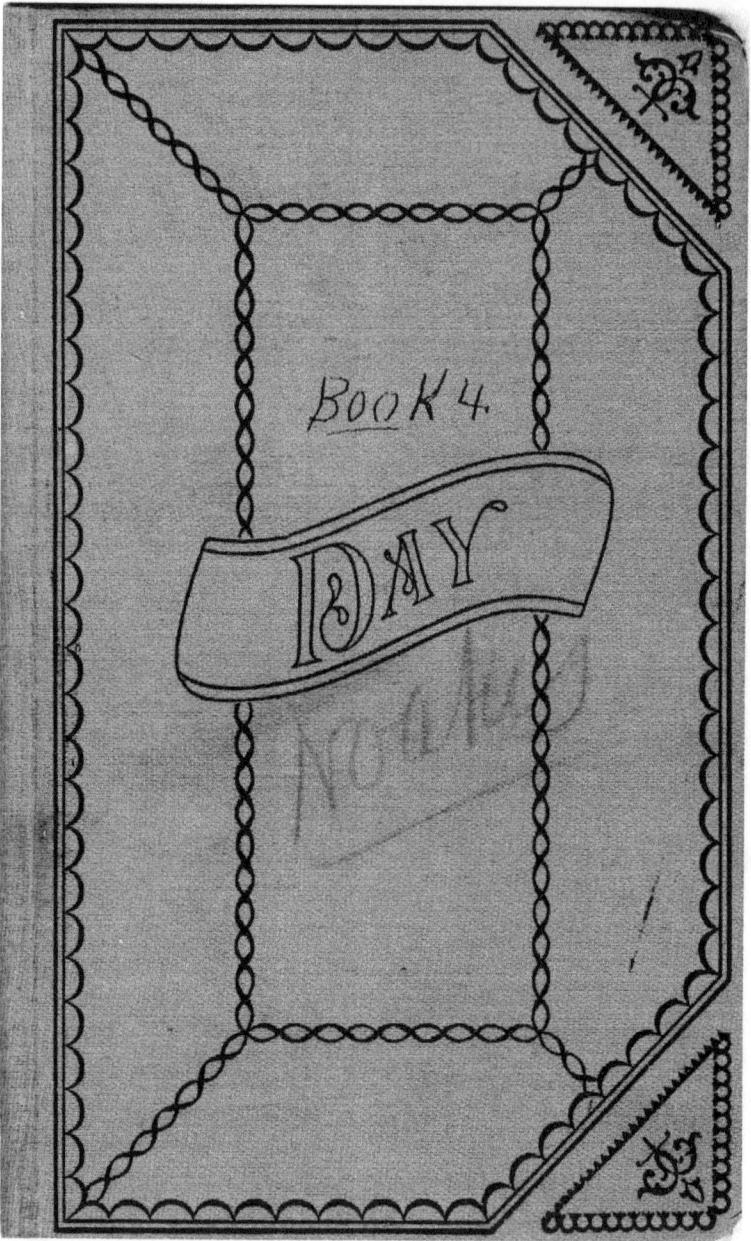

A cover of one of Noakes' journals from the 1860s.

October 1860

Fri 5. I and Ned Taylor rode out to Banquette
Creek and I skinned at caw that have
died during the night.

Sat 6. I rode to Corpus and stop at Adams.
sold my horse cart to Cannon.

Sun 7. I settle with Cannon about the cart
and dine at Almonds. and after seeing
Adam again, I returned home.

Mon 8. At home most of day.

Tues 9. Geese, and Sand hill cranes flying over
this week. the up country people were
down to the mills and we help them
round up their cattle

Wed 10 Jobbing at home.

Thurs 11. Started to Corpus when about half way
it began a pour down rain for three
hour I took shelter in a new house belong to Mr Biller. after the rain I rode to
Adam and staid all night.

Fri 12 - I then went in city and did by bussi
and took dinner at Adam and returned
home.

Sat 13 - I busy myself at home.

Sun 14. - I pass day alike I do every sunday
along.

Mon 15. About a dozen of us started on last cattle hunt

*A copy of a page from one of Noakes' journals, showing entries
from Oct. 5 to Oct. 15. 1860.*

Thomas Noakes' painting shows the high point of the battle of Corpus Christi on Aug. 18, 1862. Union ships fired at a Confederate battery of three guns located near where the ship

channel is located today. Union forces landed and were repulsed by Confederate cavalry (lower left). Noakes was a member of Capt. John Ireland's infantry company, which participated in the battle.

Thomas J. Noakes' watercolor painting of the of the Battle of Corpus Christi Pass on Dec. 7, 1862.

The burning of Noakes' store during the bandit raid on Nuecestown on March 26, 1875.

An old bull has bothered me greatly for the last
week. He would break through my pen fence
anywhere he pleased, then break out again. I
made myself sick working to keep the fence in
repair. Early this morning I heard him crashing
through the fence again. It made me so mad I
rammed a ball into my gun and went out
and killed him.

—Sept. 14, 1865

AFTER THE WAR
1865

July 9 (Sunday)

After breakfast Mr. Price, a Welshman who recently
married in this town, called to get me and two others to go
down to Padre Island to see if we can go pick something
up, so I have been preparing for the trip. Price is lending
me a horse. We started at noon, four of us, with Price, an
Irishman named Fields, and a young man named Hooper,
Price's brother-in-law.

We encountered our first difficulty at the mouth of the
Oso. The water was nearly deep enough to swim our horses
and very boggy. We made it without more hurt than a little
wetting of our provisions. We continued our journey till we
reached the crossing of the Laguna Madre, which divides
Padre from the mainland. It is a good six miles across.

After dark we saw two men on foot coming towards our
camp. They had just crossed over from the island, having

been left there by a boat, without anything to eat or drink. We gave them their supper and they went on.

July 10 (Monday)

Weather hot. Last night I got no rest or sleep, the mosquitoes being so hungry and troublesome. We saddled up at dawn and crossed the lagoon, which was unusually deep. The water for about a mile splashed over our saddles. It seemed doubtful whether we could cross over it at first. We took our breakfast on a sand hill near some willows which were full of heron nests. Most of the nests were occupied by young birds. I saw a pair of sandhill cranes flying around, the first I have ever seen here in the summer.

We rode over to the beach and continued on for 20 miles till we reached a spot that was opposite a deserted hut called Curry's Ranch.[196] We rode across the island till we reached it, where we camped. We found the place most desolate looking, occupied only by mosquitoes and ants. One of the boys shot a hog, which accidentally came too near the house.

July 11 (Tuesday)

Weather fine. The mosquitoes last night were awful. This morning our horses looked jaded out. We protected ourselves against the insects by getting in the hut and smothering ourselves with smoke and want of air. I got very little sleep. After getting our breakfast from the pig that we killed, we continued our journey down the beach.

Our discoveries yesterday consisted of 20 bales of cotton, most of them buried in the sand, and today we saw nothing more valuable than empty barrels, bread boxes, water cups, a can of spoiled vegetables, two boxes of spoiled tea biscuits, and a cask containing about four

---

[196] The Curry Settlement was a family enclave started by a Baptist preacher from Alabama named Carey Curry. His large family settled on Padre Island, 17 miles below Corpus Christi Pass. Preacher Curry had two sons, Joe and Uriah and two daughters with husbands and their own families. The Curry Settlement, or Curry Ranch, was sometimes called The Settlement.

gallons of good vinegar. We passed the wrecks of two vessels, several boats, a good deal of rigging, and other things belonging to ships together with a dozen chairs.

We took our dinner at a water hole on the island which we had a good deal of difficulty in finding. We rode and rode till after dark, trying to find water at a place to stop for the night. Our horses were so tired that we had to walk and drive them before us. But being unsuccessful in finding water, we had to turn down on the beach and content ourselves with a dry biscuit for supper. We tied our horses up for the mosquitoes to feed on during the night, after a ride of 30 miles.

July 12 (Wednesday)

Weather fine. We were dreadfully tormented all night from the mosquitoes even though we laid ourselves as close to the surf as we could get. We have the burning heat, fleas and ants to torment us during the day, when we stop, and mosquitoes and sand crabs during the night. Last night one of the crabs got under my blanket and bit me on the face till it bled. One of our party accidentally discovered water behind the sand hills, so we watered our horses.[197]

We thought we should have reached the boat yesterday that we had been assured was beached on the island. About noon we met a man named Murdock, a Yankee renegade with a light wagon and a yoke of steers, and another man returning with him.[198] They told us we were eight miles from the boat but they did not think we could do anything with it.

---

[197] People who lived on Padre Island learned there was a shallow layer of fresh water three to four feet down, between the sand and heavier salt water underneath. Relatively fresh water could be found almost anywhere on the island with a little digging.

[198] The year before, in June 1864, Noakes on a salt-gathering trip stopped at a house on the Oso where the women were without their husbands who had "gone over to the Yankees." Noakes helped bury one of their children who had just died. It seems probable that that was the family of William Murdock, whom Noakes and friends met on the island returning from the border.

239

We reached the boat about four p.m. and went to work on it. The first thing we did was to dig a shallow well with barrel staves and put in a flour barrel [to reach the water table and shore up the sides to keep out sand]. The island here was nothing but loose white sand with a coarse grass which the horses would not eat. We decided that Hooper would drive the horses to the nearest place where they might feed while the rest of us worked on the boat.

We made a shade as best we could with a small sail Fields brought along for the boat. We went to work. Price and Fields caulked it and mended the holes with cotton. With only a dull hatchet for a tool, I had to supply a mast boom, rudder and tiller. For nails, I salvaged them from boxes found on the beach. Getting out spikes and nails, I broke my hatchet handle three times and had to make a new handle each time.

July 13 (Thursday)

Weather hot, no breeze. We worked closely on the boat and by night I had the mast boom and rudder ready. The mast I made out of a piece of a ship boom I found a mile from the boat and the boom I made from a stick of willow left by the tide. The rudder was made by chopping up a narrow plank and spiking it together and hanging it by means of staples which I extracted from a hatch cover on the beach.

For the last two days we have been on short rations, with no meat and our bread nearly gone. Our prospects are that we shall be entirely without, or we are obliged to allow ourselves only two meals a day, and very little at each meal. By sundown the boat was nearly ready to launch. We concluded to launch her in the morning.

July 14 (Friday)

Weather very hot with a little wind. We commenced before day to get the boat ready for sea, bending on the sail. The mosquitoes last night allowed us no rest. I never went to sleep. This morning we were all worn out. We got the boat down to the water on rollers, saddled up the horses, and were prepared to start when we found that the mast was too large. We had to hunt for smaller sticks, which Fields succeeded in doing. As I was hunting along the shore, I found a bone, or part of one, which by its size must have belonged to some extinct animal. It was larger than any now in existence.

We divided the provisions and found that we had, for breakfast, three biscuits apiece and a little coffee, which we had enough left to make a few cups, and that was the allowance with which we have to start to travel 75 miles up the island. Two of the horses were about to give out.

Price and Fields agreed to take the boat while Hooper and I were to take the horses. We launched the boat without much trouble, the wind being fair and the sea calm. Hooper and I followed along the shore. We agreed to try to get to Curry ranch that night if possible and lay up a day to rest the horses and kill some meat to save ourselves from starvation. After noon we could not get the horses out of a slow walk and at dusk we came up to Murdock, who was camped. He told us we were 20 miles from Curry's.

As I expected that the boat had made a good run and would be waiting at Curry's, I intended to keep going, but one of the horses could barely stand and Murdock persuaded us to camp with him. I told him of the state we were in; we had eaten our second biscuit, intended for our supper, as we rode along. I felt exceedingly hungry and low. I pulled off the saddle.

Murdock gave us a handful of hard bread, or tea biscuits, and after staking the horses we made ourselves a cup of coffee. Never did bread taste so good before as did those tea biscuits. The wind blew strong enough to keep down the mosquitoes and after a short talk we threw ourselves down on the sand and I got the first night's sleep since I started the trip. I woke up chilled and wet, with the heavy moisture of the night, but felt stronger after sharing about two dozen tea cakes from Murdock, and he gave us a drink of liquor.

We started on our journey and traveled about 14 miles when we met Price and Fields coming to meet us. They were nearly famished for food and water. We kept on till we came to the boat which they had beached. We were within four or five miles of Lively's place.[199] Fields and I took the boat. Price would go no more, having been seasick the day before. I felt very low, without nourishment of course, and we were nearly capsized by the surf, which came in very heavily.

We saw a horse in the distance and when Price and Hooper came up with the horse, we were overjoyed that they had had the luck to shoot a good-sized redfish as they came along. After getting out of the boat, we stuck a stick lengthwise through the fish and roasted it for supper. Price lost his saddlebags and Hooper's roan several miles back and we could not find them.

July 16 (Sunday)

Weather cooler, a fresh wind and heavy surf rolling in. Fields and I made an attempt to get to sea in the boat. We knew if we could only get through the breakers, we could make Corpus Pass by night where we expected to obtain provisions from a Mexican who lived there. But a heavy sea struck the boat, throwing her on her frame ends, and the gunwale hitting me as it flew up knocked me into the water. It was not very deep and I was in no danger of drowning. I made for the boat again, which by this time was half full of water. We baled her out and ran her ashore and worked her up on blocks to wait for a more favorable time.

Fields and I walked across the island to Lively's empty house and hoped to kill some meat on the way. The others followed with the horse. We could see no signs of getting

---

[199] A Mr. Lively, a schoolteacher from the North, resided near the Curry Settlement after the war. Ref. "Padre Island" by Writers' Round Table.

anything to eat. We had had no breakfast and were getting weak. We kept one man on top of the horse all day so as to be on the lookout for hogs or cattle, but none were seen. In the evening Price and Hooper took the two best horses and rode out to hunt something to kill, but returned after dark without having seen anything.

Being too weak to fight off the mosquitoes, we climbed up on the roof of the house and laid there, it being very flat. The mosquitoes did not trouble us much up there. Before we laid down, we turned out all our wallets to see if we had any old biscuit pieces that had been overlooked. We ate up all the crumbs we could find and the little coffee we had left.[200]

July 17 (Monday)

At daylight I fancied I saw two hogs near the place and we all turned out in a hurry. It was a delusion. As our horses were too weak to carry us home, we concluded that our only chance was to get back to the boat and see if Murdock had not gone far and if possible, to catch up to him and purchase some provisions at any price. I took the best horse and a wallet and after riding four or five miles found him. As luck would have it, they had just brought him a hog they had killed.

I only had a dollar and a half but Murdock sold me a dollar's worth of flour, one-half dollar worth of ground coffee, gave me a leg of the hog and lent me a frying pan. I was not long in getting back to camp, where I was received with joy. We soon had a good meal cooked, and didn't we eat!

---

[200] A wallet was a bag sewed up at each end with a slit opening in the middle that could be slung on the back of a horse with the weight distributed evenly on each side. Robert Adams described it in his memoirs: "A wallet was a rectangular sack of cloth, the opening being down the middle. You would put your cup, coffee, and clothes in it, or just anything and everything, and hang it on behind your saddle."

We could not get the boat off. We would have to wait till the sea settled down. Near sundown Murdock passed again and he let us have a little more flour.

July 18 (Tuesday)

The sea was still running high. We decided to try and kill some kind of meat. But we got nothing. When we got back to camp, we found that the other two, instead of saving the provisions, had wasted them, so that we should be compelled to abandon the boat and return home. Seeing that such was the case, I considered the partnership at an end and determined to try to get the boat through the breakers. I suspected that Fields wanted us to abandon the boat and by doing so would relinquish any claim to her. Then, in a few days, he could return with a chum of his to get her off and claim the whole.

But since he was the only one of us who could hope to manage her in the breakers, we had to trust him for getting her back. After a while we got him to make a reluctant start. I went with him, but he purposely ran her ashore and said it was useless trying, that we would have to leave her, and he began taking out the oars and other things and carefully laying them out of sight on the shore.

This confirmed my belief in his intentions, and I made this known to Price. We made up our minds not to be out-generaled by him. We told him that if we left the boat that we would not return for her, as it would not pay, but that if he wanted our claims to the boat he would have to pay us what was reasonable, and then we would help him pull the boat high out of the water and surf. Then he could return for her anytime he wanted. But no! He wanted her but he did not want to pay us for our shares. I proposed to put it to a vote whether we should break her up and leave her or leave her intact for others to reap the benefit of all our toil and suffering. All but Fields was in favor of breaking her up. We again made him the same offer, but he refused.

244

We used a pole to knock a hole in her bottom and left her to the breakers. We packed up our horses and reached the end of the island a little after dark. We found the Mexican gone and no water.

July 19 (Wednesday)

We were not troubled by mosquitoes but we had no water, for ourselves or our horses. We managed to get enough water out of a hole to make some coffee and wet some flour. We crossed the island and the lagoon, the crossing of which reminds me of going to sea on horseback. You can barely see the opposite shore when you start across. After not finding water where we had camped, as we came out of the lagoon we had to continue on.

The horse I was riding could barely move; it belonged to Price and was in poor condition when we started. We crossed the Oso, leading our horses for fear of them getting bogged, and then we found water sufficient for them and ourselves. We stopped and finished up our flour and coffee. We wet the flour in a sack and then twisted the dough around a stick and baked it.

Fields caught up with us, having been to a friend's at Flour Bluff. He told us about the Yankee being in Corpus so we concluded that it would be best to slip into town after dark, since our appearance was by no means prepossessing, not having had a wash for 11 days.

When we came in sight of the town, sure enough, there were the [N------s], two regiments of them and more said to be coming. However, no one molested me and I rode straight to my yard and was glad once more to be back. Like all my Texas trips, the experience I had gained was my only remuneration. Supper was soon ready and I was satisfied in that respect. Mrs. Ludewig was there. Before going to bed I had a good wash.

July 20 (Thursday)

Weather fine and windy. I stayed indoors, wrote up my journals, and kept quiet. The town is full of [N------s] and scandal. Towards night I went into town, but there was nothing but [N------] troops, turn which way I would.

July 21 (Friday)

Weather fine. After cleaning up my saddle I went into the town, calling at Mr. Schubert's store where I met Mr. Staples and some others.[201] We went into a discussion in regard to the taking of an oath that is required of us by the Yankee. We came to the conclusion that, being whipped, we would have to conform to their measure sooner or later so we considered it the best policy to do so at once. I went to the provost marshal's office and performed the ceremony. Mr. Ludewig was down and took dinner with us.

July 22 (Saturday)

Weather very hot with thunderclouds and rain in the morning. I was busy all day covering a saddle tree for Dr. Britton.[202]

July 23 (Sunday)

Weather fine and hot. I remained in the house most of the day. My face and neck are blistered and sore from the effects of the sun that I am ashamed to be seen. I went over to Schubert's store a little before noon to hear if there was any excitement stirring but could hear of none. Nor could I get any papers. If we go out on the streets, we see nobody but the colored troops. I believe there are over two regiments here now with more coming. Up to the present time it has been quiet. Mrs. Ludewig is here yet. The money now in circulation is entirely greenback. More boats bringing [N------] troops arrived this evening.

---

[201] Waymon Staples came to South Texas from Alabama in 1857 and established a grocery and produce business in Corpus Christi. He was appointed mayor in 1866.

[202] Dr. Edward Britton was the oldest son of Sen. Forbes Britton, a former army officer who was pro-Union at the beginning of the war when he died. Dr. Britton joined the Confederate Army as a surgeon while his younger sister, Anne Elizabeth, married Judge Edmund J. Davis, who was also pro-Union and became the Reconstruction governor of Texas. Ref. Frank Wagner's Research Papers and "Maria von Blucher's Corpus Christi."

July 24 (Monday)

Weather fine and hot. I loafed around town, having nothing to do. I purchased some sulphur to take as medicine. All of us have been troubled with a skin condition resembling chicken pox. I went to the army sutler's store where I was kindly treated. I spent most of the evening talking with Mr. Robertson.

July 25 (Tuesday)

Weather hot and dry, needing rain. Having nothing to do, I loafed around town, waiting for something to turn up. I heard Mrs. Swift would be here in a few days. On Sunday last the house of Dunn's was robbed by [N------s] and today the Dunn boy caught some of the thieves, killing one and capturing another, with some of the stolen property still on them.[203]

July 26 (Wednesday)

Weather the same. I passed the day in the same unprofitable manner. I thought it best to move back to the Motts so I spoke to Mr. Burks about his moving us out, but afterwards changed my mind. Mr. Ludewig was down yesterday and Mrs. L. went home with him. There was a row at the upper end of town last night, occasioned by a man, supposed to be a [N------] soldier, disturbing Mrs. McCabe by getting into her house. I spent the evening at Schubert's store.

July 27 (Thursday)

Weather cloudy and about 10 a.m. a squall blew up from the south and we had a small sprinkle of rain. I was talking with Mr. Robertson till the squall blew up, then I went to

---

[203] The incident happened at the home of John Dunn, four miles west of town. An account is related by Dunn's nephew, who said the soldiers entered the home while the family was at church. They returned to find guns and uniforms left behind and property missing. One of the boys, Matt, traced the two black soldiers to the reef road crossing Nueces Bay. Matt charged the two, shot one and killed him, and took the other to the soldiers' camp. Ref. "Perilous Trails of Texas" by John "Red" Dunn.

our house. I passed the evening between Schubert's and home.

July 28 (Friday)

Weather as yesterday, with a squall coming up about the same time, and from the same quarter, only we had a little more rain. I took the saddle I covered for Dr. Britton over to Schubert's, where I stayed till noon. I bought a watermelon and went home to eat it. I am loafing away my time till I can hear of some way of using it. We cannot buy even the necessaries, and those things that are not necessary are selling at a higher rate than they were during the war.

July 29 (Saturday)

In the first part of the day, and in fact all day, I did nothing. I felt dull and miserable, seeing nothing that I can do which will do us any good. I am tired of loafing about town. I am tired of the suspense of being told every day that Mrs. Swift is coming in a day or two. But still she does not come and I do not hear from her. I am making nothing and we have to buy everything we eat and drink at high expense. I try to read but cannot. I try to sleep away my time, but with no better success. My mind is too unsettled to paint and, besides, I have received no encouragement whatever since the strangers in the military service left. People here cannot compromise their dignity so much as to call to see my painting.[204]

I turned my attention to covering saddle trees, one of which I was paid for, another I took out in hides, which I spoiled, and the other one I will never be paid for. I would like to go up to my place at the Motts and see if I have anything in the shape of cattle left. But I have no horse and the cost of hiring one for that purpose will not pay. I could ride for a month and not do myself one dollar's worth of good. I feel myself checkmated, look which way I will.

---

[204] He no doubt means his painting of the bombardment of Corpus Christi by Union warships.

This evening Gen. [Charles] Russell, commander of the federal forces here, sent a polite request to see my paintings. I sent them and they were soon politely returned, with many thanks. Afterwards, having occasion to visit the quartermaster's office, I met Fitzsimmons.[205] He was acting as clerk, and being an old acquaintance, I was speedily introduced to the quartermaster. Fitzsimmons expressed a wish to see my painting, so he accompanied me back to the house. Nothing would do but that we should take them back to the office, which we did, with results that were very satisfactory for my feelings. The paintings gained me an introduction which, without them, I could not hope to obtain.[206]

Mr. Ludewig was down with his cart. I took the opportunity of sending out some of our things, as many as he could take, along with the boy. I expect to send Marie out on Tuesday next, and the balance of our things. But I do not intend to remain at the Motts myself, if I can possibly help it. After seven years of living at the Motts, a long time, I have seen the absurdity of doing so without friends who can lend me assistance that is necessary at times to manage a ranch, and without money sufficient to procure that assistance. My cattle and horses have gone to the wind, my place has been turned upside-down, with no riding horses, no steers, no cart, although I own the best part of one and can use it only as a favor. All the labor of fixing up the place, pens, well, which I have done so many times before, is a prospect hard to consider.

---

[205] Joseph Fitzsimmons moved to Corpus Christi after the Mexican War. He was a Union supporter during the Civil War and was appointed county clerk by occupation authorities.

[206] Besides the more famous painting of the bombardment of Corpus Christi, Noakes also painted a scene from a skirmish at Corpus Christi Pass, which was near the present-day Packery Channel. The date of this skirmish, Dec. 7, 1862, coincides with a gap in the Noakes' diary but he was believed to have been an eyewitness to the skirmish as a member of John Ireland's company. Ref. "War of the Rebellion," report of Confederate Capt. H. Willke to Maj. E. F. Gray.

Then I should be surrounded and crowed over by people whom I look upon as my inferiors, though they are better adapted to withstand the fatigue and experiences of Texas Life, being possessed of great elasticity, never wishing for the luxuries and refinements of civilized society. They live happily and make money under circumstances sufficient to drive a person with any taste for refinement to despair. And for that reason — while I have seen myself becoming poorer and poorer — I could not stoop to do as they do. They have been amassing wealth and at the present time look down upon me with a jeering kind of pity . . .[207]

July 30 (Sunday)

Thought I would attend church, but was too late. Loafed at Schubert's till dinner time. Idled away the rest of the day till sundown. Then I went to see the [N------] dress parade. I was surprised to see them drill so well.

July 31 (Monday)

I painted a small picture representing "Rabbit Hunting on the Prairie."

August 1 (Tuesday)

I wrote a letter to Capt. Alsbury, the former Confederate quartermaster at Banquete, which I got forwarded through the quartermaster here. A government steamer came in today bringing forage. Everything is still in suspense. Mrs. Swift does not make her appearance.[208] I can see no prospect of doing anything by remaining here.

---

[207] There was another quarter-page of despondent self-pitying sentiment, with Noakes using his diary to vent his frustration, but the tirade is not worth anthologizing. We should keep in mind that he never intended anyone to read his journals except perhaps members of his family, so he was mainly communicating with himself.

[208] A later entry revealed that Noakes had approached Mrs. Susan Swift, who owned a boarding house in Corpus Christi, about starting a sheep venture with her putting up the capital. He was in suspense waiting for her decision.

August 2 (Wednesday)

I took the letter to Capt. Alsbury to the quartermaster's and called on a captain about a table he had taken from me and then went to see the general about getting a pass to go to New Orleans. I have a notion to go there and get photographs made of some of my sketches and try to sell them. Mr. Ludewig was down but did not bring his cart to the house.

August 3 (Thursday)

Reynolds was down with his team and I intended on moving out to the ranch, but hearing no more from Mrs. Swift I could not do so. I concluded to stay till she returns. The federals holding a court of inquiry in town which brings a great many people from the country. I also commenced a sketch of "The Taking of the Yankee Ship Morning Light."[209]

August 4 (Friday)

The "old man" was down and took his meals here. Mr. Beynon also dined with us.

August 5 (Saturday)

Adolph Ludewig and his wife (for he has recently married) and Ellen came down and spent the day here. Consequently, I did nothing else. I have no friends or associates in the town, where I might go to pass an hour or two for a change and no one to pass the evenings with. I mope about the house.

August 6 (Sunday)

After making breakfast and taking a wash, I went out on the wharf and remained there till noon when I went home to get dinner.

---

[209] The Morning Light was one of the Union ships in the blockading squadron. It was captured, along with the ship Velocity, by the Confederate gunboat Josiah H. Bell after a battle on Jan. 21, 1863. It's not known if Noakes was at the battle, but he was at the scene of two of his other battle sketches, the bombardment of Corpus Christi and the skirmish at Corpus Christi Pass, so it is likely that he was at this one as well. Ref. Handbook of Texas.

August 7 (Monday)

I passed the time by painting and sleeping.

August 8 (Tuesday)

I passed the morning painting and about three o'clock Mrs. Swift arrived on a schooner from the Rio Grande. Consequently, my calculations were turned into a new channel. Mr. Ludewig was here with his cart, but I could send nothing (furniture and furnishings) out, as Mrs. Swift has not a thing to use. I kept mine here for her use until she can get her place fixed up.[210]

August 9 (Wednesday)

Feeling in the way, there being so many at Mrs. Swift's, and my company not being particularly required, I spent most of the day about town and at Schubert's. Things are not working out to my satisfaction; I went and engaged a team to move our things tomorrow morning. Marie and I prepared to move.

August 10 (Thursday)

The wagon was at the door soon after sunrise. By nine o'clock I had it loaded it up. As I had no horse, I had to ride up on top of the load. The wagon was driven by an old [N------] man known as Uncle Ned. We reached my place and I unloaded about 5 p.m. I had to go up to the old folks for supper.

August 11 (Friday)

With the assistance of Adolph, his wife, and Ellen, I had the house and shed cleaned up and everything in its place by sundown.

August 12 (Saturday)

I cleaned out the well then went to the old folks, where Marie was, the old man having fetched her out the day before. I hunted up the steers and brought home such things

---

[210] In the context of Noakes' cryptic entry, it's not clear why Mrs. Swift would need his furniture or furnishings, unless she was staying with Noakes while getting her boarding house ready to re-open.

that they [the Ludewigs] had there of ours. I took back a barrel of water and there being nothing to eat at my place, I had to get my dinner there. After trifling away the afternoon, Marie and I reached home after dark.

August 13 (Sunday)

I did but little, it being Sunday. In the evening I went to see James Bryden. Samuel Couling was here today and offered to trade for my place and stock. I walked home with Ellen.

August 14 (Monday)

I was working about the place, putting up a shade to cook under, and talking to those who came along, which took a considerable amount of my time.

August 15 (Tuesday)

I was busy all day, there being a great many things to do. Everything that I have done several times before now have to be done all over again. I see nothing ahead but hard work, and I return to it with a poor heart. The question that is ever before my mind is — will it do me any good?

I finished the shade and commenced building a back gallery to the house and plaited another whip. The one I plaited a short time ago in Corpus was gnawed up by the rats. I have far more important work I should be about but the sun is so hot it is impossible to work in the heat.

August 16 (Wednesday)

I mended the calf pen, hunted for the old man's steers on foot, till I was worn out. I went to get some firewood and wood for the pen then walked over to John Williams and fetched home some things he had brought from Corpus for me. Afterwards I traded off some old corn for kershaws [cushaws]. The corn I recently bought at one dollar per bushel I had to trade at the rate of 70 cents, and take it in kershaws, because it was not fresh. I will have to buy new corn at $1.50 per bushel. I went up to the old folks and loaded the corn on John's cart, he bringing something for me at the same time.

August 17 (Thursday)

Weather excessively hot without the customary breeze. I was at John's getting my kershaws and working at home till evening when John brought my things down in his cart. I hired him to haul some firewood and haul some wood to repair the pen from the remains of the field fence.

August 18 (Friday)

Last night heavy thunder passed to the east but no rain fell here. The weather is peculiarly hot and sultry. Everything is burned up. I was repairing the pen, getting in the cows and calves with a horse borrowed from Bryden, and working on a saddle tree I am repairing for H. Couling. I have eight cows in the pen for milk. I work hard from before daylight till after dark. My health is very good and I am little troubled with my cough.

August 19 (Saturday)

I rode around and penned and branded a bull yearling, with Marie's help. He fought so that I had to rope him from horseback. I then worked on the saddle tree and on a gallery that I am making for the back of the house. Near sundown Adolph came along and we rode up together and necked a yoke of steers. We are cooking out of doors, as we find the fire unbearable in the house. I made a shade by stretching my rawhide cart cover over poles in the ground, tent fashion.

August 20 (Sunday)

I rode around a little then was compelled to sew up the cover of the saddle that I had in soak, or it would have been spoiled. I have to work, Sunday or not. After dinner Marie went up home and Adolph came down, bringing us a leg of beef. I took a bath in the river and by that time I had to see to the horses and cows.

I find myself settling down to the same old drudgery: Work, work, work, poor living, ragged clothes, no comfort, no pleasure, no society, no refinement, and no hope for

254

anything better, as long as I am fool enough to remain at this detestable spot.

August 21 (Monday)

Weather a little cooler, showers passing around. I penned three cows with young calves and rode to Tule Lake with Adolph to hunt for more. I found but one. After getting home I branded all the calves in the pen. There were 12.

August 22 (Tuesday)

I finished the gallery at the back of the house, cut the rawhide strips for a rope, repaired the doorstep of the house, fixed up my cot to sleep on, and did several other jobs.

August 23 (Wednesday)

The horse I had the last few days, the one I borrowed from Bryden, was gone this morning, having broken his rope. I did not feel well so did not do much till noon, when the horse came back to the well for water and I caught him. I plaited two calf ropes and spliced my stake rope.

August 24 (Thursday)

Weather fine although showing for rain. I branded a nice black heifer nearly two years old, and by the time I had finished with her the rain commenced and continued till noon. After dinner I was digging a ditch in the pen and mended a table. Heward and Stevens came to see me about teaching school at the Motts. All the people are anxious for me to start a school. I thought it was the last thing I should come to, but I expect I shall try it, as I must do something to get along.

August 25 (Friday)

We are very low in the housekeeping line. We have one meal of flour left and we shall soon be out of everything. There is nothing to be bought in the county. I believe the Yankees intend to starve us, like some people will starve wild horses so that they can be more easily broken.

Most people here, before the Yankees took possession, were looking forward to the time when they might be able to procure anything they might want to eat or wear, at cheap rates. But up to the present time they have been sadly mistaken. We have been worse supplied with the necessities of life since the Yankee occupation than we were before.

Flour is $30 a barrel, when it can be bought at all.[211] I bought a bushel of corn still in the shucks the other day and had to pay $1.50. After getting it home, shucking and shelling it myself, it measured not quite three pecks. When ground by hand on my mill, and sifted, it was still less. Since I left Corpus, meal cannot be bought. There is none.

August 26 (Saturday)

Dug a trench inside the pen to make the fence higher to keep the cattle from jumping over.

August 27 (Sunday)

It rained in torrents and the bedding in the shed is wet. Cannot milk as the cows are knee-deep in mud. The flats are covered with water and the hollows are running down like rivers. Marie's shoes have given out and she has to wade through the mud in bare feet. I would do the same if could. To be kept in the house so long, with nothing to read, is unendurable.

August 28 (Monday)

Heward, Bryden and Reynolds came to get me to teach school, which I agreed to do, starting a week from today.

August 29 (Tuesday)

Worked at chores all day.

August 30 (Wednesday)

Repaired the pen fence all day. Henry Couling brought us a piece of meat this morning. Overcome by heat while working.

---

[211] The inflation calculator shows that the equivalent price, in today's dollars, would be $1,472.

August 31 (Thursday)

Rode up to Mrs. Bryden's and talked with her awhile.[212] After dinner I rode up to see Heward. I prepared myself for a trip to Corpus the next day, but a high fever set in and by bedtime it began to look serious.

September 1 (Friday)

I spent a wretched night with fever and had to stay in bed all day. Toward night Marie fetched Mrs. Bryden, who brought me such medicine that I was in need of.

September 2 (Saturday)

Still feverish and unwell.

September 3 (Sunday)

Maggie and Adolph Ludewig came down and spent the day.

September 4 (Monday)

Still sick.

September 5 (Tuesday)

Still unwell.

September 6 (Wednesday)

Still feeling very unwell.

September 7 (Thursday)

I have been mustard-plastering and blistering my neck, which is still raw. I am in a jumble mentally and can write no more.

September 10 (Sunday)

Weather the last few days has been cooler, with a strong breeze from the south. I feel better today, but not being able to get the things I require from Corpus, I am slow in recovering. I find I am not strong enough to start school tomorrow, so shall have to put it off. I consider myself fortunate in getting a sack of flour yesterday. Samuel

---

[212] Noakes apparently turned to Janet Bryden for advice and it seems that Janet, along with her husband James, was a driving force behind re-opening the school and encouraging Noakes to teach.

Couling got it for me from some teams passing on the road. I paid $10 per hundred for the flour.

September 13 (Wednesday)

Weather cooler for the last three days. I have been too unwell to do anything and have passed most of my time on my cot. Yesterday I put a rawhide bottom in a chair and the day before I glued a stool for the boy. Today I feel better, but low and weak. I am taking my old bitters and although I have only used them two days, I feel a great benefit from them already. I ought to, for I had to pay $2.50 for the bottle of liquor. I have been fishing today, without success.

September 14 (Thursday)

Thundershowers passed around all day. I was trying to fish without any luck. An old bull has bothered me greatly for the last week or so. He would break through my pen fence anywhere he pleased, then break out again. I have made myself sick working to try to keep the fence in repair. This morning early, I heard him crashing through the fence again. It made me so mad I rammed a ball into my gun and went out and killed him. After dinner, it being cloudy, and Adolph being here, we took off the old bull's hide so the buzzards could get at him better.

September 15 (Friday)

Weather showery. We had one hard shower and several small ones. I can catch no fish although I try night and day by keeping a line in the river. I did nothing but peg out a hide and watch the fish line.

There are great numbers of toads everywhere. It is astonishing to see how dexterous they are at catching flies. The toad will hide and if a fly lands within two or three or even four inches, he will snap him up before you can see how he does it. The toad does a great amount of good in destroying insects. Even mosquitoes who overgorge on blood and cannot fly fall prey to the toads who are always on the watch for them.

September 16 (Saturday)

Weather still showery and still no fish. Henry Couling brought us a nice piece of beef so we shall do nicely today. I am gradually getting my strength back, but it returns very slow. The country looks beautiful. The grass is high and green, but the mosquitoes are always in like proportion. As yet, we can buy nothing to eat or to wear. I cannot buy Marie a pair of shoes. She has to wear a pair of mine. I expect the Yankees think that if we can starve for five years then we can stand it for any length of time. We get no account of what is proceeding in the world, we get nothing to read, nothing to wear, nothing to eat or drink, nothing besides what we can make ourselves.

September 17 (Sunday)

I walked to Mrs. Bryden's to see about commencing school but the walk there showed me that I am still too weak so I postponed the commencement of it.

September 18 (Monday)

Towards sundown a thunderstorm passed from the east to the west but we got none of it. I tried to repair the fireplace in the house and commenced at it, but was soon glad to lie down on my cot. I have no strength. And bread and butter, and mush and milk, with some coffee, is not the kind of diet to build up one's strength.

September 19 (Tuesday)

Weather fine, although nearly every day and night we hear thunder passing around. I did nothing but look over some school books. In the early morning the dew is so great that I cannot leave the house. But as soon as the dew is gone the sun is too hot for walking and, as I have no horse, I cannot ride. Even if I had a horse, I have nowhere to go. Consequently, I stayed at home and laid on my cot.

September 20 (Wednesday)

The wind for the last three or four mornings has been from the northeast and quite cool. I made another attempt at the fireplace (which has to be done) and did considerable work at it, but tired myself very much. Near sundown I went to the river to try to gig a fish but saw none. We have great difficulty getting meat while I am sick.

September 21 (Thursday)

Weather fair and hot. I finished the chimney and fixed a chain on which to swing the kettle.

September 22 (Friday)

Hot and foggy. Marie and I went hunting cats and killed two, the house and shed being infested with them. After dinner I did nothing till nearly sundown when I tried to gig a fish.

September 23 (Saturday)

Cool, with a morning fog from the north, which cleared up and was followed by a fine day. I had the old folks' colt on stake. Adolph brought a message from Corpus to the effect that if I went down as soon as I can I might get a clerk's situation in the adjutant's office. Towards sundown I rode up to the old folks and, as we needed meat, Adolph and I killed a small beef.

September 24 (Sunday)

Hot and fine, although we had lightning during the night. I cut up and salted a little of the meat and jerked some of it. Reynolds came by to tell me he had heard of my little roan horse Tony and he knew where he was and that if I would give him an order he would try and get him for me. I did so and am in hope of getting him again. I am making preparations to go to Corpus tomorrow. Those merchants who have been to New Orleans for goods have returned without any and our prospects of getting the necessities of life are as bad as they have ever been. We have not starved before and I suppose we shall not now.

September 25 (Monday)

I started for town before sunrise and reached Corpus about 8 a.m., stopping a short distance from town and munching a piece of bread for breakfast. I went to the adjutant's office but the vacancy for a clerk was filled. I then went to the commissary to apply, but with no better success. Seeing that there was no chance of getting a situation, I made up my mind to try the school, which I should so much have liked to have escaped.

I inquired for books and hunted up a schoolteacher by the name of Carroll.[213] I spent the afternoon at his school trying to gain an insight into the manner of classing pupils. I found him very obliging and quite willing to impart all the information he could. I dined at Mrs. Swift's.

September 26 (Tuesday)

This was one of the fall winds that seem to affect my lungs so much and this morning I had my old cough and was expectorating bloody mucus from my lungs. Marie and I had a regular clean-up of the house, moving our bed from the shed to the house. After dinner I rode around to see the parents of the pupils which I am promised. I let them know that I intend to open the school on Monday next.

September 27 (Wednesday)

In response to an invitation given to me by Mr. Carroll, I arrived at Corpus at eight o'clock, the time he begins school, in order to see him go through the morning exercises. I find that the greater part of the exercises is given at the blackboard. The writing lesson is copied on the board, either from the grammar or the arithmetic, by the teacher. The lesson is recopied from the board by the pupils. After this each pupil has to recite what he has written down and the teacher examines the writing at the same time. By this method, the pupils learn to write, cipher, and speak grammar in the same exercise.

The first is the spelling class. This includes all the pupils. The next is the geography, which includes part of the

---

[213] William Carroll, known as "Little" Carroll to distinguish him from his brother, "Lawyer" Carroll, was one of two teachers at the Hidalgo Seminary in Corpus Christi. His niece was Mary Carroll, who would one day become superintendent of the school system and namesake of Carroll High School.

students. Then comes the arithmetic. The pupils go over the multiplication tables and do exercises in addition. The teacher writes two or three sums on the blackboard and, commencing with the top of the class, each boy does his part. The teacher does the figuring on the board as the pupils direct him. Each pupil copies on his slate the sum as it is written on the blackboard. When the sums are completed, the students take their slates to the teacher or he goes around the class and inspects the manner in which they are written. The sums are merely copied and ready for the students to work on. The students take their slates to their desk and complete them in the same manner as the teacher did on the blackboard. After they finished doing those sums, they did some other sums from their arithmetic [book] till noon.

The afternoon exercises commenced with a spelling and reading class. Each pupil in his turn reads a short passage while the one next to him stops him (as they term it). That is, at a comma the student next to him exclaims, "comma one," or "period one," and so on through all the stops as they occur, counting the number according to what the stop may be.

After being examined and cross-examined on previous lessons, the pupils get their copy books, which have not yet been examined, and each one reads his writing and they get out their slates and parse and cipher till school is out. I left my horse and saddle at the school house.[214] I went into the town, calling on Mr. [Henry] Taylor to try and buy his blackboard.[215] He would not sell but agreed to lend it to

---

[214] The Hidalgo Seminary was on the bluff on the corner of Lipan and Tancahua.

[215] Taylor had been the teacher at the Motts, when he arrived in 1860. He moved to Corpus Christi where he was appointed postmaster of the town by the occupation authorities. Ref. "Handing the Mail at Corpus Christi" by Jim Stever.

me. I executed all my business and reached home after dark.

September 28 (Thursday)

I fixed a fastening to the back door and this morning I went to John Williams and bought one-half bushel of corn and a dozen kershaws [cushaws]. I gave the bull's hide, which I staked out a short time ago, to Mr. Doakes to use to cover his wagon.

September 29 (Friday)

I fetched home the kershaws from John's, rode up to the old folks, then to Bryden's after dinner. I put together a small bedstead for the boy and studied my school books. Little George Reynolds came bringing me — who? what? — you may ask. Tony! My little roan horse! How glad I was to see him. Mr. Reynolds had succeeded in getting him for me and only charged me what he paid the Mexican who accompanied him.

September 30 (Saturday)

I went up to Reynolds and necked Tony to a horse in his remuda.[216] This was to accustom him to them so that he would stay with them. I also helped Reynolds brand a horse and, in the afternoon, I went up to the schoolhouse with Jimmy Bryden and George Reynolds and we cleaned the place and prepared for the coming Monday. Geese and sandhill cranes arrived today.

October 1 (Sunday)

I rode Billy, the old folks' colt, up to Reynolds' and from there to the schoolhouse, after which I wrote a letter for Reynolds to Rev. Orchard.[217]

---

[216] Necking was the method of yoking a wild outlaw horse to another more tractable animal so that he might learn how to behave in a civilized manner. The practice was also used to tame unruly cattle. Remuda was a vaquero word for horse herd or string of extra remounts.

[217] Rev. Stephen Orchard moved his family from Nuecestown to San Patricio in 1861, then to Goliad and from there to Luling, where he died in 1895.

October 2 (Monday)

I now commence with another chapter in my changeable life, that of teacher or schoolmaster. I began at nine a.m., came home for dinner at twelve, and quit at four p.m.

I experienced much less difficulty from my pupils than I had expected. I found them anxious to learn. I experienced the greatest difficulty for want of books, slates, everything required to conduct a school. I found the schoolhouse as much deficient as the pupils. The windows are gone, sashes and all, and the blockings which support the concern have given up their situation. However, I managed to get through, to the satisfaction of all concerned.

October 3 (Tuesday)

I am troubled by my old cough. It returns every fall with the east winds. But I kept school and after four went out with the colt and brought home a cow.

October 4 (Wednesday)

At school till half past four, fixing the blackboard. Came home and worked on the well till dark. I have 14 scholars with the prospect of three more.

October 5 (Thursday)

At school for the usual time, from nine till four. After school I took a ride to Blucher's Prairie and saw a gang of turkeys.

October 6 (Friday)

Today I went over the lessons of the week, repeating what had been studied during the previous four days. I have thus far experienced much less trouble than I anticipated at first. My pupils are attentive and anxious to learn.

October 7 (Saturday)

This being a holiday, I went to town in quest of books for the school and shoes and clothes for myself. I found everything very dear [expensive] but more reasonable than they have been. I spent over twenty dollars and could see nothing for it. I rode home with Mr. Wilson.[218] He is the father of four of my pupils.

October 8 (Sunday)

I wrote the copies that I have to set each day for my pupils. Then I took a walk up to Reynolds and saw John Williams. After dinner Adolph came along and as we had been without meat for some days we were compelled to kill some. I rode up with him and we did so and I brought half of it home.

October 9 (Monday)

Before school I was cutting up the meat to jerk and salt. I attended school the usual time and after school I called at James Bryden's and then came home to work the hide that I had buried.

October 10 (Tuesday)

When I reached the schoolhouse this morning Mr. Wilson met me and paid me three months schooling in advance for four pupils. This looks very much as though they are satisfied with my teaching. After leaving school I called at Mr. Stevens and came home to work on the hide.

October 11 (Wednesday)

A great many people are sick and from what I can learn sickness prevails all over the country. As to my own health, I have nothing more to complain about than my cough, which is troublesome at night but most particularly so of a morning. I am still taking bitters for it. I attended school the usual hours (nine till four).

I am getting over the principle difficulties of teaching and becoming more accustomed to my new pursuit. I find that it requires more patience than education to qualify one for the situation. After school I brought home a bushel of meal from Stevens, which goes to help pay my bill, and I

---

[218] U. B. Wilson and his wife Martha came to Texas in 1860 and settled at Nuecestown. He was from Virginia and she was from Indiana. Their daughter Louisa later married Henry Couling. Ref. Old Bayview Cemetery web site.

have agreed with Stevens to school two of his children on condition that he supply me with dinner every day that I keep school. I rode up to the old folks and got the candle molds for Marie.

October 12 (Thursday)

After school I rode out to see after Tony.

October 13 (Friday)

I had three pupils on the sick list today. After school I rode up to Hinnant's on business.

October 14 (Saturday)

With the assistance of Hinnant, I brought home a stray mare of mine from a ranch about 12 miles up the river, the Rancho Grande.[219] She was wild, never having been on the rope and after penning and throwing her, we fixed the rope in a way to lead her, and in that way brought her home. I suffered from the heat of the sun. From what we saw and heard at the places we stopped on the road, nearly everybody is or has been down with fever of some kind. We reached home at sundown and necked the mare we brought home to one of the others to adjust her to the bunch.

October 15 (Sunday)

In the morning I remained at home, writing copies for the school and studying to prepare for next week's exercises. After dinner Matson called.[220] He brought a letter for me which proved to have come from mother, enclosing her photograph, which I was very happy to receive.

October 16 (Monday)

I kept school as usual, taking dinner at Stevens' house, which is close to the schoolhouse. In the evening I took a short ride.

---

[219] Rancho Grande was Robert Love's ranch, across the river from the village of San Patricio.

[220] Jacob Matson bought the Thomas McCoy ranch seven miles west of Corpus Christi, and Matson was also in the Confederate militia with Noakes, the Nuecestown Precinct 2 company.

266

October 17 (Tuesday)

I was at school all day.

October 18 (Wednesday)

I kept school. Nothing occurred worth noting. I was feeling unwell and did nothing after getting home.

October 19 (Thursday)

I kept school and after getting home found that Mr. Ludewig brought us some meat and, having more than they could use, I rode up and got some more.

October 20 (Friday)

I cut up and salted the meat, attended school, and after four o'clock took the fishing line to the river to try and catch a fish. On Friday at school we go over the lessons of the week.

October 21 (Saturday)

This being my holiday, I worked a small hide and did various jobs at home till dinner, after which I took a long ride down the prairie among the cattle and horses. I brought in my little roan and two horses of Reynolds.

October 22 (Sunday)

Adolph came down about ten a.m. and wanted me to ride out with him to help find his horses. I rode to Blucher's Ranch when, feeling the sun too hot, I returned home. After supper I walked to Bryden's to see him about the school.

October 23 (Monday)

I attended school and did not get home till dark, being detained at the schoolhouse.

October 24 (Tuesday)

I did nothing but my daily morning work before going to school and my evening work after returning, which consists of attending to the cows and horses, and getting up water. I have no time for anything more.

October 25 (Wednesday)

Last night was a rough one. We had thunder and lightning, wind and rain. Today it has been fair and warm. I have three scholars on the sick list, which I take to be about the average at the present sickly time. I kept school as usual.

October 26 (Thursday)

Weather fine and warm. I kept school, repeating the grammar and geography lesson for the month. I have an application for a saddle tree.

October 27 (Friday)

Weather warm in the morning but a light norther came up at noon and the rest of the day was cool. We went over the exercises for the month at school. I find that my pupils, as well as their parents, are perfectly satisfied with me as a teacher. If we can continue as we have commenced, we shall do very well. The parents agreed to repair the schoolhouse and to make my salary equal to that of twenty scholars a month, which I shall be able to procure that number.

October 28 (Saturday)

Weather cool, wind from the north. Ben Gibbs called and I tried to make a settlement with him about the flour.[221] I offered to pay over half what he said he paid for it, 30 dollars in Confederate bills, which at that time was worth ten cents on the dollar. His previous assertion was that he paid 20 dollars, not 30. He set the value of the money at the time at 20 cents on the Confederate dollar and I set it at ten. I offered to split the difference and pay him for half the flour at 15 cents per pound, but he changed from what he had paid for the flour to what he had received for it from his father and set the price that I was to pay at much more

---

[221] The argument with the James Gibbs' family began in December 1863. Gibbs claimed that a supply of flour Noakes had obtained from Corpus Christi was rightfully his, that his son Ben bought it and sold it to him. Noakes refused to turn over the flour since, he said, Gibbs had no proof it was his. See entry for Dec. 22, 1863.

than what had previously been set.[222] I told him the offer I made was the only way I could settle it. In justice to myself I considered that I had no right to pay him anything. The whole mistake was due to his carelessness and since I had received no benefit from the flour, then I ought to have no loss.

After dinner I rode out and met the cattle hunters from the Motts with a herd of cattle. I returned to Reynolds' place and helped them. They had a cow of mine with a large calf.

October 29 (Sunday)

Weather cool. A steady rain commenced at nine and continued till noon. I remained in the house till dinner time and it continued to be cold. I did the same till night.

October 30 (Monday)

Weather cold and misty in the morning, but cleared off. Adolph came down, bringing us a letter from William in Illinois. I kept school and walked up to the old folks.

October 31 (Tuesday)

Weather cool. Last night it was cold and misty. I kept school as usual. I have 17 scholars.

November 1 (Wednesday)

Weather cold and wet. I did nothing but attend school and things at home.

November 2 (Thursday)

Weather damp, cold. Wind has been from the north all week. I kept school, which takes all day.

November 3 (Friday)

Weather very cold. I kept school, but the windows being without glass, and there being no firewood, we had a cold time of it. We need a broom to keep the floor clean, an axe to chop wood, and a bucket. The teacher's desk has only

---

[222] Noakes offered $3 for the flour, Gibbs wanted $6, Noakes countered with $4.50, but they couldn't agree.

half a lid and the chimney smokes badly. The broken windows allow a passage for the smoke. The tall weeds and bushes around the schoolhouse supply a place for a privy and a playground.

November 4 (Saturday)

Weather cold. I was at home till noon when I walked up to Reynolds to borrow a horse on which to hunt my little roan Tony. After dinner I rode down to Blucher's Prairie and, falling in with Reynolds and Joe Wright, I found mine (which I had penned) with them. We drove them together till we came to the timber and Tony and some others made a break into some bushes and we lost them.

I called to see how Mrs. Ludewig was doing. She was very sick. I returned home, having (as is usual in my aims) accomplished nothing. I received a kind letter from Mr. E. P. Alsbury today.

November 5 (Sunday)

Weather cool. I remained home till near night when Hinnant sent me word that he had my horse. I went up and got him and then rode over to the old folks and brought home some meat.

November 6 (Monday)

Weather fair but cold. I was at school all day.

November 7 (Tuesday)

Weather cold. I kept school all day.

November 8 (Wednesday)

Weather warm. Wind from the south again. I kept school, which takes the whole day.

November 9 (Thursday)

Weather fair. At school.

November 10 (Friday)

Weather cloudy. Wind from the north again. At school all day.

November 11 (Saturday)

Cold and windy. I rode to Corpus to get some things we needed. I paid 50 cents a pound for coffee, 30 cents a pound for sugar, flannel for $1 a yard. Finding no one to talk with and the sky looking like rain, I started home, after trying in vain to speak to a photographer about making photographs of my drawings. As usual I had no dinner, but tied my horse to a post, did my business and left. I had a dark, disagreeable ride, as it rained most of the way.

As I was going into town, I met the funeral procession of Dr. Britton who died the previous day. He was followed by most of the town, together with Yankee officers.[223]

November 12 (Sunday)

Weather warmer. I was at home till dinner when I rode up to the old folks' and to Hinnant's.

November 13 (Monday)

Weather warm, foggy in the morning. I attended school and mixed paint for the blackboard.

November 14 (Tuesday)

Weather as yesterday. I painted the blackboard in the morning before school. Today I had a supply of firewood brought to the schoolhouse by Mr. Hinnant.

November 15 (Wednesday)

Weather fine and quite warm, but a dreary fog from the west in the morning. I attended school and, when returning on my horse Tony, I found and penned a large unmarked yearling. My shoe has again irritated my heel; it is so sore I can hardly walk.

November 16 (Thursday)

Weather fine. Marie and I marked and branded the yearling, after dressing a wound he had in the flank. I

---

[223] Dr. Edward Britton, the son of Sen. Forbes Britton, died on Nov. 9, 1865. By a strange and tragic coincidence, his young son, who was traveling with his mother in Virginia, died on the same day. Ref. Research note, Old Bayview Cemetery web site.

attended school as usual and gave the blackboard another coat of paint.

November 17 (Friday)

Last night thunder passed around and the first of the morning was misty. About 11 a.m. a cold norther came up, accompanied by heavy rain, thunder and lightning. We had one close strike. With the windows of the school out, the wind and rain beat in and made it very disagreeable. After dinner I made a fire and blocked up some of the windows, but it was very cold and with most of the children being thinly clad, I dismissed school at 3 p.m., an hour early.

November 18 (Saturday)

Weather cold and windy. I did nothing in particular till noon when I took a walk up to Bryden's, after which I went to the schoolhouse and put in eight panes of glass and fixed the windows.

November 19 (Sunday)

I took a ride down to Blucher's Prairie. I fell in with Hinnant, Reynolds and Ned Taylor driving horses and cattle and I turned back with them. Finding a maverick, I put it with their herd, along with a cow with a calf. We penned at Hinnant's where they branded the maverick for me, and I brought home the cow and calf. After dinner I went back to Hinnant's, where they killed a beef and I brought home some of the meat.

Country very sickly, numbers of people being sick. Three teams that left here awhile back to go upcountry for provisions returned yesterday and all of the hands are sick but one.

November 20 (Monday)

Weather fine. After school I went to Couling's to get some bacon.

November 21 (Tuesday)

Weather fine, morning foggy. After school I went up to George Reynolds' place to see John Williams, who was very sick. He was senseless and reduced to the last stage of exhaustion from having eaten and drunk immoderately of improper food and liquor while having the chills and fever on him. I offered to stay with those watching him but found there were plenty there on the vigil without me.

November 22 (Wednesday)

Weather fine and warm, morning foggy. Before going to school, I rode up to see John Williams but found him no better. The doctor has given him up. But to judge from what I saw I thought there was hope for him yet. I rode up again after school but found him no better.

November 23 (Thursday)

Weather warm and pleasant, morning foggy. Before going to school, I rode up to see John again but found him no better and left with less hope than I had before. I am afraid he is so exhausted it will be impossible for him to recover. I rode up again after school and offered to sit up with him, but the neighbors would not allow me to do it, lest, as they told me, it might make me sick and prevent me from keeping school. They seemed to think that the worry of the school was as much as I should bear. It is gratifying to find everyone so anxious for me to continue the school. So far, I have received every encouragement.

November 24 (Friday)

John seems better. After school I watched him until 2 a.m. We have greater hopes for his recovery.

November 25 (Saturday)

Rode up to see Samuel Couling, who is also sick, then to John, and found him better, then to the old folks, where Mr. Ludewig is also sick with the prevailing fever. Brought home some flour, two hundred-weight, from Hinnant, with 22 pounds of bacon, to offset the school account. Weighing and sifting the flour till dusk.

November 26 (Sunday)

Rode around to see the sick folks. After dinner Marie and I and the two boys went fishing in the river. Marie caught a fat turtle full of eggs and two catfish, which we cooked for supper. Afterwards I went up to Hinnant's and got him to exchange a good sack of flour for the bad one I got yesterday.

November 27 (Monday)

At school. After supper I walked up to the Motts and stayed a short time at a dance which the young folks got up. John Williams is getting better.

November 28 (Tuesday)

Kept school as usual.

November 29 (Wednesday)

I heard a loud boom last night from the Hinnant place. It was caused by the explosion of a bottle containing gunpowder, which was carelessly being used as a candlestick and when the candle burned down it slipped inside the bottle and detonated the gunpowder.

My best pupil, a young girl of 15, was the nearest to the explosion. She was engaged in writing and was hit on the face and arm by flying fragments of glass. She was badly cut besides suffering burns. After school I rode up to see her and was distressed to see what had been a pretty face so badly cut, burned and swollen. I hope her eyesight may not be damaged.[224] I now have four pupils sick with fever and one wounded from an explosion. John Williams had a turn for the worse and is dying.

November 30 (Thursday)

Last day of the month. Reynolds was at my house before daylight and asked me to assist in making a coffin for John Williams, who was dead. A man named Kinghorn came

---

[224] The injured girl was Mollie Hinnant, born in 1850, the second child of John and Nancy Hinnant.

down, bringing the lumber from Samuel Couling.[225] We went to work and made the coffin in my shed. Reynolds brought the lining and cover at noon. We took dinner and finished the job and at 4 p.m. we buried him. After the burial I went and had a talk with Reynolds about John's property, offering to become the administrator of the estate.

December 1 (Friday)

Some [N------] troops passed through the Motts. They were very saucy in their behavior. I kept school and, in the evening, I walked up to see how Miss Hinnant was getting along.

December 2 (Saturday)

Reynolds came down as I was getting up the calves and wanted me to apply for the administration of John Williams' estate. I rode down to Corpus with him as soon as I had eaten breakfast. We went to see Mr. [John] McClane, one of the county commissioners, and I had no difficulty in getting my application approved.

I had to write out the form of application, together with the form of a $1,000 bond, with Reynolds and McClane going my security. After being sworn in, Mr. Taylor, the county clerk, handed me some paper posters which have to be posted in different locations. After getting through with the business, I made some purchases and took supper with McClane at his place.[226] I returned home by moonlight.

December 3 (Sunday)

The first thing this morning I went up to Reynolds' and took possession of John's papers and the key to his house and should have made a list of things in the house but

---

[225] Robert Kinghorn from Scotland settled at Nuecestown in 1856. He was a blacksmith and sheep man. Ref. 1870 Census.

[226] Noakes' official business would have been conducted at the 1854 courthouse on Mesquite Street. Across the way, on the east side of the street, was John McClane's home where Noakes went to supper.

Adams has some things there of his and not knowing which was which, I had to quit making the list.

In searching John's place, I found no money or papers, except an old receipt or two and some Confederate bills. I tacked up the notices and called at the Wright's for a law book, for which I had an order, but they did not have it. After dinner I rode up to see Mr. [J. W.] Littig to try to borrow his but with no better success. I walked up to the old folks to see if they had a book of forms, but they could not find it so I had to relinquish the idea of drawing up the forms I will need, until I can get the copies.

December 4 (Monday)

I inspected John Williams' premises all through the night. I had just enough time to get home for school before the norther came up. I had two new scholars today.

December 5 (Tuesday)

We kept a good fire at the schoolhouse, having firewood. Some days school-teaching goes very much against me and this was one of the days. I sometimes feel as though I must get on my horse and ride away and leave everything. Then there are moments when I feel more satisfied.

December 6 (Wednesday)

I kept school and came home by way of Williams' place to see if it was all right. I think the most revolting traits in human nature exhibit themselves in the case of a person dying without relatives or friends who cared for them than at any other time. In this case in which I am the administrator I see everybody around watching with anxiety to get what they can and at the same time prevent anybody else from getting a chance.

December 7 (Thursday)

Kept school.

December 8 (Friday)

Kept school and attended to my administration affairs.

December 9 (Saturday)

I walked over to the house of the late John Williams. I made a list of the goods and chattels in and around the house. I exchanged some flour at Mr. Hinnant's, which I had received from him as school pay, but it was too black for my use. I fetched home some meat, as they had killed.

December 10 (Sunday)

I rode to McKenzie's and borrowed a law book to help me relative to the estate of John Williams. I rode up to Bryden's and remained there till late (near night). I received two letters at home, one from my brother Edmond and the other from Capt. Alsbury requesting me to send him his trunk. I found an alligator on my line, which was about six feet long. I wrote a letter to Edmond.

December 11 (Monday)

I kept school and, in the evening, I drew up some papers (the inventory and the form of my bond) relative to my administration affairs.

December 12 (Tuesday)

I kept school as usual.

December 13 (Wednesday)

I did nothing during the day but attend school and inspect the premises of J. Williams, deceased. I commenced a letter to mother, after writing my school copies.

December 14 (Thursday)

Weather very cold. Ice on everything. I kept school, however.

December 15 (Friday)

I kept school but it was a cold job, as we were short of firewood. After supper I went to Bryden's to see him about different things.

December 16 (Saturday)

I went up to George Reynolds to get a horse on which to go to town but was informed there by James Bryden that he and Reynolds intend to take the administration of the J. Williams estate into their own hands. As I was only appointed pro tem, they can do so. At the same time, it shows me plainer than ever what I have long seen, that I have no right to remain in this part of the world another hour, as I have not a friend here.

The only reason these people can possibly have in behaving in this way towards me is that they begrudge me the small percentage that I should be entitled to from the estate as administrator. They hate to see me make a cent and if they can keep me poor, I will be dependent on them. By allowing me to keep a small school, they intend to keep me from starving, while they get their children educated. But should I have the slightest prospect of getting a good school so as to enable me to live comfortably, they will immediately withdraw their patronage and thus keep me at what I am now. I conclude that I had better stop right here. I will not ride to town.

December 17 (Sunday)

I made up my mind to go to Corpus tomorrow if possible. I rode around to tell the neighbors I would not keep school Monday. After dinner I finished a letter to Orchard, requesting him to furnish me with all the information he could relative to the estate of J. Williams. I am also writing a letter in retaliation for the usage I have received from Bryden and Reynolds. I intend to exert my utmost to prevent their contemplated self-appropriation of John Williams' estate so that it will fall back on their own heads.

December 18 (Monday)

Rode down to Corpus to see about sending a trunk of Capt. Alsbury's to Lavaca and to see parties in relation to the affairs of John Williams. I dined at Col. [Charles] Lovenskiold's [an attorney] and returned home without accomplishing anything. I mailed a letter to Edmond and one to Mr. Orchard, relative to the Williams' estate.

December 19 (Tuesday)

Kept school as usual.

December 20 (Wednesday)

I kept school and wrote a long letter to Capt. Alsbury at Lavaca.

December 21 (Thursday)

Kept school.

December 22 (Friday)

Kept school as usual. At 4 o'clock I told my pupils that I was compelled by circumstances to give up the school. I then dismissed the children. I had intended to say more but so many sorrowful-looking faces turned on me quite overwhelmed me and I had to thank them for their attention to me during the short time we were together.

I felt hurt and dejected that my evil genius should follow me in every pursuit. Samuel Couling and Judge Doakes called to hear about the school.

December 23 (Saturday)

Rode to Corpus in preference to staying at home, a prey to all the troublesome thoughts that racked my brain. I first went to a sale of furniture being held at Ohler's store. I mailed a letter to Capt. Alsbury and left a specimen of my handwriting at the adjutant general's office as a recommendation for a clerkship. I made some purchases — 60 cents a pound for coffee, 50 cents a pound for sugar, 10 cents a pound for Irish potatoes, 10 cents for onions and $1 for a small tin of preserved peaches.[227]

December 24 (Sunday)

After getting my breakfast and having an interview with Col. Lovenskiold, I rode home. I had no sooner reached there than I wished myself away again. My mind is so

---

[227] The inflation calculator shows that the 60 cents Noakes spent on coffee would be equivalent to today's value of $9.41 and the $1 he spent on a can of peaches would be equivalent to $15. 68.

disturbed that I hate to think and I need excitement to divert my attention.

December 25 (Monday)

Christmas day. Everything went crooked and everybody was cross. I passed a wretched day, thinking of the unjust treatment I have received at the hands of that avaricious and malicious lump of ignorance, Bryden, that I had no appetite so I just moped around.[228] After dark I brought Marie home, who had been up to supper at the Ludewigs, a meal which, as is usual for me on high days and holidays, I went without.

December 26 (Tuesday)

I moved out my school belongings, fixed my writing desk, and in the evening, I rode up and had a talk with Hinnant and Wilson about my giving up the school. After supper I was getting my administration papers together to go to town tomorrow.

December 27 (Wednesday)

I rode down to Corpus and gave an account of my administration of the estate of J. Williams to Chief Justice [John] Dix, and praying for a release from the same, which was granted and I withdrew my application for the administration. Bryden and Reynolds were in town but I did not give them an opportunity to display their satisfaction at having, as they imagine, taken the bread out of my mouth. As soon as I made a purchase or two, I left for home. In these people we see the old adage verified, that if a beggar gets on horseback he will ride to the devil.[229]

---

[228] In his depressed frame of mind, Christmas was no holiday for Noakes.

[229] Whatever the details were of the dispute, or rather collision of interests, over the administration of the John Williams' estate, Bryden and Reynolds were men of power and influence, not only in the Motts but in Corpus Christi as well, mainly through their connections to Richard King of King Ranch. These were men who were listened to and Noakes came out on the short end.

December 28 (Thursday)

I did nothing in particular, feeling disheartened and dejected. I remained close at home.

December 29 (Friday)

I amused myself by making an ax handle. Mr. Doakes was down. He is succeeding me as the school teacher. Mr. Doakes is a young man from Louisiana with a young wife, who has been brought up in refinement and luxury. Judge Doakes, of whom I have frequently made mention in this journal, is the father of this young man. He came here thinking that his father was rich and could assist him but the judge is otherwise. The judge depends on a [N------] boy named Harrison.

They [the young couple], not being able to agree with the situation, have left the judge and have been living with Couling, working on the place to earn their board and shelter. Young Doakes is the only person around here they could get to teach at the school. They prevailed on him to start it, without any questions about his qualifications. Mrs. Doakes lost her home and nearly all her relations in the war. Mr. Adams was here to supper and stayed for some time.

December 30 (Saturday)

I remained close at home. I wrote out a little deed for S. Couling and a form of agreement about the school for Mr. Doakes. I did nothing besides but talk to Mr. Ludewig, who came down, and S. Couling who took supper with us.

December 31 (Sunday)

This is the last day of another unprofitable year. The only gain I have made during this time has been confined entirely to experience and that may be good pay for future purposes but it is a very poor article to live upon. On the whole, I suppose I should not grumble. I have a good many around me who have enriched themselves and as far as matters go, they can carry their heads above me, yet I doubt if the enjoyment of their wealth will compensate for the loss of their conscience, and the enemies they have made, to acquire it.

Now that I have given up school-teaching I wonder what fate has in store for me next. The last copy my scholars were given as a writing exercise was — "Compelled to part, let us part as friends" and "Maliciousness may have its ends" which I wrote on the blackboard for all to copy, as a finish to my episode of school-teaching.

I am told that my giving up the school caused quite a commotion in the neighborhood and that all the patrons were put out about it. I cannot help thinking that those who have acted against me in such a manner as to compel me relinquish the school have injured themselves more than me. I was taking every pain in my power to get my pupils on.

Perhaps the next teacher they may have will take pains for nothing but getting his pay. This Mr. Doakes, who starts the school tomorrow, I have reasons to think is short-tempered, a failing that will go very much against his success as a teacher, but time will tell.

I remained at home in the morning and after dinner I rode out a little. George Reynolds was down about sundown and paid me my account against him for schooling. He produced his administration paper and tried to get the deed to J. Williams' property but I would not give it up. I want to keep it as security so that I will get my pay for what I have paid out during my administration pro tem. The balance that is owing to me for my trouble I would be willing to wait for.

Some of the manners and customs of cattle hunting are worth notice. The excessive cruelty practiced by cattle hunters toward horses and cattle is enough to upset anybody with common feeling. Cows get killed and small calves are trampled to death in the pen. A man must leave his feelings at home when he starts cattle hunting and those with anything like a sensitive stomach had better not start.

—*June 10, 1866*

AFTER THE WAR
1866

January 1 (Monday)

New Year's Day. I walked over to make my final inspection of J. Williams' premises and found everything in place then walked up to Couling's to have a talk and remained till sundown.

January 2 (Tuesday)

I rode out on Tony and cut a load of firewood for the house. We have been tearing the fences up for firewood. After cutting a load, I borrowed a yoke of steers from Couling and brought the cart down from the old folks ready for the next morning. Marie and I cut up a fallen tree near the house.

January 3 (Wednesday)

I took Couling's steers and fetched home the firewood I cut yesterday, blistering and tearing up my hands badly. I brought the dead tree up to the house and after dinner rode out to the woods on Tony and cut another load for tomorrow. The severe work of chopping wood comes hard at first, not having done hard work for so long, but I feel thankful to think that I am able to work at anything yet. And thankful that I am able to keep myself independent of those who thought they had got me into a place where I was bound to remain, taking all the slights and insults they would have taken such pleasure in heaping on me.

For the last three months, my mind has been at rest on the matter of provisions for the house, but we could get no firewood. Now the tables are turned. Soon we will have plenty of firewood but no flour, coffee or sugar. Such is life in Texas, always something different.

January 4, 5 (Thursday and Friday)

I cut and hauled firewood. On the latter day, in the evening, I called on Mr. and Mrs. Doakes and did all in my power against an election being held at the Motts on Monday.[230] I delivered the property of the estate of J. Williams to Reynolds this morning and took a receipt.

January 6 (Saturday)

I rode down to Corpus and procured a written permission from George Pfeuffer and Fitzsimmons to graze sheep on their lands within five miles of the Motts. I fell in with quite a jovial crowd and the treats came around pretty fast.

I bought some sugar and returned home with Mr. Frank Byler, after making an arrangement to sell some beeves. Like all my arrangements for that purpose, I expect it will fall through. The colored troops have nearly all been

---

[230] Noakes doesn't say why he was opposed. The election in Precinct 2, Nueces County, would have been held at the school house at the Motts. Noakes himself voted while he was in Corpus Christi.

withdrawn and Corpus begins to look very much as it used to look before the war. No mails have been established yet.

January 7 (Sunday)

I was at home till the evening when I walked to Judge Doakes and obtained his permission to herd sheep on his land around the Motts.

January 8 (Monday)

I rode down to Corpus to see Mr. Schubert and have a talk with him in regard to our going into the sheep-raising business as partners. I found him recovering from a short sickness and quite agreeable to the proposition I made him on the sheep question.

I have known Mr. Schubert ever since I have been in this country and I know him to be no other than an honest and straight-forward man. Added to this, he is closely acquainted with [Felix] Blucher, the surveyor of this country, and can procure a good choice for a location. I believe Schubert to possess good knowledge of business.

Our present plan is to purchases a flock of sheep and start a store at a place called San Diego, 50 miles west of Corpus. We would keep our sheep as near there as we can find a suitable place. He would keep the store and transact the business of selling and buying for the ranch and I would manage it. I only hope we may get at it, as it is high time that I was doing some good.

After coming to an agreement about sheep, I made an affidavit to an account I have against the J. Williams estate and then voted at the election being held in the town for a delegate to a convention.[231] There were two steamers and several schooners in. The steamers arrived to take away the

---

[231] The election on Jan. 8, 1866 was held to choose delegates to a convention to form a new constitution to allow Texas to re-enter the Union. The turnout statewide was low, with less than half the number of voters who voted in the secession referendum in 1861. E. J. Davis was elected as a delegate to represent Nueces County at the convention. Ref. Carl Moneyhon, "Texas After the Civil War" and "City by the Sea" by Eugenia Briscoe.

285

[N------] troops. The town looks more like old times again, with fewer [N------s] and more old faces.

January 9 (Tuesday)

I rode up to the old folks, penned a cow and a calf, and brought home their work steers. Marie and I rode out and penned a beef at their pen and killed it. They helped us to skin and cut it up. After leaving them what meat they wanted, Mr. Ludewig took the balance down for me in the steer cart, leaving Couling a leg as we went down.

January 10 (Wednesday)

Marie and I were busy all day, cutting up and salting the meat, rendering the tallow, and so on. Toward night I rode up to the old folks and found that Adolph was sick.

January 11 (Thursday)

I rode the old folks' colt down to Blucher's Prairie to hunt among the cattle for young calves but found none. I saw my mares and returned home. After dinner I rode into the Motts but called nowhere, the people having no more use for me since I gave up the school.

January 12 (Friday)

I rode out with Henry Couling but found nothing to bring home. Couling came along toward sundown when he let me use his old horse to get close to a flock of wild geese that were feeding in the flats below the house. I managed to kill one. I rode down the river to hunt the old man's steers for him. I did not find them till after dark. I drove them to his pen and stayed awhile at the house.

January 13 (Saturday)

After doing various jobs at home I rode into the Motts and had a talk with Mr. Wright. After dinner the cattle boys brought home a herd of beeves. A cattle buyer was here purchasing beeves. While they were on the salt flats by my place, I put in a fat beef I had at home.

I am so disgusted with cattle hunting that I now pay for my calves being branded and my beeves sold, rather than

286

waste my time and health in hunting them. Within the last few days I have heard of several of my calves, which were nearly old enough to wean, having been lost by getting out of the herd, being killed, and it is not in my power to help. I intend to dispose of my cattle soon as possible.

January 14 (Sunday)

It is frustrating, this state of things. After having so much cold weather all winter, when it did us no good, since last Monday I have been waiting at home to get the coming norther over with before I can start on a trip up the country to make enquiries about the sheep, besides being put to all the trouble of killing and salting my meat for nothing. It is useless for an unlucky man to try to do any good in this world.

January 15 (Monday)

I tied up the meat — a considerable quantity of which was spoiled — and rode up to the old folks to get a horse for tomorrow. After dinner I was making ready for a trip up the country.

January 16 (Tuesday)

I started early to ride up to the Lagarto Creek to make enquiries about sheep. I made the Kinto Motts where I got my dinner.[232] An hour later, by the sun, I reached the sheep ranch of Jacobs and Smith. I found them living as they were before, like dogs.[233]

I found the sheep sickly. We cooked and ate our suppers by the creek and then squeezed ourselves into the little shanty [jacal] where they slept. I found them bent on getting rid of their sheep by spring, at any price. Smith has plans to go back to England after some small property he has there and Jacobs was tired of herding sheep.

---

[232] Noakes called it Kinto Motts, Joseph Almond in his diary called it Kinte Motts, and Oscar Edgerly in his diary called it Kinton Motts. Neither made clear where it was located.

[233] Noakes made a similar trip in September 1863, according to Almond's diary, so he may have visited Jacobs and Smith then.

January 17 (Wednesday)

Weather fine. About 10 a.m. the wind shifted from north to south. After breakfast, and after inspecting the sheep, Smith offered to sell me the sheep at two dollars a head. I said I would let him know a week from the next Saturday.

I struck out for the head of the Agua Dulce Creek to find Adams and see his sheep. I had little difficulty in finding him and at his invitation stayed in a house he had covered with raw hides in which he and the children slept.

He had two small boys, one girl and a grown son with him.[234] I passed the day talking about sheep and looking at his sheep. He also wants to sell out as soon as his time expires for keeping the flock, as he took the flock on halves.[235]

January 18 (Thursday)

Weather warm, wind from the south. I passed a better night than the night before, when I slept on a bed in the shanty that was very cold and with too many fleas to allow sleep. But last night I laid down by the fire in the bushes and was comfortable. I was awake at dawn and soon saddled up and started for home. I reached the Motts about sundown. I saw Mr. [Sam] Glenn and [Samuel] Couling about some mares.

January 19 (Friday)

Rode to Corpus, bought some potash to make soap, and had a talk with Schubert about the sheep. I agreed to remain at home until I heard from him. I returned home after dark,

---

[234] Robert and Maria Adams had seven children: Elizabeth, whom Noakes once courted, was born in 1844; William was born in 1846; Robert Jr. in 1847; Harry in 1850; Ellen in 1853; Mary Ann in 1855; and John in 1858. Adams would have likely had the four youngest with him; his wife died in 1861.

[235] Later that year, in the fall, Robert Adams Sr. took his young son John back to England for a visit. On their return, their steamship "Raleigh" caught fire off the coast of Georgia. Some passengers were rescued, but the elder Adams and his son were lost at sea. Ref. Robert Adams' memoirs, "Learning by Hard Licks," Corpus Christi Central Library.

288

where I received a letter from E. P. Alsbury about his trunk. He wrote me a very complimentary letter.

January 20 (Saturday)

Was boiling soap all day. Made five boilers full. I hung up the salt beef and cleaned the shed.

January 21 (Sunday)

I cut out the soap and walked to the Wright's and back.

January 22 (Monday)

Cut out the last box of soap and wrote a bill of sale for S. Glenn and S. Couling. I passed the evening at Couling's.

January 23 (Tuesday)

I wrote out a power of attorney from S. Glenn to S. Couling for him to dispose of Glenn's land. I weighed the soap and put it away. Out of 30 pounds of tallow I made 163 pounds of soap by means of concentrated potash. After dinner J. Wright called and paid me $10 for a beef he had sold for me, deducting the difference for my calves he had branded.

January 24 (Wednesday)

I rode down to Tule Lake with several others to hunt among the cattle. We brought home a yearling each along with some wild steers of Couling's which we penned in my pen. We first roped and threw the steers, which fought like the blazes before we could neck them. Then we roped, threw and branded the yearlings, except for one which we killed for meat, then let the cattle out of the pen. But when the wild steers regained their feet, they made a break and smashed everything in their way, tearing down my fence gate, besides breaking several posts in the pen, and for this I get nothing.

January 25 (Thursday)

One of the steers we necked choked itself to death, having run around a tree by my well. I cleaned the hide of the yearling and put it in the river and rode with Couling to hunt among the cattle. We saw some unbranded yearlings and, as is the custom now, we branded two apiece. Some of the hunters since the war have branded 20 apiece.

A man who does not brand any loses all his own calves and gets nothing in return. It's a horrible way of spending one's life but fate has me here and keeps me here. I must get a little of what I can or make nothing.

I have tried for the last 10 years to live without using such means but I have fallen behind and to save myself I must take to it or leave the country. If I sold out, I could not get enough to take me somewhere else, so I have to stay and do as others do.

I took supper at the old folks' where I met Mr. McDonald, father of my brother-in-law's wife.[236] He has just arrived from Lake Michigan to see his children.

January 26 (Friday)

I went to the Motts and paid my state and county taxes. Brought home four bushels of corn for my horse and commenced a saddle tree.

January 27 (Saturday)

Worked on the saddle tree. Ellen, Adolph and his wife, Mary Bryden and Maggie called and we had a jovial time.

January 28 (Sunday)

Couling came down early and wanted me to ride with him and Hinnant down the prairie, so I went with them. To amuse ourselves we roped and branded a yearling apiece. On the way home I found a dead yearling, which I skinned and brought the hide home. After dinner I cleaned the hide and put it in water. Marie not coming down at dark, I started up to meet her. As I was passing Couling's he called me in to take a glass of egg nog, which suited me precisely. I soon met the whole party and we came home together.

---

[236] He was the father of Adolph Ludewig's wife.

January 29 (Monday)

Attended the sale of personal property of John Williams, deceased, but bought nothing. After dinner I worked on the saddle tree.

January 30 (Tuesday)

Worked on the saddle tree and went to Tule Lake with Adolph, but found no cattle.

January 31 (Wednesday)

Last day of the month. I cleaned and staked out one of the hides in soak. Worked on the saddle tree and did odd jobs. I watered several head of cattle at the well.

February 1 (Thursday)

I covered the saddle tree.

February 2 (Friday)

Couling came down and asked me to ride down the prairie with him and Hinnant, which I did. We brought home five yearlings and killed one for meat. Couling, Hinnant and Mr. Beckham took dinner at my house, after which we branded the yearlings. I was allowed two yearlings for my share.

February 3 (Saturday)

Hunting cattle with Couling, found none, and worked at odd jobs at home.

February 4 (Sunday)

I did nothing but sit by the fire and read, after taking a walk to Couling's where I met J. Polk and Hinnant. I left and went to my own fire and amused myself by studying arithmetic. I can get no new reading matter so lately I have found profitable amusement with fractions and decimals.

February 5 (Monday)

It being too cold to work, I remained in the house. Mr. Beckham called and I completed a trade with him for a horse, paying him $10 and the saddle tree, which I had just made.[237] To teach Marie how to do it, I made a real old English Sussex beef pudding, the first we have had since we were married. Also, in the way of a flourish, I made a small meat pie. After dinner the misty rain still continued. I cut a strand for a lasso, or lariat, out of rawhide.

February 6 (Tuesday)

Watered cows at the well, as yesterday's rain didn't amount to enough to make water. I rode out and brought home my new horse, penned and branded him, watered him and one of Couling's that he runs with. Then I turned him out to get fat. In the evening I rode by Blucher's Ranch to hunt a tree fork to make a saddle tree.

February 7 (Wednesday)

I took my ax and saw and rode out to Blucher's and cut some forks from an elm tree that had lately been washed into the creek. Returning home to dinner I found Mrs. Swift there on a call. She took dinner with us then she and Marie and Mary Bryden went up to the old folks. I cut the strands of a rope and after getting my supper I walked up and fetched them home.

February 8 (Thursday)

I hunted up Mr. Ludewig's steers, then he and I brought home the elm forks together with firewood. He took dinner with us, after which I plaited a rope.

February 9 (Friday)

After doing various jobs, I went up to Mrs. Wright's and repaired her clock. I returned home for dinner, rode among the cattle, and plaited another rope. After supper I went up to Couling's to write a bill out for him, where I met Hinnant. We agreed to go out next day and hunt something to eat.

---

[237] William W. Beckham moved to Nuecestown and lived near Noakes. He was originally from Alabama (1870 Census) and he and his wife Sarah had seven children. One daughter, Fanny, married "King" Hinnant and another, Laura, married John McIntyre. Sarah was buried in Old Bayview and William Beckham was buried in Collins Cemetery in Live Oak County.

February 10 (Saturday)

Mr. Beckham, who bought my saddle tree, came down with the leather to rig it, so I could not go out. I worked all day and up to past midnight before we completed the job, he looking on.

February 11 (Sunday)

Beckham stayed all night and this morning I finished his saddle. I rode out with Hinnant and his boys.[238] We rode down the prairie and around by Tule Lake, bringing home a beef to kill, which we penned in Couling's pen. Couling was tight and there were several people there, so I put for home as soon as I could. I have just finished a song about the fight at Corpus Christi, which I have been composing.[239]

February 12 (Monday)

I went up to Couling's as soon as I had finished breakfast and helped kill the beef we penned yesterday. In the evening I went up to Reynolds and got the money he owed me on the Williams estate. I made a handle for our water cart.

February 13 (Tuesday)

Hinnant, Couling and myself took a hunt up the river to get cows and calves. We returned home about sundown, bringing two or three cows and eight unmarked yearlings, which we penned in my pen. We had a good deal of running to do today.

I saw a three-year-old heifer with four proper legs and from the right foreleg another grew out above the knee joint, but was not used for walking on. I also saw an animal of about the same age with no tail whatever, in fact the

---

[238] John and Nancy Hinnant's sons were William Ancelon, called "King," and Henry Monroe, called "Tobe." King Hinnant was 14 years old in 1866 and Tobe was 12. Ref. "Lagarto, A Collection of Memories" by Hattie Mae Hinnant New.
[239] The lyrics of Noakes' song, "The Two Twelve-Pounders," are printed past the main body in Appendix 6.

backbone didn't appear to reach so far as the place from where the tail should start.

February 14 (Wednesday)

Hinnant, Couling and Henry came down at breakfast when we went to work and branded the yearlings. I got two. Jack Polk came by and we sat by the fire and talked till near dinner time. I sung my new song. After dinner I worked a cow hide and put new strings in my saddle. It was too cold to do anything in the wind.

February 15 (Thursday)

The wind was excessively cold, so much so that work of any kind was out of the question. After seeing to things at home, I went up to Couling's to have a talk but returned to dinner. In the evening I wrote out my new song and studied arithmetic.

February 16 (Friday)

I commenced another saddle tree, the cold not being quite as great as yesterday. The rain continued up to night.

February 17 (Saturday)

I worked all day on the saddle tree. At sundown I walked to the Motts and brought a letter home from Judge Doake's, which proved to be from Edmond. I tried to reach home before opening it but could not resist the impulse to do so on the way. In the middle of the mist I read it throughout, the whole description of his trip to England. It so carried me away mentally that it was only when I was through that I remembered that I was standing in the cold wind and mist in the middle of the salt marsh which I had to traverse in going from the Motts to home. I also found enclosed his own photograph and that of his wife and family. What exquisite things these photographs are. Next to reality, nothing surpasses them in representing to us our distant friends as they are. After seeing to my horse and cows, I was glad to get in by my warm fire and read Edmond's letter again.

February 18 (Sunday)

I milked the cows, attended to my horse, then remained by the fire reading some Galveston papers I brought home last night from a neighbor. There is a report that Ben Gibbs, whom I had the fuss with over the flour, was drowned, he and his brother having run a boat to Corpus since the war. He was said to have been on Corpus bay when the norther struck last Wednesday and capsized the boat. He and several more with whom I am acquainted perished. Couling came down towards night and I walked back with him.

February 19 (Monday)

I worked all day at the saddle tree. We hear today that Ben Gibbs was not drowned, that all on the boat were saved but old Mr. Runge.

February 20 (Tuesday)

I worked most of the day on the saddle tree, having it ready to cover toward sundown. I rode out to find my new horse but could not. After supper I was seeing to the hide I had in water and preparing to go to Corpus tomorrow.

February 21 (Wednesday)

The morning being fine, I rode down to Corpus to get several things for the house and to see about sending E. P. Alsbury's trunk to San Antonio. I tacked the address on the trunk and Cannon agreed to take it. I completed my purchases — a dress for Marie, 10 milk pans, concentrated lye for making soap, alum for tanning hides, extract of coffee, bread soda, and glue. A drizzling rain commenced just as I was starting for home but it didn't amount to anything.

February 22 (Thursday)

I worked the hide for the saddle tree and had everything ready to cover it. What hide was left I saved for a rope. After dinner I read the paper then rode up to Wright's to see Joe about a beef hunt. I called on Judge Doakes and Blackwell on the way. I returned home, bringing some meat I had in salt and started to smoke it.

February 23 (Friday)

I worked all day covering the saddle tree. Mrs. [Hester] Couling came down and took supper with us. I walked home with her and stayed a little while with Couling.

February 24 (Saturday)

Soon as I had breakfast, I took my gun and walked up to Hinnant's. He sent word that he had penned a beef and wanted me to come and shoot it for him. I went up and did so and he sent me half the hind quarters to pay back what he got from me the last time I killed. I then took a newspaper to McKenzie's.

In the afternoon I worked on the saddle tree, salted meat, made soap, and read while the soap was boiling. I tried something to see if it made any improvement to the soap. I had the soap made and poured out soon after supper.

I invariably pass my time of an evening reading or writing. I have no companions and none with whom I can exchange ideas on any subject other than those of a local nature, such as cattle or the scandal of the neighborhood.

February 25 (Sunday)

To pass the time, I cut the soap into bars, made a smoke in the shed for the meat, marked and altered the calves, chopped firewood, talked to Couling, wrote up my journal, hammered down the hide on the saddle tree I covered on Friday, commenced a letter to E. P. Alsbury, and salted some of the meat.

February 26 (Monday)

I made ready to start down the country with S. Couling to hunt for cows and calves, but Couling couldn't find his horse so were kept waiting till two o'clock before we could get off. We came across the Banquete cattle hunters at the ranch of [J. T.] James and learned from them where they were going to hunt.

Since they would sweep the country of everything not marked and branded, we thought we would take our share in advance of them so, not letting them know our business, we continued on after dark to the Oso Ranch.[240]

Nobody was living there but a family that had gone in to take care of it, that is to destroy what the war times have left. We made ourselves some coffee at their fire and took our supper and then crossed the creek and rode about a mile and camped in some bushes. The night was beautiful, with moonlight. A young man named Smithwick was with us, hunting for Hinnant. We took corn along for our horses. I had a slight fever on me today.

February 27 (Tuesday)

We hunted through the cattle around Ball's Motts.[241] We got some cows and calves. Couling got a steer that needed branding. We were hunting over the ground that the crowd we passed yesterday will hunt tomorrow. We gathered up what unmarked yearlings we could find, having to be in a hurry. We were compelled to get home that night with what we drove, as we could get no pen. We reached home two hours before sundown, with three yearlings each. We never stopped all day, but kept going. We drove as far as it has generally taken us two days to drive a herd. Ellen was with Marie. I watered cattle at the well till dark.

February 28 (Wednesday)

After seeing to the things at home, I went up to Couling's, where we penned the cattle yesterday, and branded three yearlings. I came home and worked at repairing Marie's guitar and a picture frame.

March 1 (Thursday)

I rode around and fetched in a young calf, which I had to rope from the horse. After dinner I commenced to plait a

---

[240] The Oso Ranch of Alden McLaughlin who died in 1860.

[241] The precise location is unknown, but Ball's Motts was probably northwest of Nuecestown, along the river, and named for longtime resident William A. Ball.

strip for the horn of the saddle tree I am rigging. I glued Marie's guitar and the picture frame.

March 2 (Friday)

I varnished the guitar and picture frame, penned, branded and marked a yearling, killed and skinned a young calf that was deformed in a foreleg. In the morning I worked at a headstall I was making to use to break one of my young horses. Couling brought home my new horse and I staked him.

March 3 (Saturday)

After doing my morning work, which takes about three hours, I went to work on the headstall, plaiting it out of my new hide. I finished it about two p.m. then cut the strands for a rawhide rope. I did my morning's work all over again. After supper I finished writing the letter to E. P. Alsbury.

March 4 (Sunday)

I did my morning work, rode around a little, and after dinner finished a letter to mother, walked up to Couling's to see him on business, then returned to attend to the horses and cows.

March 5 (Monday)

Cool and misty. I intended to go to Corpus but did not like the weather. I plaited a rope, varnished the guitar, worked on the saddle tree, and took a ride up to the old folks.

March 6 (Tuesday)

I rode to Corpus. The country is getting delightful. Most of the shrubs are in bloom and there is a profusion of spring flowers, with the air fragrant to the highest degree. The spring birds are also making their offerings. I purchased guitar strings, got rings for my saddle, glass for a picture, coffee, sugar, and a piece of cheese. I did not leave town till dark, passing some time at Mrs. Swift's. I took her a smoked beef tongue as a present.

March 7 (Wednesday)

I rode up to the Motts and called at Mrs. Bryden's for a letter.[242] She was so kind and gave me some newspapers to read. I cleaned a small calfskin and went to work with Marie and spun horse hair into a cord and with the cord I made a saddle girth.

March 8 (Thursday)

I rode out and brought home the four-year-old colt, which was running with Hinnant's mares. I penned, roped and threw him and with Marie's help I put the rope and headstall on him. I let him up. He was very wild. After tying him to the post in the pen, he threw himself several times, but I succeeded in reaching a good understanding between us. By dinner time he would let me rub him. About three p.m. I concluded I had him quieted and would lead him out on the hill, but as he came out of the pen gate it made a loud cracking noise which scared him and with a mad dash, he tore away from me and went running off at his hardest.

I saddled the horse I had staked and went after him, through the brush and mesquite. In about two miles I headed him, but somehow, in moving at such a tremendous speed, the rope he was dragging caught on a stump or something and jerked his neck out of joint.

I soon had him down, with his head hanging, seemingly unable to lift it. I got hold of the rope and determined either to break his neck or get it back straight again. I used the full length of the rope to tie him a tree. As soon as he had become a little still, I jumped at him, with a loud yell, and he tore off at the top of his speed till he came to the end of the rope and the sudden impact fetched his neck back straight.

---

[242] This was Noakes' first mention of visiting Janet Bryden since his falling out with her husband and George Reynolds over the administration of the John Williams estate two months before.

To keep it that way, I threw the rope over a high limb and drew him up as tight as I could and went to get Couling to help me to get him home. When I reached home with him, his neck was still crooked. I tied his head to a tree and kept him there all night.

March 9 (Friday)

Marie and I found the colt's neck was back in place. I hobbled him so that he could not run out on the rope and twist his neck again. I tied him to a log near the house, to keep him from straying too far, and taught him to drink from a bucket and by night I could handle him. I framed and glazed a sketch of Warwick House which I brought with me from England.

March 10 (Saturday)

I rigged my saddle tree and finished it. Marie was coming from the house to watch me work at the shed when a rattlesnake began rattling close to her. It was too dark to see him but after hearing him I ran out with a stick and hitting at random I gave him one blow but not enough to kill him and I could still hear him rattling angrily under the shed.

March 11 (Sunday)

I put a sack on the colt [to cover his eyes] and walked him about. I read some papers that were sent to me.

March 12 (Monday)

The colt got away again. I hunted him all day. I found him four miles down the Oso Creek and ran him across Blucher's Ranch and caught him at Turkey Creek. I put my rope on him and with one end tied to the saddle horn I dragged him home and tied him in the pen. I ate something while Marie caught and saddled up Tony and I hunted till dark for my plaited rope.

March 13 (Tuesday)

Skinned a bull yearling and this morning I pegged out the hide. Made a new headstall for the colt and put it on him. I tied a rope to the headstall and the gate post. I tied another rope to his head to lead him out of the pen, expecting him to play the same trick he played before.

Sure enough, when he came to the end of the tied rope he turned a complete somersault and landed on his back. He repeated this trick several times before he learned that it would not pay. I fastened him to a log by the tree.

By this time a norther came up and I went into the house and took Couling's clock to pieces, which he wanted cleaned and repaired. After finishing the clock, I varnished my best saddle tree.

March 14 (Wednesday)

Put a piece of hide in soak to make another plaited rope. Bought some potatoes from Mr. Wright. I took some papers to Mrs. Bryden and she lent me some more and gave me a nice piece of fresh pork. Everything looks beautiful. The shrubs and flowers fill the air with perfume and the lovely green of young leaves on the trees and beautiful spring buds render the present appearance of the prairie and woods magnificent. Geese and sandhill cranes are still here in large numbers.

March 15 (Thursday)

I plaiting a rope and hunted my mares.

March 16 (Friday)

Henry Couling offered to ride down my wild colt so I let him take him home. I helped saddle him. We had to throw him and tie up his forelegs. Samuel Couling and I got on our horses and young Couling got on the colt and we all rode off together, the colt not trying to pitch Couling. After dinner I worked on some stirrups I was making for Henry.

March 17 (Saturday)

Mr. and Mrs. Couling spent the evening here. We passed the time singing songs to the guitar. I sent Mrs. Couling's clock home this morning and went up and regulated it. Couling and I rode down to Blucher's Prairie and brought home a yearling to kill. I ascertained from little George Reynolds that Mrs. Blackwell's jack [a stud donkey] killed one of my colts. I rode up to inform her of it and urge her to take steps to prevent a repetition, which she promised to do.[243]

I helped Couling pen the yearling, as the cattle in the pen began to fight us. I rode into the pen on my horse and lassoed the yearling from the saddle. We killed it and I took home a quarter, with the head and the hide. I dressed the head for cooking and put the hide in water to slip the hair. I cut up and salted some meat, branded a yearling, and the old folks came down.

March 18 (Sunday)

I crushed some salt and alum then read most of the day. I have three Harper's Journals.

Young Henry Couling took my colt to visit his lady lover; he's getting married today.[244] I received an invitation to the wedding but excused myself, my services not being required. I can turn down an invitation to a wedding without giving offense, but at a funeral they have use for me without having to put out any expense. To even attempt to excuse myself from a funeral would bring down the wrath and indignation of the whole community on my head.[245]

March 19 (Monday)

I rode all day to find my cattle but returned empty-handed. After supper the wedding folks came down and I had to sing my new song and Marie played several tunes on

---

[243] Margaret Blackwell was the wife of Charles Blackwell. They are listed in the 1850 Census but not the census in 1860 or 1870, though they did reside in Nuecestown. Joseph Almond also mentioned Mrs. Blackwell in his diary.

[244] Henry Couling, born in England in 1845, married Louisa Wilson on March 18, 1866. Couling was the son of Samuel and Hester Couling and Louisa was the daughter of U. B. and Martha Wilson.

[245] I presume that Noakes meant that he was usually asked to make a coffin for the deceased.

the guitar. Having nothing good to eat or drink to offer them, they soon left.

March 20 (Tuesday)

After dinner I rode up to Wright's with Henry Couling, who was riding my colt. We branded a colt and a mare that had been brought in from a horse hunt.

March 21 (Wednesday)

I rode my colt for the first time. Tied up some salt meat to smoke and worked on stirrups until night. The river is salty and rain is badly needed. The long-tailed flycatcher has arrived for the summer.

March 22 (Thursday)

Rode up to the Motts and hunted with Thomas Beynon. After dinner I went to talk with Charlie Shaw. My colt nearly ran away with me.

March 23 (Friday)

After dinner I rode the colt down the prairie.

March 24 (Saturday)

Last night I caught a ring snake and put it into a box. This morning, to find out whether it was poisonous, I caused it to bite a kitten, which died in 10 minutes. These snakes are called King snakes here. They are very beautiful in their markings and coloring, having yellow rings around the body at one-inch intervals, with the space between alternating with red, black and greenish blue. A yellow band crosses the head.[246] I made the stirrups for Henry Couling and repaired my clock and set her going.

March 25 (Sunday)

Thunder and lightning all day but no rain. Passed the day reading.

March 26 (Monday)

I rode up to Hinnant's then rode among the cattle.

---

[246] Noakes was describing the Texas coral snake, which has a banding pattern of red-yellow-black, with vibrant colors. It is considered shy but highly venomous. Ref. Handbook of Texas.

March 27 (Tuesday)

Found a large unmarked maverick and drove it home, having an unusual amount of trouble. Penned and branded it. It was two years old and fought like mischief. Worked on the stirrups.

March 28 (Wednesday)

Last night we went to Samuel Couling's to a dance, having been invited to celebrate his son's wedding. We had a very pleasant and special night, everybody being there. We danced and sang till broad daylight. Came home, milked the cows, rode the colt, and worked on Couling's stirrups.

March 29 (Thursday)

Price came and fetched away their jack. I worked on the stirrups. Henry Couling took his away when I finished.

March 30 (Friday)

Took back some journals to Mrs. Bryden she sent me to read, together with a piece of smoked beef as a return for the meat she gave me. When I returned, Charlie Shaw was trying to pen two of his cows in my pen so I helped him and branded the calves.

March 31 (Saturday)

Last night at 10 p.m. the moon was totally eclipsed. My health is better now than it has been for years. I am stronger than I ever was.

April 1 (Sunday)

Did nothing special today.[247]

April 2 (Monday)

Put salt and alum on the hide I had in the river and rolled it up.

---

[247] For much of March and April, 1866, Noakes was one day behind on his dates; perhaps he was using an old calendar. I followed each day's entry in the journal but put them under the correct date. For example, Noakes has Sunday as March 31 rather than April 1, which was the correct date.

April 3 (Tuesday)

We hunted the pens throughout the town, getting quite a herd of cows that people were milking. We hunted home and penned at Reynolds' pen. We made two roundups at Tule Lake, stopping a little while to eat. I found nothing but a dry cow whose calf had been stolen and I put in three yearlings. I left tired and went to bed early.

April 4 (Wednesday)

After breakfast I took my rope and branding iron and walked up to Reynolds' pen, where all the boys met to brand up. After roping and branding for about three hours, among a good many cattle that would fight, we dragged out a yearling, killed and divided it out and then went home to dinner.

April 5 (Thursday)

I fixed a new hind tree to Hinnant's saddle tree. In the evening I worked with the colt and Marie and I had a rat hunt in the old house. I put the hide to soak to cover the saddle tree.

April 6 (Friday)

It was so cold that no one could work outdoors.

April 7 (Saturday)

Weather cold for the season. Still using oak bark for tanning. Killed a beef and skinned it in an hour. Henry Couling and Adolph came by and got quarters of the beef.

April 8 (Sunday)

The morning was frosty and the evening cold. I covered the saddle tree and penned and branded a bull yearling. I put the hide in salt and alum and a strong ooze to color.

April 9 (Monday)

I rode around and gathered up a yearling bull and fine heifer, put them in the pen. After dinner Couling came and helped me brand them. Marie went up to the old folks and I rode down the river. I found another heifer which I drove home, but the pen was shut and the heifer too wild to pen. I tied a loop in the rope I had on the horse (I left my lasso at home) and roped her from horseback. I took her to a spot on the river bank and tied her, went home and got my brand, threw her and branded her.

April 10 (Tuesday)

I found a yearling bull, ran him home and into the pen. But he fought so that I had to ride into the pen and lasso him from my horse. Marie and I soon had him branded.

April 11 (Wednesday)

Most of the cranes and geese have left.

April 12 (Thursday)

Rode up the river to Hind's Bend and found three yearlings each, which we branded in my pen. Hinnant gave me one of his for the saddle tree I had covered for him. It is very dangerous work, catching and branding bulls and calves.

April 13 (Friday)

Worked on hides, rode on the prairie, and jobbed about the house.

April 14 (Saturday)

The same as Friday.

April 15 (Sunday)

Jobbing about the house.

April 16 (Monday)

Jobbing about, cutting firewood.

April 17 (Tuesday)

The cattle hunters returned from a cattle hunt, bringing home 120 yearlings, which they divided among them. I made a lasso in the afternoon.

April 18 (Wednesday)

I rode down on the prairie and found the mare that Capt. King gave me. She had a mule colt. I drove home two yearlings and we killed one for meat and took a quarter up to the old folks.

April 19 (Thursday)

Jobbing around the house till night.

April 20 (Friday)

I rode out and found Mr. McKenzie's horse and he insisted on me taking a dollar as a present to the boy. After supper I wrote a letter to Mrs. Glenn for S. Couling.

April 21 (Saturday)

Asked Mr. Hinnant to bring me four pounds of alum from Corpus Christi.

April 22 (Sunday)

I worked on the hides to keep them from spoiling. Worked at tanning a hide till night. The country has a beautiful appearance after the rain. The grass is green, flowers blooming and blackbirds, hummingbirds, bluebirds, large white pelicans and long-tailed flycatchers have been seen.

April 23 (Monday)

Jobbing around the house.

April 24 (Tuesday)

I rode down the prairie to help Hinnant and Mussett hunt a horse. We couldn't find him. I hunted for cattle on the prairie all day.

April 25 (Wednesday)

William Rhea was here last night and wanted me to join him and others at the head of the Oso so this morning we went to the place and worked among the cattle till afternoon. We penned in Reynolds' pen and branded the calves. I branded a young bull and heifer.

April 26 (Thursday)

Jobbing around the house.

April 27 (Friday)

Attended an auction in Corpus Christi. Mrs. Swift loaned me a book to read.

April 28 (Saturday)

Went out riding after horses and cows all day. I came back to Hinnant's. He had killed a beef and I got as much meat as I wanted, and the hide.

April 29 (Sunday)

Visited with the Coulings and Hinnants all day.

April 30 (Monday)

Jobbing around the house.

May 1 (Tuesday)

Worked on hides all day. Marie and I went to Bryden's in the evening.[248]

May 2 (Wednesday)

Some Mexicans came by to see my leather and saddle tree.

May 3 (Thursday)

Went on a cattle hunt to Glenn's Ranch with Frank Byler, Joseph Wright, and John Scott.[249]

May 4 (Friday)

Hunting cattle all day.

May 5 (Saturday)

Killed a calf every day and had meat to cook.

May 6 (Sunday)

We rounded up the cattle at Ball's Motts and branded them.

May 7 (Monday)

We rounded up the cattle near the lagoon and returned to camp with a hundred yearlings, which we branded.[250]

---

[248] Noakes had not been on friendly terms with James Bryden after the quarrel over the administration of John Williams' estate, but in the months since then he shared reading matter with Janet. The invitation to dinner must have been a peace offering.

[249] Sam Glenn's was at Grulla Motts on the Oso, the ranch that once belonged to Mustang Gray.

[250] During the war, stockmen could not keep up with the process of branding and marking the yearly increase in their herds. Calves went unbranded and

May 8 (Tuesday)

We rounded up the cattle near the lagoon, where we found another 40 cattle hunters, but they soon left us. The cattle were so wild they would run over our horses. It was very dangerous.

May 9 (Wednesday)

Last night and again tonight we slept around the pen to keep the cattle from breaking out. But it was a dangerous place to sleep, for if the cattle stampeded, they would have trampled us to death. It began raining at daylight but we went into the pen and branded all we could. We had two Mexicans on horseback roping the animals and dragging them up to the fire. Some threw them and held them while others marked and branded them. We sent all the extra horses and wagons home. We branded 12 fine animals apiece. All were mavericks or unbranded cattle. When I got home, I found everything all right.

May 10 (Thursday)

I was roping and branding colts and horses with my neighbors.

May 11 (Friday)

I found two more mares and their young colts. I made hobbles for the young colts and hobbled my young horse. I bought a good-looking mule for 20 dollars.

May 12 (Saturday)

I was breaking the mule and working with the wild colt. Rode out and brought in another cow and calf.

May 13 (Sunday)

Mr. Ludewig took dinner with us. We had a heavy rain and thunderstorm after noon. I saw a constrictor snake go

---

became mavericks, unbranded yearlings, abroad on the range and available to anyone able to pen and brand them. Unbranded cattle were seen as public property. The widespread practice of hunting for unbranded yearlings far from one's home range led the Texas Legislature to enact a law in late 1866 prohibiting driving another person's livestock from its normal range. But the law was almost impossible to enforce and the search for mavericks went on.

into a hole and immediately a long rattlesnake came rushing out of the hole.

May 14 (Monday)

I worked on saddles and hobbles for my colt and tanned the hide of a beef. Marie and I threw both the colts and doctored them for worms.

May 15 (Tuesday)

Worked on the hide and horses and mules and wasted two precious hours with Stevens. Being out of meat, I took my gun with Henry Couling to help him kill a yearling. I brought a quarter home. We have seen our first mosquitoes.

May 16 (Wednesday)

Thunderstorms all day. I took some meat to the old folks.

May 17 (Thursday)

Rode out and found a cow and calf and did my morning work.

May 18 (Friday)

Rode out and found the colt that had been killed by a panther the night before. I worked on the saddle and made a stake rope.

May 19 (Saturday)

Took up the floor of the shed to kill rats. The river is running full but within its banks. A few days ago, a Dr. Allen, an Irish surgeon, was drunk and intending to wrong a widow woman with a large family in Corpus. When he sobered up, he took laudanum and killed himself.

I heard yesterday that a rowdy named Garner in Corpus Christi shot a merchant and killed him for nothing more than that the merchant would not let Garner have some tobacco on credit. The crowd beat Garner nearly to death then hung him. It was the best thing they could do, as the merchant was the fourth man Garner had murdered.[251]

---

[251] The slain storekeeper was Emanuel Scheuer. Other accounts say that an argument stemmed from his refusal to give Garner credit to buy a pair of boots. See Appendix 7.

Received a new paper the other day from my brother Edmond at Mobile, Ala.

May 20 (Sunday)

Rode to the Motts and talked to Mr. Blackwell and Judge Doakes.

May 21 (Monday)

Rain fell in torrents. Mr. Wilson called and talked until nearly noon. I broke a colt today.

May 22 (Tuesday)

Worked with a colt. Stretched a piece of dressed hide on a frame and plaited a rope. The mosquitoes are so bad that we have to make a smoke in the pen and let all the horses, broke and unbroke, in with the cows.

May 23 (Wednesday)

Heavy rain. Worked with my colt and on the hide I had framed. Tried in vain to shoot rabbits.

May 24 (Thursday)

I rode to Corpus Christi. As Mr. Wright was going down with his cart and could bring a barrel of flour home. I purchased ours at Headen's for 11 dollars.[252] I also bought some sugar and a bridle bit. I received a letter from William, my brother. I visited Mrs. Swift and talked with Mr. Almond about sheep.

May 25 (Friday)

Mailed some letters. Rode to Corpus to try to buy a mare from a federal officer stationed there, but he put too much value on her. Had a pleasant talk with a captain and a doctor of the company. Rode home with a disagreeable number of mosquitoes.

May 26 (Saturday)

Worked with my colt till dinner, after which I rubbed a hide I am dressing. I must work for my supper. While all

---

[252] William Headen's large store was in a two-story frame building on the corner of Chaparral and Schatzel streets.

animals are afraid of fire, even my two wild horses will neigh for me to take them to the pen and not only follow me but will crowd up close to the fire built to smoke away the mosquitoes. When the mosquitoes are bad, the horses will allow me to take off their ropes and treat them like old broken mounts.

May 27 (Sunday)

I rode up to the Motts and walked home with Couling and Ellen Ludewig. Received a letter today from sister Emily.

May 28 (Monday)

I made up mind to go on another cattle hunt. Marie volunteered to see to the wild horses while I was away. I reached the place of rendezvous at 3 p.m. at Glenn's Ranch on the Oso. I took along two horses. I ate supper with the cattle hunters.

May 29 (Tuesday)

The night was very hot and several of us went out into the open to sleep but the mosquitoes prevented us from getting much rest. A norther blew up towards morning and I fell asleep. I woke up quite chilled. We did not take time to eat but rode on to our roundup of cattle on the Laureles Ranch, where we penned them.[253]

I found a good pocketknife which could not have been dropped more than a week before. Killed a calf and got supper. The water we had to drink was muddy. In the crowd I was with there were about 17 were hands of Capt. King, John Scott, Frank Byler, and several others of their kind.

---

[253] The Laureles Ranch, named for bay laurel trees near the Laguna Madre, was purchased by Charles Stillman, the Brownsville merchant, in 1844. Mifflin Kenedy bought the Laureles in 1868 and later sold it and bought the La Parra Ranch to the south. It was owned by Stillman when Noakes and the cattle hunters were there.

May 30 (Wednesday)

We left the cattle in the pen and rode north of the ranch where we branded the calves and mavericks. I kept book of the brandings. We rode six miles in the direction of La Parra Ranch for more hunting. We killed a calf for supper and settled in for the night. The mosquitoes were so bad we could not sleep. Next day by noon we had a herd of cattle that covered about eight acres. We penned at the Laureles.

May 31 (Thursday)

We got our dinner, after which another large crowd with an even larger herd of cattle came along. We took our cattle and put them in the smaller pen and gave them the larger pen. We had two separate camps.

June 1 (Friday)

The first thing this morning we found that our cattle, which we had worked so hard for yesterday, had broken out of the pen during the night. We neglected to keep a guard, as usual. Both crowds joined and hunted together toward the south, getting a large herd of cattle and penning about 4 p.m.

June 2 (Saturday)

Some rode off to the west, some north while others stayed behind and kept on with the branding. I stayed behind. I kept an account in the pen and helped cut up a calf for dinner and made myself useful in camp. The hunters and herd returned after noon and we continued branding till night.

June 3 (Sunday)

Both parties were busy branding and herding all day.

June 4 (Monday)

We finished branding at one p.m. The yearlings were branded last. We got three apiece. I branded two of my own calves and put my mark on the cow I had from Mose, one cow and calf I lost out of the pen, and another calf was left behind, being too young to drive. We took dinner and I saddled up and came home, the others going on with the hunt. I was tired and so was my horse.

I got home at sundown and found everything all right. Marie was home and, in addition to attending to the three horses, mule, cows and pigs while I was gone, she made a pig pen out of fence pickets in a corner of the cow pen and a henhouse near the shed.

June 5 (Tuesday)

I rode into the Motts to see several people and after dinner I finished Marie's henhouse.

June 6 (Wednesday)

I rode around among the cattle.

June 7 (Thursday)

Jobbing around the house.

June 8 (Friday)

I rode up to the Motts to pay my taxes but found that I didn't bring enough money along.

June 9 (Saturday)

I agreed with Henry Couling for him to get me a hog from the other side of the river. This morning, seeing him with his dogs, I rode down and he ran the hog over to me. I roped him in the water and with Henry helping me hold him I cut off his tusks. Marie brought home three hens. We are getting an extensive establishment.

June 10 (Sunday)

I took a bath in the river this morning but had to keep my eyes skinned as an alligator took particular interest in my movement. In noting down the last cattle hunt, I had no time to dwell on details, but some of the manners and customs of cattle hunting here are worth notice. The excessive cruelty practiced by cattle hunters toward horses and cattle on these hunts is enough to upset anybody with common feeling. Cows get killed and calves are trampled to death in the pen. A man must leave his feelings at home when he starts cattle hunting and those with anything like a sensitive stomach had better not start.[254]

June 11 (Monday)

I rode around. Mr. Wright came down and brought me the Sussex paper from home.

June 12 (Tuesday)

Jobbing around the house.

June 13 (Wednesday)

I rode up to the Motts to take the Sussex paper to Mrs. Wright to look at and received the Corpus Christi Advertiser, the first number out.

June 14 (Thursday)

Jobbing around the house.

June 15 (Friday)

With the help of Henry Couling and Hinnant, I went a mile up to get a mare of mine that I heard was bogged. We hitched our horses to her and dragged her out. But we could not get her up so had to leave her. I had to get home to attend to my things. I went to talk with Mr. Ludewig.

June 16 (Saturday)

I rode out to the mare and watered her with a bucket then called at Couling's for help to get her up. After dinner, Henry Couling and his Mexican went out with me and helped raise the mare on her legs, but she fell twice and the last time we had to leave her. It was getting dark.

June 17 (Sunday)

Same as yesterday.

June 18 (Monday)

I rode into the Motts on business.

June 19 (Tuesday)

I rode among the cattle. After I reached home, I felt quite sick from riding in the hot sun.

---

[254] J. Frank Dobie concurred. The old-time cow hunt, he wrote in "The Vaquero of the Brush County," was no place for members of the Humane Society.

June 20 (Wednesday)

Jobbing around the house.

June 21 (Thursday)

Same as yesterday.

June 22 (Friday)

I jobbed around the house.

June 23 (Saturday)

I rode out on Tony to hunt the sick mare, but could find no trace of her. She must have died. I found a small plant which I have never seen or heard of before called the coma. I can find plenty of bushes but few have fruit, which is about 1/6-inch long and half that size in diameter. They have a sweet flavor. The flowers resemble a plant and are very sweet.[255]

June 24 (Sunday)

Rested all day. Marie went up to the old folks. I rode up to Mr. McKenzie's to get a newspaper.

June 25 (Monday)

I rode down to Corpus to the county and state election. The election caused quite a lot of excitement.[256] I called at Mrs. Swift's and returned a book I borrowed. We were much amused by two drunken Irishmen trying to ride one horse. Every once in a while, they would come down onto the road. They were armed with a bottle of whisky, the smell of which would kill anyone but an Irishman.

June 26 (Tuesday)

I rode to McKenzie's with some newspapers and from there to Mr. Littig's, where I found that Mr. Wright's horse

---

[255] The Coma or La Coma is defined as a spiny shrub with dirk-like thorns and blue-black fruit in season, which provide a food source for white-tailed deer in thickets and salt marshes of the Rio Grande Plains. Ref. "Trees, Shrubs and Cacti of South Texas."

[256] In the June 25, 1866 election, Nueces County voters favored ratification of the new state constitution. In the contest for governor they chose J. W. Throckmorton over E. M. Pease by the narrow margin of 146 votes to 134. Ref. Eugenia Briscoe, "City by the Sea."

had thrown him and ran off with the saddle. I went in pursuit and it took me till after the middle of the day to find and pen him. I came to dinner then went up to the old folks and killed a calf, as we had been without meat for some time.

June 27 (Wednesday)

I rode and penned a maverick and hunted among the cattle. The beef-hunting crowd came and camped at the well. Their horses stampeded my colts, who ran off in a different direction dragging their logs behind them. I expected that my horse arrangement was broken up, but luckily, I got them all back in an hour or two.

The beef-hunting crowd have about 60 head of horses about my place. I have to supply the hunters with firewood to save my place.

June 28 (Thursday)

I rode off with the beef-hunting crowd and helped to make one roundup, but getting disgusted I came back home. I was busy till sundown helping Henry Couling pull a horse that was bogged in the river.

June 29 (Friday)

My horses were gone so I had to hunt them. I also had to watch the river for cows, as the cattle are coming in in great numbers. I fixed a bell on the old mare with a chain so it cannot be cut off.

June 30 (Saturday)

I hunted in my horses, then among the cattle that came to the river. Couling and I penned a yearling for meat. In the evening Couling came down and we killed the yearling and I took a piece up to Reynolds' and after supper a piece up to the old folks.

July 1 (Sunday)

Day of rest spent jobbing among the horses and cows. I would not grumble about the work if we could only get some kind of compensation, but we work hard, night and day, Sunday and all, but never realize anything.

July 2 (Monday)

I rode among the cattle.

July 3 (Tuesday)

I went across the river with Henry Couling to hunt for a cow, which was across on Sunday. But I hunted till noon and could not find her. That will be the last of her. Couling lent me a mare to ride and we pulled a mare of his out of the river. After dinner I cleaned out the well and rode down to the river. While I was gone, Tony and the mule which were necked together got out and I hunted in vain till dark to find them.

July 4 (Wednesday)

I hunted all day for the horse and mule. It seems as though some evil demon hovers over me. I am losing everything while my neighbors grow rich. They take no pains or trouble themselves about anything, while I am working myself down. It is useless for an unlucky man to try.

July 5 (Thursday)

Tony and the mule came down the river to water with a gang of horses, so I was up on foot to drive them home, thinking that they were still hobbled. But they had broken off their hobbles and were able to run off again. I returned home to get the bay colt to get them back. Adolph, Marie and I ate some watermelon, which we fetched down from the old folks.

July 6 (Friday)

Jobbing among the cattle.

July 7 (Saturday)

Same as yesterday. Marie caught a mess of fish for dinner.

July 8 (Sunday)

I rode up to Ludewig's and brought home some meat, they having killed. I left a quarter of the beef at Couling's. After dinner I spent the time reading, writing and seeing to my horses.

July 9 (Monday)

Rode to Hinnant's and fetched home some watermelons.

July 10 (Tuesday)

I cleaned and pegged out a hide.

July 11 (Wednesday)

I took a ride by Hinnant's then went up to the old folks and got some melons and cut out leather to make leggings.

July 12 (Thursday)

Judge Doakes called in the morning with an old Mexican and they stayed all day. I worked at the leggings again.

July 13 (Friday)

I worked at the leggings and finished them two hours before sundown. I brought home a piece of meat from Couling and some melons from the old folks.

July 14 (Saturday)

Marie and I had a fine job at milking, the mud in the pen being knee-deep. The rain didn't allow me to hunt my horses. I had to stay in the shelter. I made a quirt, mine being broken.[257]

July 15 (Sunday)

After getting through with the morning work, I rode out and drove home the horse, which I found was all right. I went up to the old folks and got some melons.

July 16 (Monday)

After dinner I rode up to the old folks and put some rivets in the cart wheel then rode over to Hinnant's and helped him fix a sugar mill to crush the juice from Chinese sugarcane.

---

[257] Quirt is an American adaption of the Spanish cuarta for whip or riding lash.

319

July 17 (Tuesday)

Same as yesterday. Near sundown McKenzie sent me a bundle of newspapers to read.

July 18 (Wednesday)

Same as yesterday.

July 19 (Thursday)

I rode down to Corpus. I subscribed to and advertised my brand in the Corpus Christi Advertiser, paying eight dollars for the two. I found Corpus improving, with new houses and fences being erected. I bought lime for hides, rivets for hoops, and iron wire.

July 20 (Friday)

I jobbed around the house. After dinner I commenced on a saddle tree.

July 21 (Saturday)

I went up to the old folks to select some lumber to make a bedstead. After dinner I reframed a looking glass, sharpened a saw, and commenced making the bedstead for the old folks.

July 22 (Sunday)

I was writing most of the day, commencing a letter to Emily and writing a piece for the Corpus Christi Advertiser about Hinnant's sugar mill.

July 23 (Monday)

I worked most of the day making the bedstead for the old folks then on the saddle tree.

July 24 (Tuesday)

I worked all day on the saddle tree.

July 25 (Wednesday)

I received a Mobile, Ala., paper from Edmond.

July 26 (Thursday)

I worked with the horses. I have Adolph's horse Billy to attend to for him, he having taken his wife and gone to Corpus to work at the saddling trade. I commenced a letter home last week and every night since have been going to finish it.

July 27 (Friday)

Worked all day on the saddle tree.

July 28 (Saturday)

I had the saddle tree ready to cover and sharpened my tools.

July 29 (Sunday)

I rode up to Hinnant's and got some meat, he having killed, and after breakfast took a piece up to the old folks. I then finished the letter to mother.

July 30 (Monday)

I got a gallon of molasses from Hinnant. After dinner Couling and I rode down to the Oso Creek and camped with the cattle hunters from the Motts.

July 31 (Tuesday)

We left the herd in the charge of two hands and made a hunt down the West Oso and back, where we took our breakfast, or rather dinner, having killed a calf. We started home with the herd, in which I had six cows and calves. The heat was so great that the calves couldn't travel and I had to leave some of mine. We didn't get to Reynolds' pen till sundown. I had a fuss with the crowd because they objected to stopping the process while I took out my cows, but I took them out. I found that two of mine were without their calves so I had to put them back in the herd again. Couling helped me drive home the three, which I penned safely.

August 1 (Wednesday)

I rode up to the herd penned at Reynolds' to get the rest of my cows. The two cows there had lost their calves. I tried to drive them home, but only got one of them penned. The other one ran about in every direction and stampeded my horse. Then it rained hard but I managed to get home at night. This cattle hunting is horrible work, fit only for Mexicans and Texans. Nothing but charging, cussing, and the moment they are out of the saddle, the men are gambling.[258]

August 2 (Thursday)

I am making a saddle tree to sell to buy some flour.

August 3 (Friday)

I covered the saddle tree, taking all day.

August 4 (Saturday)

I worked all day on the saddle tree. The piece I wrote last week for the Corpus Advertiser was published.

August 5 (Sunday)

I wrote a letter to E. P. Alsbury in San Antonio. Marie has been up to the old folks. I roped and branded a calf and turned it out.

August 6 (Monday)

I worked all day on the saddle tree.

August 7 (Tuesday)

Same as yesterday.

August 8 (Wednesday)

I rode to Corpus and mailed a letter to Emily in England and one to E. P. Alsbury and sent the Corpus paper to Edmond in Mobile. I took one of my paintings to get it photographed, but the party was not fixed up for it. I called on Mrs. Swift and I had a pair of girth irons made for a saddle tree. I also made an affidavit at the revenue collector's office, which required no task on my memory since my income last year did not exceed $4.00 dollars. Corpus is rapidly improving. Goods of all kind can be

---

[258] One description of a cattle hunt explained that poker games were held every night. "They played for unbranded cattle, yearlings at 50 cents a head and the top price for any class was $5 a head, so if anyone ran out of cattle and had a little money, he could get back in the game. For $10, say, he could get a stack of yearlings." See Appendix 1.

bought for money but everything is very dear [expensive] since the war.

August 9 (Thursday)

I filed the saddle iron a little into shape.

August 10 (Friday)

My hands were too sore to work so I rode up to the old folks.

August 11 (Saturday)

I amused myself by writing some verse called "Cowboy Lament" while Marie rode up to see her mother, who is sick, but returned for dinner. I feel very bad and bilious.

August 12 (Sunday)

Last night I took a dose of James Pills and feel better today. I am also taking a big dose of bitters three times a day. Mr. Ludewig came at daylight to borrow the mule to ride to town, Mrs. Ludewig being worse. Marie went up to help and I worked a small hide and cooked dinner and amused myself writing.

August 13 (Monday)

It rained hard. Marie and I finished the hog pen.

August 14 (Tuesday)

Worked all day on the saddle tree.

August 15 (Wednesday)

Worked on the saddle tree, having it ready to cover.

August 16 (Thursday)

Worked till noon covering the saddle tree, then cut a hide for a rope.

August 17 (Friday)

Saddled up my horse and he threw himself several times and broke the saddle rigging, which took me till dinner to fix.

August 18 (Saturday)

I rode up to the old folks, penned and killed a yearling, took them some of the meat and brought home a quarter, and the hide, which I put in lime. McKenzie was down. He wanted me to paint a likeness of a buck.

August 19 (Sunday)

Rain, rain, rain. I had two hides to work and I worked them on Sunday, as our barrel of flour is nearly out and I depend on the hides and saddle tree to get another. After dinner I wrote out some verses to send to the Corpus Advertiser.

August 20 (Monday)

I worked on the hides and saddle tree.

August 21 (Tuesday)

I finished the saddle tree and put a new bottom in a wooden bucket and a new handle on another.

August 22 (Wednesday)

Worked on a pair of shoes, using my own leather.

August 23 (Thursday)

Worked all day on the shoes, getting them nearly completed, making a satisfactory job of them. I have now satisfied myself that I can make shoes.

August 24 (Friday)

It rained so hard that the mud was knee-deep and filled up my boots to walk through it. I do not do as Marie, who has gone without shoes all summer. I finished the shoes I was making for her and commenced on a pair of boots for myself.

August 25 (Saturday)

After my usual work, I finished the boots and after working into the night I started on another pair for myself, but my right hand was so sore I couldn't use it without pain.

August 26 (Sunday)

I feel unwell and my hand, which one of the calves mangled, pains me badly. I laid down after getting through with my morning work till dinner. Marie walked up to the old folks and I was left alone to my meditations, which as usual soon gave me the blues. I saddled up the gray colt and rode out, but the mosquitoes drove me home again. My hand prevented me from using my usual remedy for the blues, working to keep from thinking. I put some salt and turpentine on my hand and the pain was relieved.

August 27 (Monday)

A thunderstorm passed over but we did not get much rain. I worked all day on a shoe last and another pair of shoes. Mrs. Brown spent the evening with us.

August 28 (Tuesday)

A norther came up last night and it is cooler today. I finished my shoes, varnished my saddle tree, and read the newspapers McKenzie brought. Rode out on the gray colt and penned a cow and calf and commenced making a hat for the boy.

August 29 (Wednesday)

This morning Marie reported that the flour barrel is empty, coffee and sugar are nearly out, no meat and nothing in the house but milk. I concluded to go foraging, since I had no money. It requires considerable tact but by dinner time I succeeded in getting half a bushel of corn, sweet potatoes on credit and borrowed a bag of flour from the old folks. In the afternoon I rode out on the gray colt and penned a yearling to kill for meat and left it in the old folks' pen for next day.

August 30 (Thursday)

I rode to the old folks and, though feeling unwell, I killed the yearling and brought home half the meat and the hide. I worked with the colt.

August 31 (Friday)

I rode out and brought home two Yankee shells that were left at Couling's old place. Coming upon an unmarked yearling, I roped, threw, marked and altered him. I dragged home some posts, pulling them by rope from the saddle horn. After dinner I cleaned the hide I had limed and put it in the river to soak the lime out.

September 1 (Saturday)
After finishing various jobs, I showed Henry Couling how to build a skiff. After going to the old folks' and McKenzie's, I helped Couling on his boat.

September 2 (Sunday)
Took some butter to the old folks to send to Corpus. Mr. Ludewig is going to town Monday.

September 3 (Monday)
Went to Corpus, and as it was early, I had to stop for breakfast, and make a fire to keep the mosquitoes off while I ate. Carried down the saddle tree I had finished for Adolph to sell, as our flour barrel is empty and there is no money to buy more. I sold some butter to the captain of a steamboat but did not get enough for flour. I bought sugar, coffee, lamp wicks, shoe pegs, alum for hides, and left Corpus at sundown.

September 4 (Tuesday)
I must make more saddle trees to sell as we are all without clothes.

September 5 (Wednesday)
Last night my oldest boy became sick with a fever, which has risen and fallen all day.[259]

September 6 (Thursday)
Mr. Ludewig came down to see the sick boy, who is better. Helped Couling kill a small beef and brought home some of the meat and the hide.

---

[259] Thomas Jr., born Dec. 17, 1862, was almost four. The second son, Nelson Edmondson, was born June 13, 1865. Noakes rarely made observations or commented in his journals about his children. In his frequent notes of Marie visiting her parents, we assume she always took the children with her since Noakes never mentioned any parenting duties.

September 7 (Friday)

Worked on a saddle tree and hides.

September 8 (Saturday)

Made an augur handle and worked on a saddle tree.

September 9 (Sunday)

The boy is quite well again.

September 10 (Monday)

Worked on a saddle tree and fixed a singletree for Hinnant.

September 11 (Tuesday)

Got forks for four trees and started work on four more saddle trees. Cleaned mud out of the horse pen.

September 12 (Wednesday)

Worked on saddle trees and hides all day.

September 13 (Thursday)

Worked on the hind trees of four saddle trees. Tried to get some elm forks for more saddle trees.

September 14 (Friday)

Crossed the river and got two elm forks for saddle fore trees. Marie and I work night and day, but we are more in need of clothes and provisions than we were during the war.

September 15 (Saturday)

No potatoes, corn or meat, and I cannot do enough work to make do.

September 16 (Sunday)

River very high. I took a bath in it.

September 17 (Monday)

I commenced a saddle tree and worked on an ox yoke for Mr. Ludewig.

September 18 (Tuesday)

I rode down early to the Oso Creek to see an Irishman who had one of my cows milking it. I found my cow in his pen and made him turn her out and I drove her home. The grass on the prairie was six inches higher than the cow's head and in some places the prairie was covered with water. I received a letter from Capt. Alsbury.

September 19 (Wednesday)

Bought some sweet potatoes in town. Marie took the youngsters up to the old folks and we rode around to hunt for cows and calves, trying to find something to kill. We have been several days without meat and eating borrowed flour. I have no money to buy any.

September 20 (Thursday)

I covered the saddle tree and worked on some hides. I saw the first sandhill crane today. Being out of meat, Marie and I killed one of the pigs and made sausage.

September 21 (Friday)

I rode down on the gray colt and did sundry jobs till noon and then worked on the saddle tree.

September 22 (Saturday)

I crossed the river in Couling's boat and brought home some elm forks for saddle trees.

September 23 (Sunday)

Was out hunting cattle all day but only found one young heifer.

September 24 (Monday)

I attended to jobs around the house and sharpened my cross-cut saw. Rode up to Wright's and got the Corpus paper in which was published my lines called "Cowboy's Lament."

September 25 (Tuesday)

Rain, rain, rain. I wrote a letter to Capt. Alsbury, after which I finished the cross-cut saw and put a handle in it then worked to make a meat-chopping block.

September 26 (Wednesday)

Worked on some posts for my well. Marie and I and the boys went across the river and with the cross-cut saw cut down a large mesquite tree, then sawed it into blocks to chop meat on. Mrs. Couling brought us a piece of pork.

September 27 (Thursday)

More hummingbirds now than ever before. Made Marie a chopping block, which took all day.

September 28 (Friday)

I was thrown from a horse. He fell over backwards, but I caught the rope as I fell and was on him again as soon as he got up. He gave a big kick and I found myself behind the saddle. However, I stayed on as he was pitching and kicking but he was making for some trees so I let go and was thrown to the ground.

I branded a colt and trimmed the manes and tails of the mares to make ropes and saddle girths and headstalls.

September 29 (Saturday)

Marie and I branded young calves and Mr. Ludewig brought us a barrel of flour from Corpus.

September 30 (Sunday)

Judge Doakes stayed last night with us. He has been sick with the chills. Mr. Stevens came to get me to make him a whip. I finished the saddle tree, mended my shoes that were torn yesterday, and took the meat I had been smoking from the chimney.

October 1 (Monday)

Cut the whip lash for Stevens then Mr. [William] Halsey came and dined with us and remained some time. He brought a message from Col. Hobby at Galveston requesting me to paint him a picture of the Corpus Christi bombardment.[260] I found Halsey to be very friendly and he agreed to send me some wood for a saddle tree and asked me to make him one. McKenzie brought some papers from Corpus. I put a handle in an ax and fixed the yoke for Mr. Ludewig.

---

[260] Maj. A. M. Hobby, who commanded the Eighth Texas Infantry, was the Confederate officer in command at the battle of Corpus Christi.

October 2 (Tuesday)

Fixed the bottom of a wooden bucket, wrote a letter to Col. Hobby of Galveston, and worked all day on a saddletree. Sold one of my saddles in Corpus for $22.[261]

October 3 (Wednesday)

Weather fair and cool. Had two calves missing.

October 4 (Thursday)

I finished the saddle tree, cut strips to sew the cover on, stretched up the hides, and rode around on the gray colt after supper. Made preparations to go to town.

October 5 (Friday)

I started early to town. Mr. Ludewig went down with the cart and I rode Billy. I had a bite and rest a bit and Billy had a spell of pitching, which didn't help matters. Mr. Ludewig took some butter down for me, which I sold to the captain of a schooner. After getting my money from Adolph for the saddle I paid Schubert for the flour that he sent me the other day and bought some lumber, molasses, sugar, corn meal, a stone jar, a new hat, a blouse and calico dress for Marie. We took our meals at Adolph's and spent the evening at Mrs. Swift's, where Mr. Ludewig and I slept.

October 6 (Saturday)

I helped Mr. Ludewig load his cart with the things that I bought and a grindstone that he bought, then rode home, but found that Marie was at the old folks so I had to get dinner. Mr. Ludewig drove my things down and after putting them away, I put a calf hide, which Marie had skinned, into lime and then Mr. Stevens came along and I had to talk to him till Sunday.

October 7 (Sunday)

I took a ride on the gray colt, having some papers to deliver, going to McKenzie's, the old folks', and Wright's. Several complimentary remarks were made to me about the "Cowboy's Lament." I promised to send Col. Morgan one

---

[261] That would be the equivalent in 2019 of $353.

of my paintings for him to get framed to hang in his drawing room at Banquete. I also received a letter from Mr. Hogarth. I mailed one to Col. Hobby and another to Capt. Alsbury. My saddle trees are attracting a great deal of attention and I am getting applications for them from all over.

October 8 (Monday)

I cleaned the hide I had in lime then worked to fix up a grindstone for Mr. Ludewig.

October 9 (Tuesday)

After getting through with my morning work, I finished the grindstone for Mr. Ludewig and returned the flour we borrowed from the old folks a short time ago. I also skinned a calf that died in the pen.

October 10 (Wednesday)

I prepared a hide to cover the saddle tree I have on hand, worked on a barrel for the house, cleaned the calf hide I had in lime, and ground some new tools.

October 11 (Thursday)

I covered the saddle tree and fixed the water barrel.

October 12 (Friday)

I rode the gray colt down to the prairie and brought home a cow and calf to milk. Those we have are about dry. Hauled water, then rode the mule up to the old folks and churned some butter to send to Corpus to sell. I went to the prairie again after a cow but I could not drive her, it was getting too dark. When I reached home my horses were gone.

October 13 (Saturday)

Price was down wanting me to make him a pen gate, which I promised to do. Couling killed a big beef and gave me the quarter he owed me from last winter. I rode up on the mule and brought our half home and took the other half to the old folks. I worked on the water barrel and saddle tree until Price brought the lumber and I commenced on the gate.

October 14 (Sunday)

This being Sunday morning, everything was wrong. I took the mule and drove up the calves, which had been turned out at night. I hunted home the cows, which have got so they will not come up. I found the horses were scattered and gone but two, so rode till 10 o'clock to get them home. Watered the cows at the well and doctored the calves for worms, and did various other jobs. I rode out on the gray colt and returned some papers to McKenzie, then rode out on the prairie to get away from the work at home. Returned about dark, drove up the cows, then had to ride a mile to get the horses and bring them home and pen them, then turned out the big calves and penned the small ones, then to supper, after which I do my writing. That ends the day of rest.

October 15 (Monday)

I made the gate for Price and commenced on the saddle tree. I have a boil on the posterior.

October 16 (Tuesday)

I branded a big calf then make trees for saddles. J. Wright was down, wanting me to make him a saddle tree. My boil was so painful I could hardly work, but I kept on till night, then saw to the horses, riding being out of the question.

October 17 (Wednesday)

Marie and both boys are sick from colds. My oldest boy kept us up from what I supposed was an attack of croup. My boil was so bad I could hardly move. Had the boy take hot coffee and it seemed to relieve him. Nearly every calf was gone this morning and I could not ride to get them. If we do not get milk for the boys they will fall off. After breakfast Marie and I managed to get some milk for them. After doing my morning's work I made a saddle tree but I had to lie down now and then as the pain from my boil was excruciating. I worked till near night then had to give it up. Marie saw to the cows and horses and mule.

October 18 (Thursday)

I did but little, my boil preventing me, and Mr. Jack Helm was here nearly all day.[262] Mr. Flint brought his saddle tree and I put the hide in soak to cover it with.

October 19 (Friday)

The boil is still bad however I worked all day on the tree I was making and worked the hide in Mr. Flint's tree. I received a letter from mother today, enclosing a draft for 21 dollars.

October 20 (Saturday)

I covered Mr. Flint's tree and worked on the other. Threw the gray colt and doctored him for worms. My boil is much better.

October 21 (Sunday)

I amused myself a little with the saddle tree.[263] I wrote a letter to Mr. Hogarth.

October 22 (Monday)

I wrote a letter to mother. Rode out a little to see to the horses, my boil allowing me to do so. I fixed a hide to cover the saddle tree I am making. The man who has been living at Reynolds left.

October 23 (Tuesday)

I covered the saddle tree and rode a little on the gray.

---

[262] Jack Helm would become notorious. He was appointed a captain in the State Police, created by Gov. E. J. Davis to replace the Texas Rangers. Helm figured prominently in the Sutton-Taylor feud and his company of "regulators" was known for murdering its prisoners. Helm was shot to death by John Wesley Hardin in 1873 in the small town of Albukirk in Wilson County. Ref. David Pickering and Judy Falls, "Brush Men & Vigilantes."

[263] It seems Noakes didn't want to say he "worked" on the saddle tree, it being Sunday, so he "amused himself" with it.

October 24 (Wednesday)

I am making alterations on the saddle-tree shed. I rode up to the old folks and built a door on their chicken house. After dinner I commenced another tree.

October 25 (Thursday)

I worked at the saddle tree.

October 26 (Friday)

I rode down to Corpus, bought underclothes, two barrels of nails, and arranged with Schubert to get the draft I received from mother exchanged.

October 27 (Saturday)

I worked all day on the saddle tree, besides my usual work. The weather was warm and fair.

October 28 (Sunday)

I rode up to Wright's and Littig's and after dinner hunted in vain for my horses.

October 29 (Monday)

I rode till noon in the rain searching for my horses. I agreed with Frost Allen to repair a saddle tree for him.[264] After dinner I worked on the tree I am making. Ellen spent the evening with us and Couling called after supper.

October 30 (Tuesday)

I brought a yearling hide and got a whole side of beef and put the hide in lime to soak. I went to Mrs. Blackwell's and hung the gate I made for her the other day. I rode out and brought home my horses, getting home after dark. Today I received a letter from Col. A. M. Hobby. Mr. Wright brought me the barrels of nails I bought in Corpus.

October 31 (Wednesday)

I finished the saddle tree; it is ready for covering. Worked on the barrels and fetched home Frost Allen's tree

---

[264] Frost Thorn Allen and brother Henry Davis Allen came to Nueces County in 1852 from Cherokee County, Texas, and established the San Jacinto Ranch on the Oso. A son of Henry Davis Allen, Calvin J., founded the town of Calallen which supplanted Nuecestown.

from Reynolds' and a bushel of corn from Shumate, settling up with him for the corn and potatoes I got from him previously. After dinner I commenced on another tree. I brought home the horses and did various jobs.

November 1 (Thursday)
Made a new fore tree for Allen's saddle and a small boy's tree.
November 2 (Friday)
I am making a tonic of molasses and mesquite bark in place of hops.
November 3 (Saturday)
Covered a saddle tree for Leandro, a Mexican.[265]
November 4 (Sunday)
Got a bushel of sweet potatoes from Hinnant and took the two saddle trees I had finished to the old man [Ludewig] to take to Corpus. I ran an unbranded yearling home to kill, the whole neighborhood being out of meat. Mr. Doakes, the young man who succeeded me in school, left after three months and was succeeded by Mr. [John] Vining, who has now given it up and this desirable (?) situation is now vacant.

My hands are so sore from working on the saddle trees, working with the lime and hides, that I can hardly write.
November 5 (Monday)
I covered the saddle tree for Frost Allen. Hinnant and Couling came down and we killed the yearling. I took a quarter up to the old folks.
November 6 (Tuesday)
I finished the boys' tree for covering. Received a letter from Capt. Alsbury.

---

[265] Possibly Leandro Bautista, who lived in that area, based on Census records.

November 7 (Wednesday)

Marie, the boys and I went over the river and brought home six forks for saddle trees and some moss for mattresses.

November 8 (Thursday)

Ellen and her father came along and after dark Mussett came with the colt from Adolph in Corpus which I agreed to buy on delivery. I was too unwell to attend to it and Marie had to see to it. Mussett stayed all night.

November 9 (Friday)

Mussett left at daylight. Fetched up the forks and moss from the river and hobbled the colt.

November 10 (Saturday)

Put four hobbles on the black colt. He kicked the others to pieces.

November 11 (Sunday)

Marie and the children and I went up to the old folks' for dinner.

November 12 (Monday)

I rode up to the old folks and brought home a suckling pig to kill. Jack Helm and a man named McCowen came and brought me some forks for saddle trees.

November 13 (Tuesday)

Jack Helm and McCowen stayed all night. I took another saddle tree to Ludewig for him to take to town. Mrs. Ludewig and Ellen were here to supper. Walked home with them and then wrote to Capt. Alsbury.

November 14 (Wednesday)

I rode to Corpus to get lumber and took dinner with Adolph. I cut up the lumber in Corpus and Mr. Ludewig brought it home in his cart.

November 15 (Thursday)

I slept at Adolph's. Mr. Ludewig took nails, paint, wash basin, etc., home. I offered myself to the beef-packing company for any kind of situation.[266] I took dinner with Adolph then rode home. I find the saddle-tree business doesn't pay and, in all probability, I will give it up. I received a letter from Mr. Goodrich of Seguin.

November 16 (Friday)

I feel disheartened and out of the notion to work. I was thinking that I made as much by reading the newspaper as by hard work.

November 17 (Saturday)

I was still out of the notion to work, knowing of nothing that would pay. I bottled some beer and have been making an experiment using molasses and mesquite bark instead of hops. I find it imparts an agreeable bitterness to the ale.

Marie and I and the two boys crossed the river in Couling's boat and sawed up a large tree into blocks. The tree was left by the last freshet and had floated down the river. I brought the blocks across the river and rode the colt.

November 18 (Sunday)

I went to the old folks for dinner, where Marie and the boys had gone to visit with Adolph and his wife Maggie and Mr. Schubert. Passed a pleasant day.

November 19 (Monday)

Spent the day as usual, and worked with the colts.

November 20 (Tuesday)

Worked on a saddle tree for Mr. Chipman. Rode to McKenzie's to exchange papers.

November 21 (Wednesday)

Spent the day riding the colt and doing the usual work.

November 22 (Thursday)

Same as Wednesday.

---

[266] Noakes was likely referring to the beef packing house established in late 1866 by Richard King and Nelson Plato on the south edge of town. Other packing houses on North Beach, at Flour Bluff and at Nuecestown came later. Ref., Briscoe, "City by the Sea."

November 23 (Friday)

Same as Thursday.

November 24 (Saturday)

Same as Friday.

November 25 (Sunday)

Brought up water for the stock, which I do every day. Same as Saturday. Busy all day.

November 26 (Monday)

Weather stormy, shook house. Rode around.

November 28 (Wednesday)

Killed a hog. Marie and I dressed it.

November 29 (Thursday)

Cut up and salted the hog and made sausage. I took a piece of pork up to Couling's and to the old folks.

November 30 (Friday)

Rode the black colt up to Mr. Littig's, who paid me $11.50 for a mare he sold for me. Rode around and worked with horses all day.

December 1 (Saturday)

Rode to Corpus to get lumber to finish roofing the old house. Mr. Schubert told me that the draft he cashed ($21 dollars from mother) had been refused in New York. We soon fixed it all right. I bought nails and other things for Mr. Ludewig to bring home in his cart.

December 2 (Sunday)

Worked on hides and tanning and riding horses.

December 3 (Monday)

Killed a yearling for meat. Mr. Ludewig brought me the lumber from Corpus and I gave him half the meat. Marie has to go to Corpus; Adolph's wife is sick.

December 4 (Tuesday)

Marie started early for Corpus. Mrs. Ludewig came down for the little ones. I was left alone with all the work.

December 5 (Wednesday)

Spent the busiest day and until midnight doing a little of everything, cooking beef and coffee.

December 6 (Thursday)

Marie came home and brought some money for the two saddle trees.

December 7 (Friday)

Penned cows and a beef to kill in the morning. Rode around as usual.

December 8 (Saturday)

Henry Couling came early and we killed the beef. Got two elm trees as support for the beams in the old house.

December 9 (Sunday)

I had to catch the bell mare and tie her up. All the horses and cows got out during the night. Cut up and salted the beef. A day of riding and rounding up cattle and horses.

December 10 (Monday)

Hung up the hog meat to smoke and made a last to make the oldest boy a pair of shoes. He has none.

December 11 (Tuesday)

Same as Monday. Finished the shoes for the boy, repaired my own and made a pair for the younger boy. Mr. Lively called to get an ax handle put on.[267] Couling brought me 50 posts for the well fence.

December 12 (Wednesday)

Rode after horses all day.

December 13 (Thursday)

A man I hired made the post holes and I worked on the fence around the well.

December 14 (Friday)

I worked all day with the man to fence the well.

---

[267] Amos Lively was a farmer and stockraiser from Alabama. He and his wife Mary had six children Ref. 1860 Census.

December 15 (Saturday)

I received a summons to go Corpus to serve as juryman. I did all kinds of jobs around the house, smoked bacon, cut up the beef, and took care of the cattle and horses.

December 16 (Sunday)

Mr. Lively called and I had to repair a saddle tree for Mr. Nickerson.[268]

December 17 (Monday)

I rode to Corpus to attend court but wasn't chosen for the jury. I went to Adolph's and after taking supper at Mrs. Swift's I borrowed a book and rode home.

December 18 (Tuesday)

Repaired a saddle tree for Mr. McLaughlin and made a mallet to drive wedges.

December 19 (Wednesday)

I feel out of heart. Everything seems to go against me. It presses on my mind the thought that I would have to spend my life in the same pleasureless routine, never having time for the least recreation. I had the chance for a little pleasure the other night in town but I returned to my drudgery.

I received a letter from Emily telling me of the sale of my land at a good price. It is strange that I have, before this, felt the same depression just previous to receiving good news.

December 20 (Thursday)

Answered Emily's letter and wrote a letter to Mr. Schubert and sent them to Corpus by Mr. Ludewig. Attended to my horses and worked a piece of leather.

December 21 (Friday)

Covered a saddle tree, attended to my horses, and smoked some meat.

---

[268] E. J. Nickerson, a rancher, originally from Massachusetts. Ref. 1870 Census.

December 22 (Saturday)

I wrote a piece called "Rules for Stock Raisers" and read till midnight and smoked a pipe or two. I was alone. Marie went up to stay with her mother. There's nothing I hate more than being alone. I mended my shoes.

December 23 (Sunday)

I worked on my tanning till dinner. I rode around the rest of the day.

December 24 (Monday)

I found the old man's steers and bought some oysters from a boatman and rode up to Couling's and got some beef. The oysters I cooked in my own way and the old folks came down to partake of them. Mr. Lively and young Hinnant came down and chatted awhile.

December 25 (Tuesday)

Christmas Day. Hinnant and Couling came down and I gave them an eggnog and some cake. Mr. Moore was with them.[269] He is living where Reynolds used to live. Reynolds sold out and left.[270] Maria went home with the old folks and I spent the evening up there, a Texas Christmas.

December 26 (Wednesday)

I had a few oysters left and did various jobs till dark.

December 27 (Thursday)

Henry Couling came down for some butter. His wife was confined during the night. I worked on my leather all day.

December 28 (Friday)

Mr. McCowen brought me a fork for a saddle tree. After eating dinner, he left for Corpus. I blackened the shoe leather and Mr. Helm came and stayed the night.

---

[269] Willis B. Moore moved to Texas from Alabama. He and his wife Sarah had three children. Ref. 1870 Census.

[270] George and Hannah Reynolds moved to a ranch on Agua Dulce Creek in northwest Nueces County in late 1867.

December 29 (Saturday)

Spent the day looking for horses and cows.

December 30 (Sunday)

Cool wind. Mr. Helm left for Corpus. To get away from the drudgery I rode up to the bluffs and spent the day hunting in vain for fossils among the different strata left exposed.

December 31 (Monday)

Couling came down with his wagon and we cleaned around the well.

I walked up to Willis Moore's place to a dance.
I stood in the dark looking into a dark room
from which came the scraping of a fiddle.
There were males and females going through
the motions of what they consider dancing.
I talked with my neighbors for five minutes in
the dark, and my cup of enjoyment being about
as full as it would get, I walked home.

—Feb, 20, 1867

AFTER THE WAR
1867

January 1 (Tuesday)

New Year's Day. Last night we had a blusterous night, with the wind blowing a gale from the north and it was excessively cold. At daylight it began to freeze and it froze all day. Even the dishwater, which had been left out, was covered with ice only a short distance from a large fire. The wind was strong and cold. Put on as much clothing as you like, you soon became numb out of doors. About noon it commenced to sleet and from that to snow. By sundown everything was white and the wind excessively cold as I saw to my horse, hog and calves. Today, water froze close to a large fire. My hands are so cold I can hardly write.[271]

---

[271] Helen Chapman wrote in her diary, "Unheard of weather; water freezing solid near the fire." Maria Blucher also described the rare snowfall in a letter to her parents. "We had a strange winter; no cold or disagreeable weather at all until the first of January and then all of a sudden a strong north wind came and

January 2 (Wednesday)

The snow continued to fall all night and didn't cease until 2 p.m. when the wind changed to more westerly and the clouds cleared away, leaving the ground covered with snow, to a depth of four inches, with drifts in places that were two or three feet deep. I had Tony in the pen by the old house and fed him on corn. I was barely able to face the excessive cold to see to the cows and hog. I walked up to the Wright's to get the newspaper but it was not there.

January 3 (Thursday)

Everything froze. The river froze to a depth of three-fourths of an inch. I rode down the prairie and brought home my horses.

January 4 (Friday)

After skinning a yearling that died and liming the hide, I rode out and saw to my horse and then called at the old folks. I killed and cleaned a hog for them, Marie being there to help. I skinned a calf that was dead in their pen and we passed the evening there.

January 5 (Saturday)

I rode up to the old folks and cut up and salted their hog. I then returned hungry, my boy Tom riding behind the saddle. I watered the horses and rode up to the Motts to get a paper that I had been told was there for me. But it was left at the house while I was gone. It proved to be a Sussex Express from home and a letter from Capt. Alsbury. Last night I was sick and today feel unwell. I read the paper during the evening.

January 6 (Sunday)

Wrote a letter to Mr. Goodrich of Seguin and passed the afternoon talking to Couling. Rode out on my horse. During the last three or four nights a lobo wolf has been

---

within a few hours we had one-half foot of snow on the ground." Ref. Bruce Cheeseman, "Maria von Blucher's Corpus Christi."

howling close to the house. They are large and dangerous to a man on foot.

January 7 (Monday)

Rode to Corpus and took Mr. McLaughlin his saddle tree. Saw Mr. Schubert about our future proceedings. Mailed Mr. Goodrich's letter and was complimented by several people for my song "The Two Twelve Pounders" which made its appearance in the New York Vindicator. It was sent to the editor by Capt. Alsbury. I bought a coat and stayed all night at Adolph's. I called on Mrs. Swift and took a piece called "Rules for Stock Raisers" to Mr. Maltby, who promised to publish it.[272]

January 8 (Tuesday)

Came home, hunted cows, and went to Wright's for my paper.

January 9 (Wednesday)

Pulled two cows bogged in the river with a block and tackle. Got my horses from the prairie.

January 10 (Thursday)

Pulling cattle out of the river with Marie's help and watering the ones nearly dead.

January 11 (Friday)

Still pulling my cows from the river.

January 12 (Saturday)

Fixed the cart wheels for Ludewig and rode out to get a steer and horses.

January 13 (Sunday)

Marie went up to her mother's and our boy Tom went to Corpus with Mr. Ludewig. I not only have more than I can do with my own work, but it seems as though Ludewig thinks I am compelled to do his drudgery too. Between the two I get no peace or rest and time for pleasure is out of the question. I hate to neglect my own affairs to help others

---

[272] William Maltby was the editor and publisher of the Corpus Christi Advertiser.

when I always have to do my own work by myself. I am tired of the way things work here and hope soon to be away from it. It is impossible to get along with people here unless you let them take advantage of you in every way. They get all they can out of you and ensure that you get nothing out of them by making you welcome to all they have, which is nothing, and pride themselves on being good neighbors and call you stingy.

I heard today that Jack Cook, a murderer and desperado, was shot and killed by some Mexicans a few miles from the Motts. He owed the Mexicans and intended to cheat them out of it so they killed him.

Jack Cook is supposed to have killed a preacher who preached two years in Corpus and soon afterwards was found murdered. Jack became possessed of his effects in some mysterious manner. But a trifle like that is never investigated here. He also stopped and robbed a Catholic priest between here and Corpus, taking every cent.

January 14 (Monday)

I cut out leather for shoes. Mr. Ludewig came home from Corpus and brought me a parcel from England containing a letter from Mr. Gill, the lawyer, and the title deed of the Polegate land and an agreement which had to be filled in, signed and returned.

January 15 (Tuesday)

Rode to Corpus and had a talk with Mr. Schubert about our future proceedings. I took supper and slept at Adolph's.

January 16 (Wednesday)

I bought a steelyard [a portable weigh balance] and a kettle and left town before noon. When I reached home, I donned my buckskin and went to work, after eating some bread and cold meat by way of dinner. Marie, as usual when I leave home, was up at the old folks. The big lobo wolf is still howling tonight. I mailed a Corpus Christi Advertiser containing my "Rules for Stock Raisers" to E. P. Alsbury.

346

January 17 (Thursday)

I cleaned the hide I had in the river and ground up some alum. Ellen and Adolph's wife were down for supper. I walked home with them.

January 18 (Friday)

I wrote a letter to Mr. Gill and Mr. Wooley, the lawyers, acknowledging the receipt of the documents. Commenced on a pair of shoes, worked with Billy the horse, and watered the cattle.

January 19 (Saturday)

I finished the shoes, working on them last night till midnight. I attended to the cattle and pulled two calves out of the river.

January 20 (Sunday)

I rode out to see my horses. Called at Ludewigs, where I returned to take dinner. Adolph and Mr. Schubert were out. We passed a pleasant evening.

January 21 (Monday)

After doing my morning work, I cleaned a piece of hide and put it in alum. I rode nearly all the morning looking for my horses. In doing so, I came across a cow of mine dead. I caught the mule and rode out to skin her, but found her too far gone. I found another cow that had just calved, but the calf was too young to drive.

January 22 (Tuesday)

Marie and I concluded to kill a hog. We got some salt from McKenzie and commenced preparation. Ellen and Maggie came down and by night we had him cleaned and I drew him up (by blocks) into a tree by the old house and we killed him.

January 23 (Wednesday)

I received a letter from Martha together with a small book on New Zealand from Emily. How pleasant to find yourself kindly remembered. I cut up and salted the hog and had a talk with an old man named Victor on tanning. I rode out for the cow I saw the other day but could not find her. After dinner I rode to Wright's for the papers. I went down to the prairie to hunt Mr. Ludewig's steers, without finding them. I rode home in the dark, without a trail or road, traveling by instinct. It must be past midnight, the evening having passed so pleasantly in the perusal of my mail matter.

The cow I have been attending to on the flats was killed by a big lobo wolf. I watched by her carcass last night but did not get a chance to shoot him. This morning I pegged out the hide. She was a fine young milk cow. I expect I have already lost half of my last year's calves.

January 24 (Thursday)

The hog is spoiling, all the meat not preserved by the salt, and if this weather lasts till tomorrow, we will lose it all. I have sacrificed ten or 12 calves to get milk and laid out about seven dollars for corn and watched over him for nearly a year, and now I may see it all spoil. I rode to McKenzie's for some saltpeter [a food preservative] which I ground up with salt and rubbed on the pork. Rode out and brought home a cow and watered my horses.

January 25 (Friday)

Last night the desired norther came up and today it has been cold. Although the pork will be strong, it will make bacon. I attended to it first thing and then nailed up a half hide I had cleaned. By this time Victor came along and as he wished to stay, I let him, as he promised to teach me his system of tanning.

The rest of the day was trifled away talking to him till I took a ride down the prairie and came home at dusk. I found a turkey roost. I passed this evening talking to Victor, who is a man of good taste and information, having been in Texas over 30 years. He is an excellent tanner and dresses hides in a beautiful way. I hope we may be of service to each other, but I rather doubt it.

January 26 (Saturday)

I was fixing a barrel for dressing hides and saw to the meat and then spent the rest of the day talking to Victor. Jack Helm came by.

January 27 (Sunday)

Adolph, his wife and Ellen took dinner with us, but left soon afterwards.

January 28 (Monday)

With the help of Victor, I sawed a large willow log into pieces for saddle trees and did various other jobs.

January 29 (Tuesday)

Skinned a yearling that drowned in the river and limed the hide. Victor left for Corpus to get alum. I am preparing a saddle tree for Mr. Simons. I rode out to Blucher's Ranch to kill some turkeys, but did not get any.

January 30 (Wednesday)

I put out some poison for the big wolf that is so bold that it comes and howls close to the house. This morning the poison was gone but I could not find the wolf. I worked on the hides and leather and marked the calves in the pen. Victor returned after dark.

January 31 (Thursday)

Worked on a saddle tree and in the evening hunted again for a turkey.

February 1 (Friday)

I was starting to Corpus and it looked like rain but I went anyway. I traded a hide, some eggs and butter in payment for a barrel of flour and bought some sugar and coffee. Found a letter from brother William and from Mr. Hogarth. I mailed a New York paper to my mother, which contained my song, "The Two Twelve Pounders."

February 2 (Saturday)

Victor showed me how to dress some hides, he having a sheepskin, a wolf skin, a coonskin, and a beautiful leopard skin to dress. After dinner I killed a yearling and took half the meat to the old folks.

February 3 (Sunday)

Called on the Wright's and rode by Couling's, leaving a paper. Victor had an acquaintance come to stay all night. I allowed him to camp outside, as he was a stranger to me.

February 4 (Monday)

Worked on hides and cattle all day. Had a fuss with Victor, who is trying to impose on me.

February 5 (Tuesday)

Victor left this morning in a huff. I worked all day with the horses and cattle and hides. Smith came at dusk and had supper with us, again offering to sell me his sheep.[273]

February 6 (Wednesday)

I worked at several different jobs. There are more prairie fires to be seen at night than I can remember.[274]

February 7 (Thursday)

I worked all day covering a saddle tree.

February 8 (Friday)

I commenced another saddle tree and worked small pieces of leather. The weather was too cold to do much.

February 9 (Saturday)

All the water vessels were covered with ice. I jobbed around the house all day.

February 10 (Sunday)

The river is getting salty and the ground is too hard and dry for those who waited to plant. It looks like it will be a

---

[273] Noakes visited the sheep ranch on Lagarto Creek owned by partners named Jacobs and Smith, who offered to sell him their sheep for $2 a head. Noakes wrote then that Smith wanted to return to England and Jacobs was tired of tending sheep.

[274] Before there were fences, cattle ranchers started range fires to burn off brush. The fires had the added advantage of encouraging a fresh growth of grass in the spring. Once ranchers began to enclose their pastures with fences, the practice of range burning stopped and then the mesquite, huisache and prickly pear spread over what had once been lush grass-covered prairies.

dry spring. Rode to McKenzie's with the papers. I offered my place and cattle to Mr. [Willis] Moore. I have made up my mind to sell out if I can.

February 11 (Monday)

I rode to Corpus to get Judge Neal's signature to confirm that of the county clerk to a certificate and a deed of conveyance sent to me from England by the law firm of Gill and Wooley. I obtained all the necessary signatures, had a talk with Schubert and stayed with Adolph all night. I met a Mr. Gray from San Diego.

February 12 (Tuesday)

Went back to Corpus and took some butter and eggs but gave them to Adolph since I could not sell them. I returned home and began a letter to Gill and Wooley.

February 13 (Wednesday)

I rode up to Stevens and brought home my pig. Did the usual jobs and finished the letter to Gill and Wooley and enclosed the required documents.

February 14 (Thursday)

Went to Corpus and mailed the deed of conveyance and documents to Gill and Wooley. Took dinner at Adolph's. Mr. Maltby, the editor of the Advertiser, told me that my "Rules for Stock Raisers" had been reprinted by several papers.

February 15 (Friday)

Worked on saddle trees.

February 16 (Saturday)

Couling brought me some meat and I took some to the old folks.

February 17 (Sunday)

I amused myself the best I could. I sent another piece to Maltby at the Advertiser.

February 18 (Monday)

Worked on my hides all day.

February 19 (Tuesday)

I worked on the hides and saddle tree and repaired a chair for Mrs. Blackwell.

February 20 (Wednesday)

I worked on the hides and rode among the cattle. After supper I walked up to Willis Moore's place to a dance. I stood in the dark looking into a dark room from which came the scraping of a fiddle. There were some males and females going through the motions of what they consider dancing. I talked with my neighbors for five minutes in the dark, and my cup of enjoyment being as full as it would get, I walked home, which ended my night of dissipation.

February 21 (Thursday)

I rode out among the cattle and horses and branded a cow and calf.

February 22 (Friday)

I found one of my yearlings dead. I skinned it and worked on hides till night.

February 23 (Saturday)

I did my usual work. I pulled two dead calves out of the river. Another one I pulled out was alive. I killed and skinned it. I took the brains and boiled them and put them on a cloth to dry.

February 24 (Sunday)

I read the paper, the editor of the Advertiser having published the piece I sent him the other day. Marie went fishing and caught some fish for supper.

February 25 (Monday)

Worked as usual.

February 26 (Tuesday)

Covered the saddle tree and rode up to Wright's.

February 27 (Wednesday)

Went to Corpus to get some planks to make a table. The draft from that unfortunate legacy has now been returned three times. I believe the Yankees are trying to swindle me out of it. Bought the usual things and took dinner with Adolph, who has sold all my saddle trees. I also took a picture to a photographer but he did not have much use for it. I made an appointment with a butcher to sell him some beeves. I looked at the operations at the new beef packing company.

February 28 (Thursday)

I commenced on a table for Mr. Byler, using the planks I bought the other day.

March 1 (Friday)

Rode to Tule Lake to meet the Corpus butcher to try and sell him some beeves but I could not find one. Couling and I drove home some cows and calves which we branded in his pen.

March 2 (Saturday)

I finished the table and did the usual things.

March 3 (Sunday)

I read a paper from Sussex, England from mother and a paper from brother Edmond from Mobile, Ala. Did nothing else but walk down to the river to fish.

March 4 (Monday)

It was very cold. I put on several coats and fixed up a place in the old house to smoke the hog meat. I hung it all up and made a smoke. I began a pair of shoes for Marie, working by the fire.

March 5 (Tuesday)

Received a letter from Capt. Alsbury, enclosing a page from the Metropolitan Record in New York on which was my poem, "The Two Twelve Pounders."

March 6 (Wednesday)

I made the boy a pair of shoes out of my own dressed leather. Mr. Byler took the table home, giving me $5 for it.

March 7 (Thursday)

Did the usual things.

March 8 (Friday)

Worked as usual.

March 9 (Saturday)

Wrote to Capt. Alsbury and got some meat from Couling.

March 10 (Sunday)

Rode around all day.

March 11 (Monday)

I commenced a letter to William and worked on my hides and saddle trees.

March 12 (Tuesday)

The usual work on the saddle trees.

March 13 (Wednesday)

Wind very cold. Everything was soon covered with ice, with icicles hanging everywhere. It's the coldest I have ever known for this time of year. Made a pair of shoes for myself.

March 14 (Thursday)

I finished my shoes, put on all the coats I could get on, wrapped a blanket around me, and walked up to Wright's to get the paper. I began a letter to William.[275]

March 15 (Friday)

Just the usual riding around.

March 16 (Saturday)

Several dead cows and horses in the river. Hundreds of cattle are crowding into the river for water. Many of them are so jaded they look as though they have not had water for weeks. They are so weak that when they get into the mud, they get stuck and bog down and die on their feet. There are so many. Couling has been skinning cattle all day. I received six and a half dollars from Wright which he owed me from the proceeds of a sale of a beef.

---

[275] Helen Chapman in Corpus Christi noted in her diary for March 14, 1867 that the severe norther blighted plants all over town.

March 17 (Sunday)

Couling and his son Henry are still skinning cows that have died in the river. I rode around most of the day.

March 18 (Monday)

Rode to Corpus and mailed a letter to Capt. Alsbury and Edmond at Mobile and William in England. Bought lumber to finish the roof. Sold hides, butter and eggs to buy some things for the house. Took dinner at Adolph's and got home after dark.

March 19 (Tuesday)

Worked on the hides and usual jobs until I had to lie down. A coughing spell brought on a hemorrhage from my lungs. I swallowed some salt which stopped it.

March 20 (Wednesday)

I worked on a saddle tree. Had no hemorrhage today.

March 21 (Thursday)

I finished the saddle tree and worked on the hide to cover it.

March 22 (Friday)

I covered the saddle tree. McKenzie brought me 400 feet of lumber to roof the old house.

March 23 (Saturday)

Dry and warm. I marked the calves in the pen. Yesterday Marie got in two cows and I got in one. Rode around till dinner time. In the afternoon I began another saddle tree.

March 24 (Sunday)

Weather dry and cool, wind east. I killed a little calf whose mother had died in the river. I kept it and ourselves from starving, as it was in good order. I cut off the hide, dressed the head for dinner, and divided the meat among the neighbors. I then hauled up a barrel of water and watered the horses. In the evening I rode up to Marie's mother's and called on Mrs. Blackwell on the way, but she wasn't at home. I passed an old cow that needed attending to and drove it home and penned it with the milk cows.

March 25 (Monday)

Weather dry with a raw cold east wind. Worked at the saddle tree, getting it ready to cover, and watered the horses. Wrote a bill of sale for the old man who sold the horse Billy to a man named Kinghorn.

March 26 (Tuesday)

Weather dry, with a warm south wind, rain is badly needed; the ground is quite bare. Cut and cleaned the hide for the saddle tree, worked a piece of leather, sorted and sawed the lumber into suitable lengths for the roof of the old house. I rode out on the mule and cut three forks for saddle trees. I carried everything down to the old house needed to cover the saddle tomorrow. Then I attended to the cows.

March 27 (Wednesday)

Last night there was lightning in the west and this morning the wind freshened from the east and today it is a chilly wind. Covered the saddle tree, grained a calf hide, and attended to the cows. The long-tailed flycatcher has been here for more than a week.

March 28 (Thursday)

Weather fair and cool. I worked on the old house, putting on a roof, but did not finish it. Capt. Anderson took dinner with us.[276]

March 29 (Friday)

No sign of rain yesterday, but in the night, we were awakened by thunder and before daylight we had a good rain. It has rained all day, but it is not cold. I worked in the shed, commencing a stool for the youngest boy to sit on at table. Couling came down and brought us a quarter of a yearling and the hide, which he wanted me to tan and use to

---

[276] Capt. John Anderson, a bay pilot who lived on Water Street in Corpus Christi, ferried freight to and from Nuecestown on his flat-bottom scow, "Flour Bluff."

cover a saddle tree for him. I agreed to do so for two cords of firewood. I worked on another rough saddle tree.

March 30 (Saturday)

Last night we had more thunder and rain and today it rained more or less and the wind from the north was very cold. I worked all day in the shed on the saddle trees I commenced yesterday and I made some soft soap.

March 31 (Sunday)

Weather cold. Did only necessary things and stayed close by the fire.

April 1 (Monday)

Weather fair and warm. I cleaned two hides I had in the house and sawed up a log for saddle lumber and worked on the stool for the boy and rode around.

April 2 (Tuesday)

Warm and cloudy. I cleaned the hide and put it in the gully to soak out the lime. Mended the gallery floor and worked on the boy's stool. After dinner Capt. [John] Anderson came by with his boat, bringing back word of my old boat from way down the river. Was visiting with him most of the evening.

April 3 (Wednesday)

Cloudy and misty, no wind. Covered Couling's saddle. He and Capt. Anderson took supper with us.

April 4 (Thursday)

Weather warm till about two hours after noon and then the wind suddenly changed over to the northeast and blew cold with a little rain. I covered another saddle tree, put a hide in to soak to make leather, and did various jobs in the shed.

April 5 (Friday)

Wind from the east and cool, weather dry. Couling brought me two cords of firewood in payment for his saddle tree. I varnished my best saddle tree and then grained the calf hide I put in soak yesterday, but was worn out before I finished it and put it again to soak. I finished the stool for my boy Nelson to sit on at the table. Had my old boat brought home today.

April 6 (Saturday)

Weather fine and warm. I finished graining the hide and then prepared the "white water" and put it through the first process of dressing along with a small sheepskin. After dinner I rode over and brought home my horses then rigged my new saddle tree.

April 7 (Sunday)

Weather warm and rainy all day, wind south. Marie and I left the boys at the old folks and rode down the prairie and found two calves killed by a panther. One of the calves was my own. We took our dinner, but the misty rain made the ride unpleasant. I penned a cow and a calf for the old folks and brought home one of my own. My health is not as good as it has been.

April 8 (Monday)

Weather fine, but cloudy and warm. I worked on the hide and sheepskin I had cleaned and made Marie a fishing pole. She caught a mess of fish for supper. I then rode up to the Wrights' for the papers and to the old folks, taking some eggs and butter and a saddle tree to send to Corpus to sell. Mr. Ludewig was planning to go down tomorrow. Mr. Moore, my next neighbor, sent me down a yearling hide with which he wants his saddle covered. I put it in lime.

April 9 (Tuesday)

Weather very warm and quite oppressive. I was up early and rode up to Mr. Ludewig's with a note for him to carry to town. I rode among the cattle and found an unmarked yearling, I ran it home, roped it and tied it. I then rode out again and penned a small beef in Couling's pen, but he was not at home so I waited till evening when he and I killed it, as we were in need of fresh meat. I took a quarter of the meat to the old folks.

April 10 (Wednesday)

Last night the wind changed to the east and today it has been quite chilly. I cleaned the hide of Moore's and rode up and fetched back his saddle tree. I rode up to the old folks and when I returned, I prepared Moore's tree, ready for covering. Mr. Wright brought me a Sussex Express from England, a letter and paper from Edmond at Mobile, and a letter from Capt. Alsbury. I received an invitation to a party in the Motts and, for a wonder, passed a pleasant evening.

April 11 (Thursday)

Weather fine. I covered Moore's tree, cleaned a piece of hide, and cut strands for a hide rope.

April 12 (Friday)

Rode to Hinnant's and drove the old man's steers home, cleaned a hide and put it in water, and finished Moore's saddle tree.

April 13 (Saturday)

I rode to Corpus and bought some needles to sew leather, iron to work leather, a graining knife handle, a bushel of salts, and other things. I dined at Adolph's and sent my things home by Mr. Wright. I called on Mrs. Swift and was summoned by the sheriff to be in court next Tuesday.[277]

April 14 (Sunday)

Having to leave on Tuesday, I had to attend to the hide I had in water. The rest of the day I spent on an experiment on horns.

April 15 (Monday)

I put things to right in the old house, put the handle on my graining knife, Moore called and paid me for the saddle tree and I sold him my stirrup leather for $2.50.

April 16 (Tuesday)

I started early for Corpus and managed to get excused from the jury business. A murder was committed last

---

[277] The sheriff then was Henry W. Berry, who was appointed on Sept. 7, 1865 and served until Nov. 1, 1867.

Saturday night (April 13) by a Mexican whose victim was a poor white man who had been working in Corpus Christi only a short time. They had been living in an old house and it is supposed that the Mexican killed him for the little money and clothes he had.

The Mexican was dressed in the dead man man's clothes when he was taken. He killed the man with a dagger and cut him up in a shocking manner. He acknowledged killing the man and said he had killed seven men before and intended to kill more if he could get away. He advised the sheriff that if he wouldn't let him get away then to hang him at once.

I had a look at him in the cage. He was gray-headed with a keen eye and appeared to be an old sinner who looked as though he was quite capable of doing all that he has threatened to do. I rode home in the moonlight.[278]

April 17 (Wednesday)

I rode around among the cattle. I worked till night trying to discover a way to make stirrups out of horns but I have not succeeded.

April 18 (Thursday)

I rode around and worked on leather.

April 19 (Friday)

I put the hide in lime and did odd jobs.

April 20 (Saturday)

Marie went to town this morning for a pleasure trip. I worked all day on hides for saddle trees and went up to

---

[278] This was one of the more sensational murders of the time. Two drifters were squatting in the vacant Meuly house on the bluff, at the corner of Leopard and North Broadway (where the Nixon Building was later constructed). One was an ex-soldier from Brownsville who did odd job on the docks. The other was an old man from Mexico who cooked for him in return for part of his wages. They had a falling out and the ex-soldier was stabbed to death. The killer died in jail before he could be hanged. Anna Moore Schwien in her memoirs and John Dunn in "Perilous Trails of Texas" wrote about this crime.

Wright's to help him kill and skin a cow. I took tea with them, something unusual for me to eat away from home.

April 21 (Sunday)

Lonely but worked as usual all day. Wrote an article for the editor of the Advertiser about the "Eastern People Driving Off Our Yearlings." Expect Marie home tonight. Heigh ho! The youngsters bother me at times but the place is awfully dull without them. Received a letter and its duplicate from Gill and Wooley to inform me that they have received the deed to the land at Polegate which I sent them.

April 22 (Monday)

Sent the piece to the Advertiser and worked on the same old jobs all day.

April 23 (Tuesday)

Covered Henry Couling's saddle tree and filed a saw for Hinnant.

April 24 (Wednesday)

Wind but no rain. Began a saddle tree for Mr. Skinner. I work from sunrise to dark, never get through, and seldom make anything.

April 25 (Thursday)

Marie caught a mess of fish and Mr. Couling and Henry Couling took dinner with us.

April 26 (Friday)

The usual work all day.

April 27 (Saturday)

A nice rain today. The usual jobs.

April 28 (Sunday)

Rode around to see to the horses and read the "Life of Stonewall Jackson." [279]

April 29 (Monday)

Worked on the saddle tree and did the usual work.

---

[279] Probably Robert Dabney's "Life and Campaigns of Lt. Gen. Thomas (Stonewall) Jackson" which was published in 1866.

April 30 (Tuesday)

Commenced another saddle tree and drove home the horses.

May 1 (Wednesday)

Wrote a letter to the Advertiser relative to the improvement of Nueces Bay. A piece of mine was published in last week's Advertiser on "Eastern People Driving Off Our Yearlings."

May 2 (Thursday)

Wrote a letter and worked on the saddle tree.

May 3 (Friday)

The usual busy routine work.

May 4 (Saturday)

Another calf killed by a panther. Cleaned my gun. Henry Couling, Hinnant and myself took the dogs to hunt the panther but failed to find it.

May 5 (Sunday)

Wrote a letter, read a little, and jobbed a little.

May 6 (Monday)

Worked on the saddle tree most of the day.

May 8 (Wednesday)

Rode around among the cattle.

May 9 (Thursday)

Flint called about a saddle tree. Couling helped me kill the bull yesterday, which I divided among the neighbors. Covered a stranger's saddle tree and took it to the old folks to take to town.

May 10 (Friday)

Usual work all day.

May 11 (Saturday)

I went with a bunch of cattle hunters and brought back a large herd, but I got only two. I have had my fill of cattle hunting.

May 12 (Sunday)

Worked all day cutting out my one cow [from the herd brought in]. A day and a half of hard work for 50 cents. Received a letter from Emily and a Sussex Express, which were very welcome. John McGregor brought a saddle tree for a fresh cover.

May 13 (Monday)

Commenced a rough saddle tree for Flint.

May 14 (Tuesday)

The usual work with cows, horses and jobs.

May 15 (Wednesday)

Rode the wildest horse and general jobbing.

May 16 (Thursday)

I covered a saddle tree for John McGregor.

May 17 (Friday)

Worked all day on Moore's Mexican's saddle tree.

May 18 (Saturday)

I wrote a piece for the Advertiser and did the usual jobs.

May 19 (Sunday)

I had a good wash and after dinner I commenced a letter to mother.

May 20 (Monday)

Henry Couling helped me pull a cow out of the river, but it died and I skinned her and put the hide in lime.

May 21 (Tuesday)

I cleaned the calf skin and worked on a panther skin Hinnant sent down to dress for Mr. Nickerson.

May 22 (Wednesday)

Same as yesterday.

May 23 (Thursday)

I cleaned and cut a cow hide into pieces for a saddle tree. After dinner I wrote a letter to Capt. Alsbury and rode to Wright's and Couling's. He brought me home three cows and calves. And then rode to Hinnant's, where I got a piece of meat.

May 24 (Friday)

I rode to Corpus to get some flour. I bought a barrel full, some alum, a coat and pants. I sent a saddle tree down by Wright who brought back the barrel of flour.[280] There was a big rain last night and the flats are covered with water. I found the effects of the storm in Corpus severe; several buildings were struck by lightning.[281]

May 25 (Saturday)

I promised my wife a holiday today to go fishing. Ellen and Adolph's wife Maggie agreed to come down. The first thing I found was that four of my horses were gone. I had to ride hard till afternoon to hunt them, but was unsuccessful. I came home and we started down to the river. Then Shumate came along with a panther skin and we skinned it. I fished for half an hour without success then quit. After supper I walked home with Ellen and Maggie.

May 26 (Sunday)

I rode till noon as hard as I could but saw nothing of my horses.

May 27 (Monday)

I rode out 30 miles in search of my four colts, which were still away. I had to come home without the horses. When I reached home, Wilson brought around letters by Couling as Mr. Wilson had chosen me to witness for him in an arbitration case. We talked about this till near sundown. We will meet tomorrow with Moore at Littig's to decide the matter. Ellen came down.

---

[280] On many of Noakes' shopping trips to Corpus Christi he went on horseback and would have his heavier purchases brought home by Mr. Ludewig or one of his other neighbors with a cart or wagon.

[281] Maria Blucher in a letter to her parents described the "terrible thunderstorm." It destroyed a roof and brickyard of James Downing and E. H. Wheeler, ripped away the cross from the Catholic Church, and lightning struck the Cahill house and a ship in the harbor. Ref. "Maria von Blucher's Corpus Christi."

May 28 (Tuesday)

We all met per agreement but not having the form of agreement there, we adjourned till later. Mr. Grayson came along for his saddle tree, paying me $4 dollars for it and taking it down after dinner. I rode till night in a vain hunt for the horses.

May 29 (Wednesday)

I wrote a letter to Gill and Wooley and rode down through the timber and found the old mare had a colt. I continued on my way to the big prairie and finally found the young horses and started home but on the way, I managed to lose three of the four again. I looked for them, but darkness was coming on and I went home.

May 30 (Thursday)

I rode down to Corpus with Mr. Clark, a large cattle raiser. I took down another saddle tree. I found a Mobile paper from Edmond. I was compelled to go and report my income to the tax collector. I took dinner at Adolph's and rode to the prairie west of the Oso where I was in hopes of finding my horses but was unsuccessful. I returned to the old folks at sundown. I helped Mr. Wright unload a barrel of flour from his cart and passed the evening there.

May 31 (Friday)

I met the arbitration parties at Willis Moore's and by noon we brought the matter to a settlement. I then rode down to the prairie looking for my horses and came upon them and was driving them home when they made a stampede and I lost them again. I found them by hard riding.

June 1 (Saturday)

I was up at the old folks until noon talking with Mr. Flint. When I returned Mr. Nickerson was here and I rode back with him after dinner.

June 2 (Sunday)

The mosquitoes stampeded my horses during the night and the gray colt tied to a log dragged it a long distance. Shumate and Moore came along to get me to go with them on a hunt with the hounds. We killed a short-tailed tiger cat and a raccoon. I skinned the cat and staked the hide. After dinner I took the dogs and went out alone but found nothing.

June 3 (Monday)

I rode up to the Motts. Joe Wright and I drove down two cows with calves which Joe had brought for me. We penned them. I gave Joe $1 for helping with the calves. After dinner I rode to the woods and brought home four forks for saddle trees.

June 4 (Tuesday)

We have to make smoke each night and pen up the horses, which are driven frantic by the biting and swarming of mosquitoes. I am working on the tiger-cat skin.

June 5 (Wednesday)

I rode the gray colt over to see Shumate, Moore and William Ball on business.[282] I then worked on the sole leather and made a pair of boots for Shoemaker.

June 6 (Thursday)

Worked as usual all day. I rode the gray colt to Couling's and roped two yearlings, which we branded.

June 7 (Friday)

Worked all day with my cattle.

June 8 (Saturday)

Went up to the old folks, having agreed to get them potatoes from Page's, but they had already got them.

June 9 (Sunday)

Passed the day at the old folks. Adolph and Maggie came from town.

---

[282] William A. Ball, from Tennessee, moved to Nuecestown in the 1850s. He owned a ranch and was later justice of the peace.

June 10 (Monday)

I commenced on a saddle tree.

June 11 (Tuesday)

Worked all day on a saddle tree.

June 12 (Wednesday)

I made a rope and tied out the black colt. A thundershower came up and gave him a scare. He took a sudden run at his rope, threw himself, broke this doubled-up rope, and dashed off for the woods. Went to hunt him without luck.

June 13 (Thursday)

Worked as usual all day. I rode the gray colt to Couling's and roped two yearlings, which we branded. Yesterday as I was returning home, I found a cow in the thicket. Then my lead rope broke and away she went. I worked hard all day and accomplished nothing. It is useless for an unlucky man to try. I promised several saddle trees by the end of the week but I cannot get time to make them. My horse that ran off yesterday is worth more than the $10 dollars in rope, headstall and good saddle which he took away. It is enough to drive a man out of his wits. The time spent hunting unpenned cattle and horses is time wasted.

June 14 (Friday)

Same as every other day.

June 15 (Saturday)

Same as before.

June 16 (Sunday)

Same again.

June 17 (Monday)

Same as before.

June 18 (Tuesday)

Same.

***

The last of Noakes' journals that have survived ends on June 18, 1867 with the notation that he was engaged in doing the same old chores. Noakes' first journal, which covered his early years in Corpus Christi, was lost. So was his last journal or journals, which no doubt included entries from the summer of 1867 until his death. Several of his journals were believed burned in the Nuecestown Raid in 1875.[283]

The events surrounding the opening of Noakes' store would have been detailed in that last diary. Noakes sold land he inherited at Polegate, England. Perhaps the proceeds from that legacy helped finance his opening of a general store in Nuecestown. The Weekly Advertiser in March 1869 carried a note that "T. J. Noakes has opened a new store at Nuecestown, which is generally referred to as the Motts. Noakes advises that he will pay the highest prices for hides and peltries."

A post office was established in the store by 1869 and Noakes was made postmaster. Another ad in the Weekly Gazette in 1873 said, "Thomas J. Noakes, Dealer in General Merchandise, Nuecestown, Texas. Wool and Hides taken in Trade or for Cash."

Noakes' store was a central point of the community of the Motts, when it was burned in the bandit raid that began in the last week

---

[283] For the story of the Nuecestown Raid, sometimes called the Noakes Raid, see John Dunn's account, Appendix 8, and Thomas Noakes' account, Appendix 9.

of March 1875. 33 bandits from below the border stole horses at ranches near Tule Lake and took captives they encountered on the road.

When Noakes saw the bandits ride up in front of his store, and saw some of his friends being held captive, he got his Winchester. As a bandit raised his pistol to shoot a man named Smith, a customer in the store, Noakes shot the bandit in the chest. Noakes' account of the raid and the burning of his store was written three weeks after the event. Noakes was able to buy out the general store business of W. S. McGregor and continued to operate a store two miles from his original site. —M. G.

* * *

Thomas John Noakes died on March 7, 1877, at the age of 45. The cause of death was not listed, but he had only one functioning lung and had long suffered with congestive chest problems. His obituary three days later in the Weekly Gazette said, "We are pained to announce the death of Mr. T. J. Noakes of Nuecestown, which occurred on Wednesday morning at his home. Deceased had many friends and was well-known as an energetic, intelligent and upright business man and merchant. His store with contents was burned by Mexican raiders in 1874 (sic: 1875) thus destroying the accumulation of years, but deceased had recovered a good business since. Our sympathies to the afflicted family."

Noakes was buried at his own request close to the family home in a mott of trees on a hillside overlooking the Nueces River. It was on his own little patch of America, though far from his beloved England.

After the Nuecestown Raid Noakes was supposed to have buried a cache of $3,000 in gold and silver coins and told no one where it was hidden, not even Marie. He had buried his valuables before, during the war, when it was feared that Yankee troops would make a raid on the Motts. For a long time after Noakes' death, treasure-seekers in search of the cache of coins dug so many holes that the Noakes' place, said a grandson, "looked like Gopher Hill."

Two months after Noakes' death, on May 21, 1877, his widow Marie was appointed postmaster at Nuecestown to succeed her husband; she was re-appointed two years later, on May 8, 1879. She continued to operate the Noakes store and soon married a man named Walter Hipp, who had been a Union soldier during the Civil War. Marie had husbands from both sides of that war. She had two more children by Walter Hipp. Marie (who was also known as Mary) died in San Antonio on Dec. 9, 1929 when she was 87 years old.

The body of Thomas John Noakes and that of an unidentified child (probably Mary Noakes, who died in infancy) were dug up by a bulldozer during construction work on the site. They were reburied in Rose Hill Cemetery in May 1965.

I was surrounded by my work material — old copies of the diaries, notebooks, stick-it notes of stray facts — and saw amid the jumble the self-drawn portrait of Noakes. Someone, not me, had written on the bottom, "a long-suffering and tormented man." And so he was, to judge by his own words. Maybe he was happy near the end, but in the time that his diaries were written, from 1858 to 1867, he was a man who seemed always out of place, even in his own life, always up against the world. He always doubted whether he was doing any good, whether he was accomplishing anything.

On July 29, 1865 he wrote, "I do not intend to remain at the Motts if I can help it." He repeated that sentiment more than once. But he struggled on and persevered until, at the end, he finally escaped of the grinding poverty that so weighed him down.

When the body of Thomas Noakes was moved, in 1965, there was no Nuecestown, no Motts. The people all moved away, vacated the houses, and the town was emptied. The town just vanished. You can breathe on a mirror and leave a fine mist. Wait a second and it has disappeared. Like a dying breath. And so it was with Nuecestown, the Motts of Thomas Noakes. In that great length of time that is beyond our comprehension and the measurement of man, one moment it was there, the next it was gone.

APPENDIX 1
HUNTING CATTLE

Before there were roundups there were "cow hunts." Neighbors would gather and go out as a group, usually referred to as a "crowd," looking for each other's cattle that had strayed. In that unfenced world, cattle could range from 50 to 100 miles away and get mixed with other cattle.

Sometimes up to a dozen men or more would take part. Each man would take his own provisions, carried in a "wallet," a sack with both ends sewed up with a slit in the middle, and he would take along two or even three extra horses.

The cattle hunters in a "crowd" would ride over great distances, rounding up all the cattle into a large herd. They would pen the cattle at some nearby ranch and go to work cutting out and separating cattle with the brands of those in the hunt or of their neighbors. Unbranded calves would be watched to see which cow it followed, and then branded accordingly.

One description of a cow hunt after the war came from a letter by Lee Moore, a Texas trail driver, as quoted in "The Day of the Cattleman":

"We didn't call it a roundup in those days. We called it cow-hunts and every man on this cow-hunt was a cattle owner just home from the war and went out to see what they had left and brand up. I was the only boy on this cow-hunt and was looking out for cattle that belonged to my father. We would corral the cattle every night and stand guard around the corral. I didn't stand any guard but carried brush and cornstalks and anything I could get to make a light for those who were on guard to play poker by. They played for unbranded cattle, yearlings at 50 cents a head and the top price for any class was $5 a head, so if anyone ran out of cattle and had a little money, he could get back in the game. For $10, say, he could get a stack of yearlings. Every few days they would divide up and brand and each man take his cattle home."

The cow hunts could be brutal. Horses were gored, young calves were trampled to death in the pens, and cows could get their necks broken in the process of roping,

The ungentle methods of handling cattle were described by J. Frank Dobie who wrote in "A Vaquero of the Brush Country" that one way to subdue a wild steer was to shoot him through the horns. The pain would make him easier to handle. Sometimes they missed and the animal was killed. The old cow hunts, said Dobie, were no place for a member of the humane society.

Noakes criticized the "excessive cruelty" practiced by the cattle hunters and wrote that, "A man must leave his feelings at home when he starts cattle hunting. Those with anything like a sensitive nature had better not start."

—Murphy Givens

APPENDIX 2
LAND-SELLING SCHEME

The frontier settlement of Corpus Christi was the destination for English families who invested their savings and their lives on the basis of a sales scheme by Henry Kinney. Many of these immigrants settled in and around Nuecestown.

Kinney was in debt in the early 1850s though he had 300,000 acres to sell. He sent John Holbein to England and hired an agent in London, Henry Moss, to manage a sales office. Handbills under the heading of the Nueces Land and Emigration Company praised the unlimited opportunities of South Texas and the boundlessly fertile "green and verdant" land. Kinney's land agents distributed 20,000 handbills.

Kinney offered to sell 100 acres at one dollar an acre. With the purchase of 100 acres he would provide the buyer with a yoke of oxen, a horse, 10 cows, and a town lot in Nuecestown. The handbill said, "Two full crops of corn and other cereals in perfection are secured annually. Irish and sweet potatoes, with all other roots and vegetables, make huge returns. The peach, the vine, and other fruit trees thrive luxuriantly. Corpus Christi, situated in the vicinity of this property, is a town of considerable commercial activity and is fast rising in importance."

The sales pitch was fraudulent but it reached an eager audience. Families used their savings to make a down payment on the land and pay the ship's fare to Texas. Joseph Almond, John Wade, and Robert Adams Sr. paid for Kinney land. Joseph Wright tried to determine the character and honesty of Kinney and his agents, but his suspicions were put to rest and he bought 320 acres, which meant he also got three town lots in Nuecestown. Others made a down payment on land and took passage to Texas on the basis of the handbills.

The Almond and Wade families boarded the schooner Essex in October 1852. Almond had just wed Lizzie Wade. Her father, mother, and brother were also going to Texas. After eight weeks at sea they arrived at New Orleans, took a steamer to Galveston, boarded a smaller ship for Indianola, then took the mail boat to Corpus Christi. They landed at Ohler's Wharf. We can imagine their disappointment. The handbills described Corpus Christi as a busy market town of commercial importance. But it was a small frontier settlement with a few stores. That was their first shock. The "green and verdant" land was another. What they found was brush country covered with underground mesquite roots. This "mesquite land" was fine for grazing but not for plowing. If crops could have been grown, there was no market within reach. Robert Adams Sr. made a down payment on 100 acres but when he saw the land, he didn't take possession and lost his down payment. He became a tenant farmer then a butcher in town.

These were terrible times for Kinney's immigrants, but they were extraordinary people. After long years of privation and want, Kinney's English immigrants began to prosper. Joseph Almond became a wealthy sheepman. His neighbor George Reynolds established the 49,000-acre Palo Ventana ranch. The Adams' boys, Robert and William, became prosperous sheepmen, then cattle ranchers, in the Nueces Valley. The English settlers of the early 1850s did find a rosy future, though they had been conned and taken in by the glowing sales pitch in Henry Kinney's handbills. That's how so many English immigrants were found among Thomas John Noakes' neighbors at the Motts.

—Murphy Givens

APPENDIX 3
THE NOLAN BROTHERS

The Nolan brothers, Thomas and Matthew, were Irish orphans who became central figures in the early history of Corpus Christi. Matthew was born in 1834, Tom in 1836, probably in Providence, Rhodes Island. When their parents died, the young brothers joined the army as bugle boys. Matt was 12 and Tom was 10.

The brothers were stationed with the Second Dragoons at Corpus Christi in 1845 and early 1846. As bugle boys, Matthew and Tom served throughout the Mexican War until the war ended in 1848. They returned to Corpus Christi.

Tom joined the Texas Rangers and served with Captain John Grumbles. Matthew also joined the Rangers and served with "Rip" Ford. In 1858, Matthew, aged 24, was elected sheriff of Nueces County. He hired his brother Tom as a deputy sheriff.

On Aug. 4, 1860, a drunken butcher named John Warren stabbed James Barnard, the owner of the La Retama Saloon on Chaparral. Sheriff Mat Nolan and Deputy Tom Nolan found Warren in Richardson's store. Warren leveled a six-shooter and said, "Stand back or I'll shoot!"

Tom grabbed for the gun and was shot in the head. Mat winged Warren as he ran away. Other men, hearing the shots, joined Nolan and helped to chase Warren into Zeigler's Hall, where he was shot to death, his body riddled with bullets.

Thomas Nolan died 11 days later, on Aug. 15, 1860. He was 24. The obituary in the Ranchero said, "Reared in arms, educated on battlefields, the thunder of cannon and the whizzing of shells, shot or bullets was familiar music to Thomas Nolan."

When the Civil War broke out, Matthew Nolan raised a company of volunteers and served on the border in Rip Ford's command. He was at the battle of Galveston in January 1863. On Dec. 22, 1864, Nolan was shot on Mesquite Street by two brothers. As he was dying, Nolan said he knew why the Gravis boys had shot him but died before he could explain. He was buried in Bayview Cemetery next to his brother Tom. His headstone, like his brother's, cites that he was with Company G of the Second U.S. Dragoons.

—Murphy Givens

APPENDIX 4
MUSTER ROLLS

Roll of Reserve Company, Nueces County Precinct Two (Nuecestown), June 14, 1861

Frank Byler, captain; Thomas John Noakes, 1st lieutenant; John Emory Frost, 2nd lieutenant; Dennis McCoy, 1st sergeant; Thomas Beynon, 2nd sergeant; George Reynolds, 3rd sergeant; Henry D. Allen, 4th sergeant; William A. Ball, 1st corporal; James Hobbs Jr., 2nd corporal; John Wade, 3rd corporal; Thomas Charles Wright, 4th corporal; Samuel Page, J. E. Stevens, Jacob Matson, L. A. Edgerley, Oscar M. Edgerley, J. McGowan, Charles Shaw, William Gore, William Rhea, John Williams, Joseph S. Glenn, William Cody, James Mahon, William P. Terrell, William Murdock, Samuel Coling [Couling], John Hinnant, Robert Spence, Daniel McIntyre, Daniel P. Hurst, Horace Blaney, Samuel Stevenson, William Hughes, William Gibbs, Benjamin Gibbs, James Gibbs Jr., Robert Kingham, Richard Gallagher, Jonathan Vining, privates.

Capt. Mat Nolan's Company of Mounted Rangers, Feb. 23, 1861

Mat Nolan, captain; Reuben Holbein, 1st lieutenant; John Millican, 2nd lieutenant; Osborn Dalton, 3rd lieutenant; Richard Kennon, surgeon; Thomas Bradley, 1st sergeant; William George, 2nd sergeant; Peter Mullen, 3rd sergeant; William McGregor, 4th sergeant; Samuel Tinney, 5th

sergeant; William Hobbs, 1st corporal; Richard Brown, 2nd corporal; John Cannon, 3rd corporal; Samuel Clymer, 4th corporal; Peter Brodigan, 5th corporal; Juan Hinojosa, farrier; Michael Croghean, blacksmith; John McGregor, bugler; William Averill, James Brockius, James R. Barnard; William B. Burdett, William Cannon, Jordan Clark, Hugh Dale, George Drew, Peter Farrell, George Grissom, Alfred Hutchison, Michael A. Highland, James M. Hunter, James Hooper, Herbert G. Henson, George Hobbs, Russell Hudson, James Kiser, Chester Kenelly, John Kelly, Charles Kerr, Fernando Lopez, William McMahan, John McMahan, John Myers, William W. Martin, A. DeLeon Moses, Joseph Morrel, Douglas McDonald, Michael B. McGarey, William McKinney, James McKinney, Richard McFadden, James C. Nix, Arthur H. Neal, Justice S. Odom, John A. Polk Jr., James Perkins, Thomas S. Parker, Matt Roberts, Ephraim S. Spalding, John S. Swope, James G. Timmons, Edward Taylor, David Thalheimer, James H. Walker, Elias Wallace, George F. Wright, William F. Worth, Jesus Hinojosa, Martin Hinojosa, privates.[284]

—Compiled by Dan Kilgore

[284] Nolan's full muster roll shows that 44 men in his company joined at Brownsville and were mainly from the border area. Another 72 signed up at Banquete and these included men from Corpus Christi, Santa Margarita, San Patricio and Nuecestown. Only those who joined at Banquete are listed.

APPENDIX 5
GATHERING SALT

When Union warships blockaded Southern ports in the Civil War, salt became a valuable commodity. With foreign supplies shut off, the price of salt rose from 60 cents a bushel to $20 dollars a bushel. It was so scarce people dug up smokehouse floors to sift the dirt for traces of salt.

Without refrigeration, salt was essential to keep meat from spoiling. There could be no salt pork without salt and Confederate soldiers lived on a diet of salt meat. At home, salt became so scarce that it became a medium of exchange, good as gold.

The demand for salt gave South Texas, rich in saline deposits, a strategic importance. The oldest and largest salt deposits in South Texas were located in Hidalgo and Willacy counties.

Salt was also gathered on the shores of Laguna Madre. Robert Adams, an early pioneer, worked gathering salt during the war. "When the water came in high, it filled the shallow lakes; when the water receded, the salt could be gathered," he said once in an interview. "It was in small grains, the size of peas, and you had to rake it out of the water. We would pile the salt on the bank and let it drain, then put it in sacks and buckets. Wagons used for hauling the salt were pulled by six yoke of oxen. I used to carry salt on my back to the wagons. The salt was wet and the brine ran down my back. I guess I got pickled in those days."

Salt was also gathered along the shores of Baffin Bay, which was called the Salt Lagoon back then. Noakes made several trips to Baffin Bay to get cart-loads of salt to trade for food, traveling to Goliad, Refugio and Beeville and even as far as New Braunfels. He would trade it for bacon, cornmeal, sweet potatoes or Yankee dollars.

After Union forces under Gen. Nathaniel Banks occupied the barrier islands, troops left to garrison Mustang Island spent much of their time trying to disrupt the salt trade. They used small boats to try to capture salt barges on the Laguna Madre. The Union soldiers were under orders to dissolve the cargoes of salt if they could not capture it. They dissolved it by dumping it back into the sea from where it came. One might think an invading army would have higher priorities, but this was a part of the Union strategy to deprive the South of essentials, such as salt.

After the war, salt was still in high demand for to preserve meat and salt down the hides at the beef-packing houses that dotted the coast. Salt was hauled from the Laguna Madre on shallow-draft boats to a wind-powered gristmill on Water Street built by Capt. John Anderson. The salt was ground at Anderson's gristmill for the packing houses and for table use.

The salt beds of the Laguna Madre and Baffin Bay were wiped clean by the hurricanes of 1874 and 1875.

—Murphy Givens

APPENDIX 6
THE TWO TWELVE POUNDERS

On the thirteenth day of August in the year of sixty-two
The Yanks to Corpus Christi came, to show what they could do.
To teach the Texan Rebels with what valor they could fight,
By the taking of our city, and the putting us to flight.

They came up with their gunboats and their guns of largest weight
With their rifles and their pivot guns and percussion shells so great,
With which they proudly boasted they could blow us to the sky,
If we would not surrender, and to their terms comply.

Chorus

I tell you what it is, and I want you all to know,
That western Texas ne'er was whipped as I can plainly show!
We cared not for their gunboats, their cannon and their shell,
For with our two twelve-pounders we whipped the Yankees well.

We were short of ammunition and our guns were rather small
As two condemned twelve-pounders were what we had in all,
Yet Billy Mann decided in the darkness of the night
That before the Yankees should take us, they must whip us in a fight.

And so the guns by starlight were planted on the beach,
So close to where they anchored that their gunboats we could reach.
While the Yankees slept in silence we were fixing for the fray,
And at noon the ball we opened and at them blazed away.

Repeat Chorus

We fired into their steamship, the "Sachem" was its name.
And the splinters quickly flew about, and the Yankees did the same.
And we could not keep from yelling as we saw them scramble out
When our round shot broke their slumbers and smashed her hull about.

382

But soon they opened on us, and then commenced the fun,
For their shot and shell came pouring in, but each stuck to his gun,
The shells broke close around us and the long balls whistled through
But to dismount our little guns was more than they could do.

Repeat Chorus

For two long days they fought us, but our scare had not begun,
As Hobby, Ware and Ireland were not the men to run.
When they landed at the Rincon, our battery to take,
Our boys with rusty shotguns for their boats quick made them break!

And yet with all their thundering fuss, our "Confed" they killed,
Who with Shaw's dog and two old cows, was all the blood they spilled.
So finding Corpus was a place that Yankees could not fight,
They left it to us Rebels and skedaddled out of sight.

Repeat Chorus

But now the war is over and the Southern cause is done,
For the Yanks have moved too much for us but dearly have their won!
Though they claim the whole Confederacy, they never whipped this end,
But as they have taken both our guns, we too, must condescend.

Though we beat them back at Corpus and on the prairies round,
Yet our leaders have surrendered, so to do the same we're bound,
But if the Yanks spite us much, and do not treat us well,
We'll get ourselves two more old guns and again we will rebel.

—Thomas Noakes, February 1866

383

APPENDIX 7
THE GARNER LYNCHING

On May 15, 1866, Jim Garner went to Emanuel Scheuer's store on Chaparral and tried on a pair of boots. Garner and Scheuer knew each other; both had served in Capt. W.S. Shaw's Confederate militia company in 1861. Muster rolls list Scheuer as a corporal and Garner a private. At the store, Garner started to leave without paying for the boots and Scheuer stopped him, saying he wouldn't give him credit.

Garner pulled out his pistol and shot Scheuer, killing him instantly. The store where the shooting took place was in the 300 block of Chaparral in the Staples building. People came by to look at Scheuer's body, laid out on his own counter.[285]

John Fogg, who operated a stagecoach line, ran to Noessel's store on the corner and grabbed a long coil of rope. Others hustled the still-drunk killer across the street, looking for a place to hang him. Garner must have been sobering up. He pleaded with the mob, "Give me a trial, boys, give me a trial!" They might have listened except that Garner was a known killer. Ten years before, when he was 15, he killed a man named Bateman on Christmas Eve in a Helena saloon in Karnes County. He was also considered a loafer with a violent temper.

The mob looked at the sign over the Noessel store for place to throw their rope, but Mrs. Noessel stopped them. They could not use her store to hang him. The mob,

---

[285] Emanuel Scheuer was one of three brothers who emigrated to Corpus Christi from Germany. The 1860 Census lists them as Maritz, 23, Ludwig, 25, and Emanuel, 27.

dragging Garner along, went down to the next block of Chaparral and stopped at the Meuly house, a two-store home with a wrought iron grillwork. But Mrs. Meuly also prevented them from using her place for the lynching.

They came to an arroyo at the south end of Chaparral, past Cooper's Alley, where there were several stunted hackberry and mesquite trees and one of the mesquites had a limb a little higher than a man's neck. Over the mesquite limb went a 30-foot rope and a dozen hands grabbed for it, holding it stretched tight as Garner kicked and strangled to death.

Capt. John Anderson helped hold the rope and said the crowd was very quiet. W. S. Rankin said the sight of the hanged man haunted him for a long time. "I didn't sleep a wink for a week. His tongue stuck out. I couldn't shut my eyes without seeing that tongue sticking out." Eli Merriman later wrote that on the morning after the hanging the dead man's father (John Garner) came to take away the body. He didn't seem to be all that upset, said Merriman, and claimed that he had acquired a good stake rope by the operation. Helen Chapman wrote in her diary — "A terrible tragedy just enacted. An unoffending good citizen shot dead by a drunken loafing scoundrel who had killed several men before. About 50 citizens carried the murderer to the edge of town and hung him at once."

—Murphy Givens

APPENDIX 8
NUECESTOWN RAID

Red John Dunn

On the morning of the 26th of April 1875, my brother Matt and I, together with Pat and George Dunn, rode to town to look after some business. We had just returned home and unsaddled our horses when one of the Stevens boys from Tule Lake came in a run and handed us a note.

The note was from my cousin John Dunn telling us that Mexican bandits were robbing the Page house at Tule Lake. He told us to hurry up and come and that he would join us as we passed his house. He also told us to send the Stevens' boy to town as quickly as possible, as he was also sending a letter to John McClane, the sheriff, telling him to send men to help as there would be only four of us against about seventy Mexican bandits.

After starting Stevens to town, we re-saddled our horses and started in a gallop for Tule Lake. As we passed John Dunn's place, he joined us and we went on, feeling that it would be but a few moments until a company with rifles headed by the sheriff would be with us.

When we arrived at (Samuel) Page's place, we found no one there but two girls, one of them being a Miss Louisa Rains, a sister of Mrs. Charles Gollihar of Sunshine, Texas; and a daughter of Mr. Page. They told us that when the raiders had taken everything that they wanted they took all the men on the place prisoners and started toward the Juan Saenz ranch. At that time the ranch was considerably larger than it is now. We started out after the Mexican raiders.

When we arrived at Juan Saenz, we found the raiders busy rounding up the stock and the prisoners. They had the latter lined up against George Frank's store. We took a position about a thousand or eight hundred yards from them, where we could see everything that took place and also watch the road.

It had now been three hours since we had sent word to town and we had received no aid as yet. John Dunn told us that if we would keep watch he would go to town and see if he could raise a few men.

John Dunn took a shortcut and started off at a gallop. Shortly after he left, Sidney Borden, a merchant and justice of the peace at Sharpsburg, came driving up in his buggy. We stopped him, showed him the Mexican raiders and told him what they were doing and advised him to turn back. He stated that he did not think they would molest him and drove on. We saw three Mexicans ride out to where he was approaching and escort him over to where the prisoners were. It seemed that there were more people traveling the road that day than we had ever seen in a day before.

Shortly after Sidney Borden's capture, Mike Dunn, a brother of John Dunn, drove up in a buggy right into the midst of the Mexicans. The leader rode out and stopped him, taking a Sharp's carbine that Mike had in the buggy and told him to hand over his ammunition. He had only four or five cartridges in his pocket, which he gave them. The leader told Mike to tell his wife, who was with him, not to be uneasy, that she would not be harmed.

While rounding up the prisoners, the Mexican bandits drove a bunch of other Mexicans out of a jacal and started them to where the other prisoners were under guard. While on the way, one of the new prisoners wheeled around and started to run back toward the jacal. One of the raiders put his Winchester to the man's head and blew his brains out. Later we learned that the unfortunate man was an idiot.

It was now beginning to grow late. We feared that perhaps John Dunn must have been waylaid, as it did not seem reasonable that people would act in that manner, refusing to send help. When the raiders were ready to leave the Juan Saenz ranch, they rounded up all the men prisoners and drove them ahead, going straight up the old Nuecestown Road. They left the women behind at the ranch.

As soon as they moved out, we moved in. Some of the women saw us advancing and thought we were more Mexican bandits so a number of them ran into the chaparral. We caught them and brought them back to the ranch. We also caught some horses that the raiders had left and started the ladies for town, hitching the horses to the buggies that the raiders had captured. Some of the ladies were not found for a couple of days, being finally located by Charlie McKenzie and his brother.

Meanwhile, the raiders were driving the prisoners ahead of them in a fast trot, beating them with quirts and ropes and punching them with their guns and pistols.

Just as we were leaving the ranch on their trail, we met a stockman by the name of Bass Burris, who was a relative of Martin Culver's. With him was Clem Vetters, now janitor of the high school, and three Mexicans. All the Mexicans were unarmed.

We took to the trail again, still expecting help from town. When we caught up with the raiders, we were at Noakes' store at Nuecestown. It was nearly sundown, but there was still no help from Corpus.

The raiders were not seen from the store until they had the place surrounded. Most of them dismounted. Mr. Noakes was in a backroom and, hearing a noise in front, he rushed out and just as he reached the front door, a Mexican came running in with a cocked Winchester in his hand. Noakes fired at him and shot him through the breast. With that, Noakes dropped through a trap door in the floor and into some trenches underground. Another man by the name of Smith, who happened to be there, followed Noakes into the trench.

The bandits entered the store and after piling up outside all that they wanted to confiscate, they set fire to the building, hoping to burn Noakes out. But every time they would get the fire started, Mrs. Noakes would pour water on it. At last two of them caught her and held her until the fire got a good start.

In the meantime, Mr. Noakes held the trench. Finally, the smoke and heat got so bad that Smith crawled out and made a run for the river. Some of the raiders followed him and shot him down. He fell on his face and they put their carbines to his back and shot him four times, all the balls coming out of his breast. Two years ago, I heard from him and he was still alive and hearty.

As the raiders did not know that Noakes had another man with him, they thought that they had killed Noakes when they got Smith, and were, therefore, satisfied.

The bandits took the wounded Mexican that Noakes had shot and put him in a wagon, also piling in the goods they had stolen from the store. They put in several prisoners, among them Billy McKenzie, a brother of Charles McKenzie of Nuecestown, and Judge William A. Ball of Nuecestown. They started in a southwest direction, leaving the main road. The sun was almost setting.

At that time John Dunn returned from town. He had only four men with him, my brother James, Pat Whalen, a man from Duval County named Swank and Wash Mussett (his name was Washington). John informed us that the people of Corpus would not send anyone because they claimed they needed the men there. We concluded that we would not let the Mexican bandits go without giving them a slight reception.

The raiders had taken a trail into the chaparral. One of the boys informed us that a short distance away the trail forked in opposite directions and that it would be a good idea for two men with good horses to go ahead of the rest and see which trail they took. John Dunn and Swank volunteered to go.

As we rode on, a few hundred yards ahead we met John Dunn coming back alone. We asked him where Swank was and he said he did not know as he had gone in the opposite direction and had not seen him since. He told us that the raiders were congregated around the wagon in a small glade in the mesquite.

The raiders were firing off their arms, so it was not hard to trail them. When we came upon them in the glade, they were concentrated around the wagon that held the prisoners, the wounded Mexican that Noakes had shot, and the loot taken from the stores.

We were within a hundred yards of them before they saw us. The bullets were singing lullabies all around us. Among them we could recognize the sound of Mike Dunn's old sharpshooter of which he had been relieved at Juan Saenz. The lead in the end of the cartridges had been split down to the brass shell and they made a scream like the wail of a lost soul.

Before we reached the raiders, they broke and scattered like a covey of quail. At the same time, the prisoners jumped out of the back end of the wagon and ran into the brush. It was dusk and soon they were out of sight and we were out of ammunition. Some of us had two or three cartridges, and the most any of us had was five.

We returned to W. S. McGregor's store at Nuecestown but could get nothing but .44 rim-fire cartridges which would fit the Winchesters and .44 Colts but three of us were armed with .50 caliber sharpshooters. When we arrived at the store there were a number of men assembled there.

We tried to get them to come with us to Banquete, where there were several ranches at which we could probably

390

secure help, but they refused to go with us to overtake the raiders. That is, they all refused except one man, a Mr. Hunter. The others stated that it would be suicide to think of it, believing that we would be waylaid and murdered.

The names of the men who took part in the fight with the raiders were Matt Dunn, John Dunn, Pat Dunn, James Dunn, Bass Burris, Clem Vetters, George Dunn, Wash Mussett, Jesus Seguira, Pat Whalen and I. There was also George Swank who was killed.

We started with the one recruit for Banquete. We had had no dinner and no supper and were hungry when we arrived at daybreak next morning. However, T. Hines Clark, a cattle rancher, gave us a fine breakfast. Had the raiders known how we were fixed with ammunition they could have turned on us and cleaned us up in a very few minutes. One of the Mexicans that was with Burris stayed right with us during the whole time of the shooting. His name was Jesus Seguira. He was as brave as they make them. Years before he had been one of Cortina's lieutenants during that celebrated bandit's raids on the Texas border and he knew Mexican tactics to a finish. He had but one fault and that was drunkenness. When he was drunk, he was very dangerous.

Long since, some people circulated the report that the Mexican raiders insulted the women at Nuecestown, but that is a false report. The raiders must be given credit for treating the women courteously and not molesting them in any manner.

—From "Perilous Trails" by John Dunn

APPENDIX 9
RAID ON GOOD FRIDAY

Thomas John Noakes

On Good Friday, March 26, 1875, I was kept busy all day, having remittances to make to several business houses, that I wanted to send by the evening mail for goods that I had received a few days before, and if they had been sent off sooner I should have owed no man a cent.

After finishing my letters I made up the mail in readiness for the carrier who was about due, when a man named John Smith came into the store for some flour, and while in the act of handing him a parcel over the counter, I noticed three Mexicans ride up and fasten their horses to the rack in front of the store, and excitedly approach the door, heavily armed.

I said nothing to Smith of the circumstance, but walked hastily to the sitting room at the back of the store to get my Winchester rifle, thinking that things looked shaky.

I had no sooner reached my rifle into my hands when Smith came rushing into the room, closely followed by a savage-looking Mexican with his gun in the position to shoot Smith, but immediately on seeing me brought it around on me, but before he could shoot my bullet penetrated his chest and knocked the fight out of him.

In the meantime, Smith had escaped out of an open door opposite the one he had entered the room and my wife, passing in as he went out, was with me in the room. Seeing the wounded Mexican could shoot no more, I made ready for the next to follow. Having seen but three Mexicans, I felt no apprehension about my being able to cope with that number, and expected that when they heard the firing they would come to the assistance of their comrade, but none came. I stepped to the door leading into the store to see where they were, and was taking aim at the fellow nearest me when my attention was attracted by the number outside the front of the store, which appeared to me to amount to a hundred Mexicans.

Realizing at once that I was greatly overpowered (for one man cannot with much hope fight a hundred), I did not fire, but turned, expecting to see my wife in the room, and tell her to take the children and leave the house, but she was nowhere to be found.

The doors and windows looking into the room where I was, from three sides of the house all being open, and the Mexicans taking up a position so as to surround us, I was compelled to avail myself of a trap door in the floor, by which I passed into a trench that had been dug beneath the floor of the house.

The trench enabled me to pass from one part of the house to another and get into any room I wanted to without being exposed to sight. Here I found Smith, who, crawling under the house at the back, had found the trench. He was very excited and I advised him to stay where he was and to keep quiet. I told him that I would go to the front of the house and see if there was any chance to fight them and if I saw that he could do any good with it, I would furnish him with a pistol. But as excited as he was, he was best without one.

On reaching the trench from where I could see the crowd in front of the store, I noticed several Americans held as prisoners, among whom was a person named Lane, another, Mike Dunn, and one, Tom Nelson, and I came to the conclusion that they meant to take all the prisoners they could from among the Americans, and as soon as they were through robbing, have the enjoyment of a general massacre, la Peñascal.[286]

I determined at once that I would not be taken alive. I passed back to the place where I could command the store with my rifle, but to my consternation I found my wife in the store, surrounded by the raiders and two of them placed in such a way, with cocked pistols, that any shot that could be fired by an unseen party would be retaliated on her by one of the fiends. To resume firing was only to insure her being shot, and I had to remain inactive while my wife was trying to persuade them not to carry out their threat of taking me or burning the house.

Several times when they had lighted a fire in the store my wife put it out, and the first time by throwing a pitcher of water on it. I now noticed that Smith had left the trench, and hearing shots from the direction in which he must have gone, knew that he was shot down by the guards placed to keep us from leaving the house.

I could now hear the roar of fire over my head and to remain longer was certain death. My only chance lay in shooting down the Mexicans who guarded the back of the house and then escape in the smoke. But when I reached the end of the trench from which to put my design into operation, my wife called to me that the Mexicans were not there, and now was my only chance to leave alive. She helped me to tear a hole through the fence by which to escape.

When I left her, she was getting her feather bed out of the house, and in spite of the impending danger, I could not but feel amused at such a notion of getting out a bed while thousands of other articles, in my estimation, would have had the preference.

I expected every moment to be fired upon, and in such a case had made up my mind to lie flat and return fire, but I

---

[286] Four men were brutally slain during a robbery at the Morton store in the Peñascal community on Baffin Bay in May 1874.

was allowed to turn the corner of the fence without molestation and, by keeping along the angle, I reached a point where to go farther I had to pass over open ground where I should have been seen. I concluded to remain and see it out.

I passed by Smith soon after leaving the house, being on his face and covered with blood, and, as I thought, dead. The Mexicans, not seeing me leave, boasted that they had burned me with the house, as were their intentions. When reconnoitering from my trench among the crowd in front of the store, I noticed the mail rider among the prisoners. They took him as he came up to deliver his mail, and he was not allowed to do so, but both he and his two horses were carried off by them, together with the mail bags, when they left.

From the numerous murders and raids that have been made within the past two years, I had deemed it necessary to be well-prepared for such an emergency when my time came, which I always had a presentiment that it would do.

I had used all my spare time in making preparations for the event, and I had gone to great expense in planning the trench. I shaped it so that a person being in it was perfectly safe from the shots from the outside, and I could reach it from three trap doors, one in the floor at my bed, one at my desk in the store, and another from a room beside the store, and it led to a way of escape at the back of the house, which saved my life.

A trench also led to the cellar, and from the cellar to the front of the stairs. At the trap door in the front room I could reach the top of the house by means of a hook and ladder, and in the top of the house I kept a needle gun with 500 rounds of cartridges, and I had, to the best of my recollection, 16 improved pistols and about 50 boxes of cartridges distributed about the house. With sufficient warning of their approach to enable me to close the house, I considered myself, alone, capable of fighting off 12 or 15 men, and had determined never to surrender to a smaller force.

My wife tells me that when she left the house, as she ran down the hill towards the river, the two Mexicans who had killed Smith rode after her and were preparing their guns to shoot at her, but she begged them to spare her for the sake of her baby, and they let her go.

Early in the attack my wife had given the baby to my little daughter and her brother who, both together, were hardly able to carry the smallest, telling them to carry him away as quickly as they could, and the three had reached a point very near to where the Mexicans shot Smith, and at the time they were engaged in doing so, and were witnesses to the deed, and from what they saw became so horrified that they fell to the ground, incapable of moving.

In the meantime, the two older boys, who had been on the river and knew nothing of what was going on, suspected something was wrong at the house from seeing the Mexicans shoot down Smith. They caught sight of the little ones at the same time and, seeing them fall, came to their rescue, and all agree in saying that while crossing the flats, the five were fired at by the Mexicans and one of the shots that was intended for Smith nearly hit Grace, the little girl. The children reached the river and crossed to the other side in the skiff, where my wife joined them some time after.

As soon as darkness set in the Mexicans turned loose all their prisoners except the mail carrier and two or three others, among whom was W. A. Ball, our justice of the peace who, I afterwards learned, they took with them some distance before they allowed him to escape.

As soon as they were gone, I ran to Smith, whom I found alive, but with so many bullet holes in him that death seemed inevitable. I now met my wife who told me the children were all safe, which made me feel very grateful.

Smith was lying about 100 yards from the burning house

and praying for water. I ran up to the place where the house had stood, with the idea of getting water, but of course everything was gone or red-hot. I could not find anything that would hold water, but while I was hunting for something, two men, strangers, rode up to the fire on the other side, and one of them requested me to approach the fence on the other side of which he stood. As soon as I was close to him, he demanded my rifle, at the same time bringing his six-shooter down on me and threatened to kill me unless I complied.

Not dreaming of such conduct from white men, I was totally unprepared and he could have shot me before I could have raised my rifle. But I refused his request, saying that I needed the rifle for my own and my family's protection, as that was that the Mexicans had left me. However, as he insisted that he could do more good with it than I could, as he was going in pursuit of the bandits, I gave the rifle to him on his promise to return it. But, poor fellow, in less than an hour he was dead. Only through luck I recovered the rifle which was picked up near his body by F. Sims, a gentleman living near me, and it was some days before I recovered possession of it.

The man who took my rifle was named Swank, I was told, and was among the first of those in pursuit of the raiders and was reported to have been killed by them. He was a brave man, a fine example of a Texan.

I had now returned to Smith, who would not let me leave him, though I had no hat or clothes enough to keep me warm. After a while parties brought a cart and took him away. Then we hunted up the little ones, who were by this time huddled together under a fence near the river, crying and half-witted from fright.

My wife, luckily, had pulled the running gear of the light wagon out of reach of the flames and we now took the back wheels and mustered up all our possessions, which consisted of a bed, a blanket and a quilt, which she had

397

carried out while the house was burning, with her sewing machine, and with our five little ones we started down the hill to the wharf I had recently built on the river. In the darkness we took possession of the only home we now owned   but   felt   thankful   for   it.

As the house was burning, I had to stand and watch from my retreat by the fence, the huge tongues of flame shooting heavenward, knowing that they were licking up the fruits of ten years' toil, and everything except ourselves that I valued in the world, yet I never experienced so utterly maddening a feeling as came over me when I first realized that my children were crying for the want of a roof to cover them and the taste of a bite of bread.

—Thomas Noakes, three weeks after the raid

APPENDIX 10
NOAKES' NEIGHBORS

Nuecestown, the Motts as Noakes and his neighbors generally called it, was a small world and the people there lived in close proximity. What happened to Noakes' neighbors who figured so prominently in his diary?

George Reynolds was one of Noakes' closest friends until they had a falling out over the administration of the estate of John Williams. Reynolds, who got a job cutting hay for the army when he first arrived in 1854, became a wealthy rancher, with both sheep and cattle. He moved from Nuecestown in 1869 to a ranch he bought called Palo Ventana, near today's Orange Grove. His wife Hannah died in 1889 and George died in 1897.

Joseph Wright Sr. and his sons are frequently mentioned by Noakes. Wright bought 320 acres from Kinney's agents in England, which entitled him to three town lots at Nuecestown. He and his wife Seana had 12 children. Their oldest son, T. C., was one of Noakes' chums. Seana died in 1875 and Joseph Sr. died in 1893 at Driscoll.

Samuel Couling, his wife Hester and their son Henry emigrated from Oxfordshire, England in 1854. Couling was a freighter in Corpus Christi in 1860 but soon moved to Nuecestown. Robert Adams in his memoirs recalled that his father apprenticed him as a boy to a freighter at Nuecestown named Samuel Colon. He said that one day when he didn't move fast enough to hitch a team of oxen, Colon threw him across a porch and broke his leg. No "Colon" has been found in the census or historical records. It seems likely that Robert Adams' "Samuel Colon" was Samuel Couling.

Hester Couling died July 21, 1886 and was buried in the Nuecestown Cemetery. Samuel Couling died April 16, 1898 at Lagarto.

Noakes was also close to James and Janet Bryden until they had a fight. The Brydens arrived in Corpus Christi from Peebleshire, Scotland in 1852 and James managed William Chapman's sheep ranch on the Santa Gertrudis and worked for Richard King. He moved his family to Nuecestown at the beginning of the Civil War. Bryden later bought the old Diezmero Ranch near Santa Margarita. He died in 1881 and Janet Bryden died in 1889.

John Ludewig, Noakes father-in-law, died in the yellow fever epidemic of 1867, along with his son Adolph and his wife. Ludewig's widow and her daughter moved to Corpus Christi but, in 1870, she still had branded cattle on the range.

Rev. Stephen Orchard came from a family of Baptist ministers in London. He and his family arrived in Texas in 1854 and settled next door to Noakes at Nuecestown. Noakes was a frequent guest at the Rev. Orchard's home. At the beginning of the Civil War, Orchard moved his family to San Patricio then Goliad. He died near Luling in 1895.

James Hobbs Sr and wife Sarah came to Texas in 1852 from Derbyshire. She died in the yellow fever epidemic of 1854. Hobbs' daughter Sarah married Reuben Holbein, clerk of King Ranch. William, the oldest son, known as "Uncle Billy," married Harriet Wright, daughter of Joseph Wright, and established the Hobbs Ranch near Lagarto. James Hobbs Sr. died in August 1868.

John Heward, who came from North Carolina with his wife Nancy and five children, moved his family in 1865 and vanished from the local record.

"Ned" Taylor, who was George Reynolds' uncle and whom Noakes on a trip to New Braunfels called "nothing but a curse," died in 1873.

John Hinnant moved to the Lagarto area where he died in 1877. His son "Tobe" married Mary Ann Adams and built Los Picachos Ranch near Lagarto.

They all moved away from Nuecestown, which was already in serious decline when it missed out on the railroad in 1905. Rancher Calvin J. Allen gave land to the St. Louis, Brownsville and Mexico Railway for right of way three miles from Nuecestown. A new town began to grow around the railroad depot and it was named after the rancher, Cal Allen. As Calallen grew, Nuecestown declined. Noakes' son, New Noakes, who married Cal Allen's daughter Lula, moved his store from Old Nuecestown to the new town of Calallen.

In 1896, some 200 people lived at Nuecestown. In 1927, there were 50. By the 1960s, all that was left of Nuecestown was a Motts Restaurant and curio shop and by1980 all that remained was a restored schoolhouse and the Nuecestown Cemetery.

—Murphy Givens

APPENDIX 11
THE NOAKES CHILDREN

Besides his old brown diaries that crumble at the touch, Noakes left behind his children. There were seven in all, but one died in infancy and another died young. They included Thomas John Jr., born in 1862. The second son was Nelson Edmondson, born in 1865. The third son was Adolph George, named for Marie's brother. One daughter was Mary, who died in infancy. Another was Grace Amanda. New Noakes got his unusual name because he was born on New Year's Day 1873. The youngest of the children was Leona Marcella, born in 1876, the year before her father's death.

Thomas Noakes Jr. was born on Dec. 17, 1862. His birth coincided with one of the gaps in the Noakes' diaries. It is believed that Noakes was away serving in the Confederate Army. Thomas Jr. died young.

Nelson Edmondson, the second-oldest son, was born in Swift's boarding house on Water Street on June 13, 1865. He was named for Lord Horatio Nelson and Noakes' brother Edmond. Nelson married Linnie Dafron from Kansas. There is more to this story.

The third son, Adolph George, was named for Marie's brother Adolph Ludewig, a saddle-maker who died in the yellow fever epidemic of 1867. Adolph married Lillie Dafron, the sister of Nelson's wife in a double wedding.

The fourth son, New, was born on Jan. 1, 1873. He was a toddler at the time of the Nuecestown Raid. When Nelson and Adolph married the two Dafron sisters, New Noakes was supposed to marry a third sister in a triple ceremony, with three brothers marrying three sisters, but New got cold feet and backed out.

Grace Amanda Noakes was born on Jan. 21, 1870. She married John Ball of Nuecestown. She died on the Palo Alto Ranch on Jan. 16, 1908 and was buried in the San Diego Cemetery. Leona Marcella Noakes, the youngest of the children, married Charles McKenzie, a longtime justice of the peace in Nueces County.

The most notable of Noakes' children, at least from the standpoint of local history, were New Noakes and Adolph Noakes.

New Noakes followed in his father's footsteps as storekeeper and postmaster. New married Lula Allen, daughter of Cal Allen, founder of Calallen. The son of Adoph Noakes, Herbert, once recalled his uncle's store. "There was licorice in jars and groceries in barrels. I can almost smell that store. Candy, spices, foods, and other goods all blended together." New moved the Noakes store from Nuecestown to Calallen to make way for Highway 9. He later remarried, after the death of his first wife. He died on Jan. 17, 1957 and was buried in Rose Hill Cemetery.

New's older brother, Adolph George Noakes, owned a prosperous machine shop business in the 300 block of Chaparral in Corpus Christi. Adolph Noakes, like his father, was a man of many talents. He was a taxidermist, inventor, and sold and serviced some of the first automobiles in Corpus Christi. He died on Oct. 6, 1940. A grandson of Adolph Noakes (a great grandson of Thomas Noakes) was Herbert Noakes Jr., a computer scientist who worked for NASA and helped train astronauts on the lunar space module used on the moon landing in 1969.

—*Murphy Givens*

POSTSCRIPT

The original Noakes' diary is at the Corpus Christi Museum of Science and History. I did not have direct access to these journals because of the fragile nature of the pages, which can crumble at the touch. Photocopies of a few of the pages were provided at my request. The diary should be copied and made available in digital form for scholars, and I'm told that this will be done, but not in time for this project.

I relied on handwritten copies of the Noakes' diary at the Corpus Christi Central Library. I have complete copies of those volumes. They were made in the 1930s when Mrs. Frank DeGarmo was writing her work called "Pathfinders," which included some Noakes' material. Other transcriptions of parts of the Noakes diary were made in the 1960s by Caller-Times reporter Ernest Morgan, who wrote a series of articles on the Civil War, and later by historian Dan Kilgore. All of these were most helpful.

The handwritten copies were sometimes abridged and condensed. Some of the handwritten copies were all but illegible and had to be deciphered, like ancient hieroglyphics. In particularly difficult cases, the Museum of Science and History photocopied those entries and made them available.

Noakes often added extraneous words, repeated the same word in succeeding sentences, and preferred run-on sentences with conjunctions like the coupling of railroad cars. So, some editing was a must, to help the flow and clarity of the narrative. Words within a parenthesis were Noakes' own words, but if they are sandwiches between brackets, they were added by the editor. Some will go to any lengths to avoid footnotes, but they are the simplest and easiest way to add explanatory notes and comments, which were very much needed.

Finally, the task of transcribing and editing the Noakes' diary was approached from the mindset of an editor, not a lawyer, with the intent to make it as readable as possible while remaining faithful to Noakes own style and meaning.

—Murphy Givens

INDEX

Ludewig, Adolph: listed as saddlemaker on census, 102; in Ireland's company with Noakes, 137, 194, 218; sold saddles for Noakes in Corpus Christi, 326, 330, 353

Ludewig, Ellen: compared to Marie, 93; engaged to a Mr. Jones, 120

Ludewig, John: moved next to Noakes, 81-82; on census, 93; salt-gathering trip, 127; illness, 273; death, 400

Ludewig, Theresa: advertised cattle brand after husband's death, 57; census, 93; illness, 270, 323; joined daughters in serenading Noakes, 97; tended Noakes' children for Marie, 339

McClane, John 166-167, 275, 386

McGregor, Frances and Flora 55

McGregor, John Steward 55, 363

McGregor, John Steward Jr., 379

McGregor, Mary Ann 55

McGregor, W. S. 73, 369, 378, 390

McIntyre, Daniel 378

McIntyre, Donald 92

McIntyre, John 292

McIntyre, Mary 92

McKelvey, Dr. —— 37-41

McKenzie, Billy 388-389

McKenzie, Charlie 388-389, 403

McKenzie, William 47, 107, 193, 216, 277, 296, 307, 316-317, 320, 324-326, 330-332, 338, 347-348, 351, 355

McLaughlin, Alden 87, 111, 297

McLaughlin, Alden Jr. 340, 345

McMaster, John (Fink) 173

Maltby, Henry 137, 146

Maltby, William 137, 345, 351

Manahuilla Creek 175, 207

Marsh, Jane 179, 186

Matagorda Island 148, 192

Matson, Jacob 266

Medio Creek 175, 183

Merriman, Dr. Eli 212, 219

Merriman, Eli (son) 109, 123, 152, 385

Middletown 207

sisters, 92; Confederate soldier, medical furlough, 137-138, 212-213, 226; death, 369; feud with Bryden and Reynolds, 277-280; health problems, 37-44, 47-49, 155, 161, 200-204, 208, 211-213, 254, 265, 304, 358; letters from brother Edmond, 50, 67, 108, 277, 294, 359; letters from sister Emily, 13, 48, 91, 104, 312, 341, 347, 363; letters from his mother, 55, 194, 266, 333; letter from uncle Richard, 194; marriage to Marie Ludewig, 98, 101; opinions of neighbors, 78, 177-178, 249-250, 278-282, 318; partnership with Kershaw, 6-43; property sold at Polegate, England, 194, 346, 361, 368; salt-trading trips during war, 127, 183-186, 192-208; store at Nuecestown, 236, 368-369, 388-389, 392-398; tried teaching school, 256-280

Noakes, Thomas Jr. 327, 344, 402

Nolan, Mat 76, 83, 166, 174, 376-379

Nolan, Tom 76, 83, 376-377

Nuecestown (the Motts): dances at, 28-29, 34, 44, 77, 81, 83, 94, 97, 274, 304, 352; Cortina scare, 75, 116, 124, 126; grape-gathering trips, 20-21, 34, 139; Kinney's land offer, 374-375; picnics, 34-35, 58, 81, 124; raid, 370, 386-398; school at, 78, 83, 256-280; Union occupation troops march through, 275

Nueces Valley (newspaper) 14, 25, 28-29, 33, 57, 79, 120, 191

Ohler, Edward 159, 279

Ohler, Matilda 159

Ohler's Wharf 379

Orchard, Mrs. Emma 37

Orchard, John 5, 13, 37, 40, 61, 71

Orchard, Rev. Stephen 3-5, 10, 13, 15, 20-26, 32-37, 41, 49, 56, 60, 66, 74, 77, 79, 82, 88-89, 99, 106, 278, 400

Oso Creek 53, 69-70, 105, 108-109, 117, 122, 127, 189, 300, 321, 328
Oso Ranch 87, 111, 122, 297

Padre Island 84, 228, 237-245
Palo Alto Creek 166, 189, 191
Palo Alto Prairie 189
Palo Alto Ranch 119, 128, 209, 403
Palo Ventana 4, 375, 399
Papalote Creek 171, 175, 208
Parkinson, Col. H. 14, 33
Pass Cavallo 148
Penitas Ranch 159
Perham, Rev. J. P. 79, 138, 158, 209, 210
Perkins, James 166
Petronila Creek 54
Photos and illustrations 233-236
Poesta Creek 186
Polk, Jack 291, 294
Polk, John A. 379
Precenos Ranch 167
Price, — — 237-245
Priour, Rosalie 227

Quinn, Alonzo 141

Rabb, Martha 117, 119
Rachal, D. C. 119
Rains, Ned 112
Ranchero (newspaper) 75, 80, 83, 101, 103, 107, 111, 113, 122, 123, 127, 136, 146, 152, 167, 227, 376
Rancho Grande 266
Rancho Seco 183
Reynolds, George 3, 5-10, 13, 22, 34-38, 45, 48, 50-59, 62-69, 72-78, 82, 90-91, 104-105, 107, 110-111, 118-124, 126, 149-155, 159, 168, 180-182, 212-214, 263-284, 293, 305, 307, 318-322, 341-342, 378, 399-400
Reynolds, George Jr. 302
Reynolds, Hannah 3, 37, 79, 106, 157, 181
Richardson, James 210
Richardson, James (of King Ranch) 210
Riggs, John 152
Rincon (North Beach) 87, 113, 383
Robertson, George 152, 247
Rogers, William (Billy) 128, 209
Round Lake 112, 196
Russell, Gen. Charles 249

ALSO AVAILABLE FROM NUECES PRESS

1919 – The Storm

Corpus Christi – A History

A Soldier's Life

Great Tales from the History of South Texas

Recollections of Other Days

Perilous Trails of Texas

Columns   2009 – 2011

Columns 2 2012 – 2013

Columns 3 2014 – 2015

Columns 4 2016 – 2018

Streets of Corpus Christi Texas

Signed copies are available from

www.nuecespress.com